# SQL Server 2(
## Procedures |

Tony Bain
Louis Davidson
Robin Dewson
Chuck Hawkins

Apress™

# *SQL Server 2000 Stored Procedures Handbook*

# Credits

# About the Authors

### Tony Bain

Tony Bain is the founder of Tony Bain & Associates and he has worked with SQL Server for the last 6 last years. Tony is passionate about all database technologies especially when they relate to enterprise availability and scalability.

Tony spends a lot of his time writing and presenting database topics and he currently has Microsoft Certified System Engineer, Microsoft Certified Solution Developer, and Microsoft Certified Database Administrator certification.

*Thanks to Linda, Laura, Stephanie, and William for their continued support and thanks also to Craig Walker who is a .NET legend!*

**Louis Davidson**

Louis Davidson has been in the technology industry for ten years, as a corporate database developer and architect. Currently, he is serving as a Database Administrator for Compass Technology Management in their Nashville Data Center supporting the Christian Broadcasting Network and NorthStar Studios in Nashville, TN.

Davidson has a bachelor's degree from the University of Tennessee at Chattanooga in computer science with a minor in mathematics (though the minor in mathematics is more of an indication to how much math UTC required to get the CS degree, rather than any great love or skill in the subject).

The majority of his experience, with slight deviations into Visual Basic, has been spent with Microsoft SQL Server from version 1.0 to the latest version that is in Beta. Louis' primary areas of expertise are in database architecture and coding in Transact-SQL, and he has written numerous stored procedures and triggers throughout the years, though he seldom has the need anymore with the code generation tools he has developed to generate objects, with only a few procedures and triggers to code from the ground up.

Louis has published "Professional SQL Server 2000 Database Design," also by Apress. The book follows the complete arc of developing a database through requirements, architecture, and design. He has also been an active volunteer with SQL PASS as a presenter and a chairperson in their special interest groups. It has been said that in his ridiculously small amount of spare time, he tends to play a lot of Nintendo (got to save that darn Princess, she went off and was captured by the silly dragon, again!) and watch a great deal of television. Most notably, his favorites are old English programs (the Avengers, The Saint, Monty Python, and Blackadder to name a few). Quite often, this spare time is also spent with his notebook computer writing something pertaining to SQL.

### Robin Dewson

Robin has come a long way since the early heady days of the Sinclair ZX80/81 and Spectrum. He was first introduced to computers at an exhibition in Glasgow where he saw a Commodore Pet manipulate a robot and he knew instantly that computers was the route for him. Unfortunately that route initially took him into IBM mainframes.

However, he feels that this is a crucial keystone in his overall approach to computing and without this he would not be where he is today. Well, that, Scottish College of Textiles, his family and of course many, many bottles of Irn Bru (who needs caffeine?). Robin moved to working with PCs nearly 10 years ago with FoxBASE and has moved from there through Visual FoxPro, Visual Basic, Sybase, and of course SQL Server.. Robin can be contacted at robin@fat-belly.com.

*There are many people once again that I would like to thank for different reasons. All those at Wrox throughout the years but especially Cilmara, Douglas, Cath, Helen, James, and Chris for different reasons, but thanks! Andy at Pinball Mania for keeping my pinball machines working, Charlie and Debbie at Sea Palling in Norfolk for being two great friends and brilliant with my children in their arcade, Phill Jupitus, Phil (2112 rules!) Wilding, Gideon Coe, Liz Kershaw, and Andrew Collins at the BBC's 6Music, (www.bbc.co.uk/6music) for the excellent music and humor to keep me going at work, all my traders at Lehmans but especially Anthony "Jock" Jawad for his staunch support, and my good friend Jack Mason. Of course special thanks though to my mum and dad for sorting out this great life for me, my sister Carol and her family, Eleanor, Erin, and Lucas out in Australia but most of all my wife Julie who goes through hell with each book I write. I am afraid this was "not another one". But you can now go and enjoy the Donny Osmond concert. Also my 3 long suffering kids, Scott, Cameron, and Ellen. Let's go and see a movie.*

*Up the Blues. (http://www.bedfordrugby.co.uk)*

### Chuck Hawkins

Chuck is a senior consultant and database administrator in Virginia Beach, Virginia. Working for Compass Technology Management, he currently manages the daily ups and downs of multiple servers for several large ministries. He has extensive experience in T-SQL programming, replication, performance tuning, developer management, and routine server management.

Chuck has spoken at Professional Association for SQL Server conferences in Chicago, London, Denver, and Seattle. He has contributed columns to several magazines and was a contributing author for Louis Davidson's "Professional SQL Server 2000 Database Design," now published by Apress. Prior to his life as a computing professional, Chuck taught English in Japan for five years.

Chuck is happily married to Kathy and adopted Kristina from Russia five years ago on Christmas Day. When not working with databases, he likes to play with Kristina, run long distances, and read "First Things" journal. You can get in touch with Chuck at chuck@sqlserver.cc.

# SQL Server 2000

## Stored Procedures

Handbook

Table of
Contents

# Table of Contents

**Introduction**                                                     **1**

  **Who Is This Book For?**                               **1**

  **Book Outline**                                         **2**

**Chapter 1: Stored Procedures Overview**                            **5**

  **What is a Stored Procedure?**                          **6**
    System Stored Procedure                      6
    User Stored Procedure                        8
    Creating Stored Procedures                   9
    Performance Consideration                    11
    Network Consideration                        11

  **Why Use Stored Procedures?**                           **11**

  **Replication**                                          **12**

  **Designing Good Stored Procedures**                     **13**

  **Data integrity**                                       **14**

  **Calling a Stored Procedure**                           **17**

  **Rules for Stored Procedures**                          **17**

  **Modifying Stored Procedures**                          **19**

  **Parameter Usage**                                      **20**

  **Flow control**                                         **21**
    Code Blocks/ BEGIN...END                     21
    Decisions                                    22
      IF...ELSE                        22
      CASE                             23
      GOTO label                       25
    Loops                                        25
      The WHILE Loop                   25
    Pausing and Halting execution                26

  **Nesting in Stored Procedures**                         **27**

**Returning Values**   **28**
RETURN   28
OUTPUT   29
Single Row of Data   30
When an Error Occurs   30
Other Issues with Returning Values   30

**Restoring the Example Databases to their Default Condition**   **31**

**Summary**   **31**

## Chapter 2: Optimizing and Debugging   35

**Optimizing Stored Procedures**   **35**
SET NOCOUNT ON   35
RECOMPILE   37

**The Execution Plan**   **38**
Why Bother About the Execution Plan?   39
Viewing the Execution Plan   39
Graphical View of the Execution Plan   39
Textual View of the Execution Plan   40
The Execution Plan and Stored Procedures   42
Multiple Statements within the Stored Procedure   43
Understanding the Execution Plan   44
Cost   44
Benefits of Understanding Cost   47

**Common Mistakes**   **48**
Batches and GO   48
Dynamic SQL in Procedures   50
Security   51

**Error Handling**   **52**
@@ERROR   53
RAISERROR & Return Parameters   55

**SQL Server Debugger**   **57**
Finding the Debugger   57
Using the Debugger   58

**Summary**   **62**

## Chapter 3: Concurrency, Cursors, and Transactions   65

**Cursors**   **66**
Syntax   66
Special Cursor Syntax   67
Alternate Cursor Syntax   70
Accessing Cursors from Code   70
Opening Cursors   70
FETCH Statement   70
@@FETCH_STATUS   72
Closing Cursors   73

Uses of Cursors                                                          73
    Formatting a Result Set                          73
    Batch Operations                                 78
Best Practices                                                          80

**Transactions**                                                        **81**
Syntax                                                                   82
    Simple Transactions                              82
    Savepoints                                       86
    Distributed Transactions                         87
    Explicit versus Implicit Transactions            88
    Compiled SQL Server Code                         88
Best Practices                                                          90

**Concurrency**                                                         **91**
OS and Hardware Issues                                                   92
Concurrency Controls                                                     92
    SQL Server                                       93
    Coding for Integrity and Concurrency             99
Best Practices                                                          108

**Summary**                                                             **109**

**Chapter 4: Common Practices with Stored Procedures**                  **111**

**Typical Purposes**                                                    **111**
Encapsulating Logic                                                     112
Improving Performance                                                   115
Easing Administration                                                   120
    Performance Tuning                               120
Simplifying Code Deployment                                             120
Improving Database Security                                             121
Improving Data Validation                                               122
    Constraints                                      124
    Why not Build Validation in the Front-End Application?   125
    Triggers                                         126
Executing Code at SQL Server Startup                                    127

**Points to Avoid While Using Stored Procedures**                       **129**
Stored Procedure Grouping                                               129
Nesting Stored Procedures                                               131
Generic Stored Procedures                                               131
Stored Procedures with Many Parameters                                  131

**Summary**                                                             **133**

**Chapter 5: System Stored Procedures**                                 **135**

**System Stored Procedures**                                            **136**
Effect of the 0x80000000 Status Bit                                     138
    Making System Stored Procedures with the 0x80000000 Bit   140
    An Important Feature of System Stored Procedures   142

Other Features of SP_: Global Tables and Views                    144
Common Documented System Stored Procedures                        145
Other Important System Stored Procedures                          149
Mining System Stored Procedures                                   150

**Undocumented Functionality**                                    **151**
Finding Undocumented Extended Stored Procedure Functionality      152
Windows-Registry Related Stored Procedures                        152
  The Windows Registry                                            152
  XP_RegRead                                                      153
  XP_RegWrite                                                     155
  XP_RegEnumKeys                                                  156
  XP_RegEnumValues                                                157
  XP_RegDeleteKey                                                 157
  XP_RegDeleteValue                                               158
  XP_RegAddMultiString                                            158
  XP_RegRemoveMultiString                                         159
  XP_Instance_Reg extended stored procedures                      160
The File System                                                   161
  XP_AvailableMedia                                               161
  XP_SubDirs                                                      162
  XP_DirTree                                                      162
  XP_FixedDrives                                                  163
  XP_FileExists                                                   163
  XP_ReadErrorLog                                                 164

**Performing Complex Tasks with System Stored Procedures**        **166**

**Tracing Object Creation and Deletion**                          **168**

**SQL Mail**                                                      **169**
Best Practice Tips for SQL Mail                                   170
XP_SendMail Recursion                                             170
XP_SendMail Bullet-proofing                                       172
Breaking the Exchange Umbilical Cord – XP_SMTP_SendMail           172

**Summary**                                                       **176**

**Chapter 6: User Defined Functions**                             **179**

**UDFs**                                                          **179**
In-Built Functions                                                180

**Creating a UDF**                                                **181**
Types of Functions                                                181
  Deterministic Functions                                         182
  Non-Deterministic Functions                                     182
Computed Columns                                                  182
Example of Creating a UDF                                         183
Converting a Non-Deterministic Function to Deterministic          183

**Scalar Valued Functions**                                          **186**

**TABLE Data Type**                                                  **188**
Single Statement Table Function                                       188
Multi-Statement Table Functions                                       190
Table Variables                                                       190
In-built Functions with Table Data Type                               192

**Schema Binding**                                                   **193**

**Stored Procedures versus UDFs**                                    **194**

**Summary**                                                          **195**

**Chapter 7: Triggers**                                              **197**

**What is a Trigger?**                                               **198**

**Why use Triggers?**                                                **200**

**Performance**                                                      **201**
Deferred Updates and Direct Updates                                   202

**Creating and using a trigger**                                     **202**
The Conceptual Tables within Triggers                                 204
Triggers Fired on an Update                                           205

**Types of Trigger**                                                 **206**
FOR                                                                   206
AFTER                                                                 206
Ordering Trigger Actions                                              208
INSTEAD OF                                                            209
Cascading                                                             210
No Rows Updated                                                       210

**Transactions and Triggers**                                        **211**

**Trigger versus Constraints**                                       **212**

**Triggers versus Stored Procedure**                                 **213**

**Replication**                                                      **213**

**Recursion**                                                        **215**

**Good Practice**                                                    **216**

**Bad Practice**                                                     **216**

**Summary**                                                          **217**

## Chapter 8: Security     219

### Increased Need for Security     219

### SQL Server Vulnerabilities     220
Misconfiguration of SQL Servers     220
    SQL Server Setup     220
    Permission Paths     223
    Putting it all together     231
SQL Injection Attacks     234
    The Problem     234
    The Solutions     237
Encrypting Stored Procedures     239
    The syscomments Table     240
    Breaking Object Encryption in SQL 2000     241
    A Strategy For Encrypting Your Data     242
SQL Buffer Overflow     243
Installing a SSL Certificate for SQL Server     244
    Importing the certificate:     244
    Using the SetCert utility     245

### Summary     245

## Appendix A: Support, Errata, and forums.apress.com     247

### Customer Support     247

### Errata     247

### The Peer-to-Peer Forums at forums.apress.com     248

## Index     251

# SQL Server 2000

## Stored Procedures

### Handbook

### Introduction

# Introduction

As well as being used for fundamental database administration, stored procedures are the cornerstone of any kind of database solution. Mastery of stored procedures is imperative to access and modify your data in the most effective way, as well as to keep your database secure and performing well. This book is a must on your road to that mastery.

This book is dedicated to stored procedures and the surrounding aspects of SQL Server 2000 that affect their operation. In here you will find many useful tips, facts, and techniques that will help you to get the most from your stored procedures. Whether you are accessing data from a client application, performing database administration with system stored procedures, or even using extended stored procedures to work with other parts of the operating system, you will hopefully find information that will make you review your own dealings with stored procedures, and ensure the continuous improvement of your database solutions.

## Who Is This Book For?

SQL Server 2000 administrators and designers will benefit from this book, as will experienced SQL Server 2000 developers who are already familiar with the basic concepts of stored procedures.

# Book Outline

Below is a detailed outline of what this book covers, chapter by chapter.

## Chapter 1 – Stored Procedure Overview

We begin by examining what constitutes a stored procedure and discuss different types of stored procedures. Then we will look at the difference between system stored procedures and user stored procedures, creating and designing stored procedures, using parameters and best practices, flow control statements, recursion, and return values.

## Chapter 2 – Optimizing and Debugging

In this chapter, we will discuss optimizing SQL Server's stored procedures. Here, our focus will not be on optimizing the SQL statements themselves, but instead, how SQL statements can be optimized within the context of a stored procedure. We will also discuss error handling, signaling error conditions, and debugging stored procedures.

## Chapter 3 – Cursors, Transactions, and Concurrency

Initially, these are three topics that might seem unrelated; however, upon deeper discussion, we will discover that they are related. Cursors are mechanisms to code non-set-based operations into T-SQL statements. In general, their use is considered bad practice, but can be useful when building stored procedures if used properly. In this chapter we will look at accessing them from code and their typical uses. Transactions are used to group together similar operations into one atomic logical operation, and we will look at look at simple, nested, and distributed transactions, and their use from stored procedures. Concurrency is related to multi-tasking of operations. In databases, we are concerned with the number of queries that can be executed at the same time, especially making use of the same resources and data. We will look at locks, which are the markers used by SQL Server to decide whether the commands can be executed concurrently or not, and also discuss methods to maximize concurrency by using programming schemes to limit SQL locking between read-only and read-write sessions.

## Chapter 4 – Typical Uses of Stored Procedures

In this chapter, we will focus on the purposes of stored procedures within our applications, such as encapsulating logic, improving application performance, easing administration, abstracting the underlying base tables away from developers, simplifying code updates, and improving database security and data validation.

## Chapter 5 – System Stored Procedures

In this chapter we will look at system stored procedures, and their implementation by Microsoft. We will also look at some of the undocumented functionalities provided with SQL Server, which Microsoft uses to make certain system stored procedures work. Along the way, we'll be giving you tips and tricks on when to use (and on avoiding) their quite useful, but obviously 'unsupported', undocumented functionalities.

If you manage a SQL Server as a part of your day-to-day tasks, you will find this chapter helpful. There's a section on mining system stored procedures that will be especially useful to those involved in T-SQL coding.

## Chapter 6 – User Defined Functions

User defined functions, known more commonly as **UDF**s, are routines called from T-SQL code to return either a single value or a rowset, providing the developer with the ability to create their own customized functions, which can then be used from other parts of their T-SQL code.

UDFs have some features that are common to stored procedures but there are a number of restrictions, as well. In this chapter, we will begin by looking at what a UDF actually is, and then move onto look at the different types of UDFs, building and calling functions that return different types of data, using schema binding with UDFs, and how UDFs differ from stored procedures.

## Chapter 7 – Triggers

Triggers are best used for enforcing business rules as well as performing validation or data modifications, when other methods are not sufficient. Triggers are typically used in two areas: creating audit records and reflecting changes to crucial business tables, and validating changes against a set of business rules coded in T-SQL. In this chapter we will look at performance considerations when working with triggers, the different types of triggers, transactions and triggers, and recursive triggers.

## Chapter 8 – Security

In this chapter we will first analyze security threats and the core security requirement of SQL Server – allowing data access only to explicitly authorized users. Then, we will look at the proper implementation of stored procedures for adequately countering these threats. Finally, we will examine some general methods for securing our SQL Server implementation, giving special emphasis on SQL Server stored procedures and the system stored procedures that Microsoft ships with SQL Server.

# SQL Server 2000

## Stored Procedures

# Handbook

## 1

# Stored Procedures Overview

Welcome to the SQL Server 2000 Stored Procedures handbook. Here, we will cover the different types of stored procedures used in SQL Server 2000 and their usage. We will also examine the working of stored procedures, the potentially tricky areas, and how to avoid them.

Accessing and manipulating data within a database is a fairly straightforward operation. We can build a complete working application with four simple commands – SELECT, INSERT, DELETE, and UPDATE, and perform all the required tasks. The skill in working with databases lies in being able to not just work with these commands, but also complete each unit of work efficiently.

To achieve efficiency, a developer must consider a number of factors during development. However, we will concentrate on running T-SQL from within stored procedures, in this book. Stored procedures can take different forms of design and implementation, but the basics of the code are similar. In this chapter, we will examine what constitutes a stored procedure and discuss different types. We will cover:

❑ The difference between system stored procedures and user stored procedures

❑ Creating and designing stored procedures

❑ Using parameters and best practices

❑ Flow control statements

❑ Recursion

❑ Return values

# What is a Stored Procedure?

If a repetitive T-SQL task has to be executed within an application, then the best repository for it is a program called a **stored procedure**, stored in SQL Server. Storing the code inside the SQL Server object gives us many advantages, like:

- ❑ Security due to encryption
- ❑ Performance gains due to compilation
- ❑ Being able to hold the code in a central repository:
  - Altering the code in SQL Server without replicating in several different programs
  - Being able to keep statistics on the code to keep it optimized
- ❑ Reduction in the amount of data passed over a network by keeping the code on the server
- ❑ Hiding the raw data by allowing only stored procedures to gain access to the data

You may have executed some ad-hoc queries for tasks like inserting data, querying information in other systems, or creating new database objects such as tables. All these tasks can be placed within a stored procedure, so that any developer can run the same code without having to recreate the T-SQL commands. Also, generalising the code for all values makes it generic and reusable.

Stored procedures are more than just tools for performing repetitive tasks. They can ensure the integrity of data (through standalone stored procedures or triggers), behave as subroutines for performing part of a task that can be called from several routines (known as user-defined functions), or even act as SQL Server routines for everyone to use.

There are two main types of stored procedure – system stored procedures and user-defined stored procedures. We will see how these differ, in the next section. We also have extended stored procedures that can reside as either system or user-defined types. Extended stored procedures give functionality that is not necessarily contained within SQL Server, like allowing DOS commands to run and working with e-mail. It is also possible to create your own extended stored procedures. This book doesn't cover building extended stored procedures, as these are written using C++ libraries.

## System Stored Procedures

Although there is an engine that runs much of SQL Server, a number of stored procedures surround this. These are called while working with **Enterprise Manager**, or through a query tool, such as **Query Analyzer**. These procedures are installed with SQL Server, and hence, we don't have to create them.

Every time we add or modify a table, make a backup plan, or perform any other administrative function from within Enterprise Manager, we actually call a stored procedure specifically written to complete the desired action. These stored procedures are known as system stored procedures, which are functions that enhance the basic functionality of SQL Server itself, either by extending the functionality of an existing system stored procedure or by creating new functionality that enhances the basics of what is already there.

For example, the sp_who system stored procedure will list connections to SQL Server, including all the system running processes, but if you do not want to see those system processes, you can write a new sp_whouser system stored procedure based on sp_who by taking sp_who as a basis, and create the new procedure from that.

System stored procedures are prefixed by sp_, so it is not advisable to use sp_ for any of the stored procedures that we create, unless they form a part of our SQL Server installation. Creating a stored procedure prefixed with sp_ and placing it in the master database will make it available to any database without the need to prefix the stored procedure with the name of the database.

Lets clarify this with an example. If we take the sp_who stored procedure, call it sp_mywho, store it in the master database, and move to another database such as northwind, we can still execute sp_mywho, rather than having to specify the procedure in the fully qualified manner as master.dbo.sp_mywho.

Although SQL Server comes with many useful and relevant system stored procedures built in, there is always room for improvement. We will discuss how we can harness the full capablities of SQL Server by inspecting these and improve the usability of SQL Server by creating our own, in *Chapter 5*.

**If you want to extend the functionality of an existing system stored procedure, do not alter the existing procedure – create your own version instead.**

If we create our own system stored procedure then we will need to place them within all installations of SQL Server (an instance of SQL Server is a separate installation, and hence a separate entity) in our organization, to ensure consistency. There are several reasons for doing this. For example, it is possible to create development, testing, and production installations as completely separate entities. We may find the development and test instance on one machine, and the production instance on a different one.

We can see that there are three instances defined in the following screenshot – a Development instance, a Live instance, and a Local instance. The Development and Local instances reside on the same computer, while the Live instance is on a remote computer. Therefore, each instance would have its own stored procedures to perform the administrative tasks:

**7**

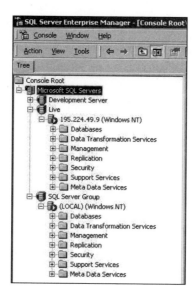

System stored procedures reside in the `master` database or the `model` database for each instance installed. Every stored procedure residing in the `model` database will be placed into any database that we create within our SQL Server instance, by default.

> **Each instance of SQL Server, even if there are several instances on the same machine, would have its own set of stored procedures.**

When we create a new database, it is based on the `model` database. Therefore, any new system or user stored procedures added to the `model` database will also be placed into each new database that we create.

It is rare to create system procedures that are specific to one database. Generally, they are implemented as user stored procedures. Now, let's take a look at them and see how these differ from system stored procedures.

## User Stored Procedures

A user stored procedure is any program that is stored and compiled within SQL Server (but not in the `master` database) and prefixed with `sp_`. User stored procedures can be categorized into three distinct types – user stored procedures, triggers, and user defined functions. Each of these types has its features, uses, limitations, and differences.

1. User defined stored procedures provide an interface to a set of processing without the need for the end user to know the structure of the tables, the business logic of the organization, or the mathematics involved, to produce the end result. They also provide a secure method, which along with other security measures, can result in a database where data is protected from malicious or accidental modifications.

2. A trigger is a stored procedure which fires when a specified table action takes place. You are also limited to certain code that you can place in a trigger, as you should not return any data from a trigger. We will see more of this in Chapter 7.

3. A user defined function is a stored procedure which can take parameters, but only return one item of information, either a scalar value or a table of data.

# Creating Stored Procedures

The creation process depends on what we want it to do – we can either build the whole procedure immediately, or build the T-SQL first (for more complex solutions), check its performance, and finally, place it in a stored procedure. Both ways require us to wrap the T-SQL code with the same CREATE PROCEDURE command.

Now let's take a look at the syntax for creating a stored procedure:

```
CREATE PROCEDURE procedurename [parameter1 datatype [length] [OUTPUT],
parameter2…]
AS
BEGIN
...
END
```

An example of a simple stored procedure follows, where two numbers are passed in and the midpoint of the two numbers is listed:

```
CREATE PROCEDURE ut_MidPoint @LowerNumber int, @HigherNumber int
AS
BEGIN

  DECLARE @Mid int
  IF @LowerNumber > @HigherNumber
    RAISERROR('You have entered your numbers the wrong way round',16,1)

  SET @Mid = ((@HigherNumber - @LowerNumber) / 2) + @LowerNumber

  SELECT @Mid
END
```

At the time of creation, SQL Server takes our code and parses it for any syntactical errors. Column names and variables are checked for existence at compilation. Even if they don't exist, any temporary tables created within the stored procedure will also pass the compilation stage. This is known as **deferred name resolution**. It can be an asset or a drawback, as we can create temporary tables that exist for the lifetime of the stored procedure execution only, which is desirable, but if we define a temporary table and get something wrong later on, such as a column name, then the compilation will not pick up this error.

While executing the CREATE PROCEDURE statement, errors will be reported. Once it is compiled, the details of the stored procedure are stored in three system tables in the concerned database:

❑   sysobjects
This table contains a row for each object that is created within the database. If you want to track an object in the database, you can use this as the main root. Apart from the object name and type, this table also keeps track of the object's owner and time of creation. This can be useful in crosschecking the contents of our source control system with our database.

❑   sysdepends
This table stores dependency information about objects. For example, when a stored procedure, view, or trigger is created, there can be references to other tables, views, or procedures within it. These references are known as dependencies. If one of the dependent objects alters, we may need to recompile the stored procedure. For example, if we alter an index on a table, we should recompile every dependent object.

❑   syscomments
This holds the original SQL definition statements of the stored procedure. It also holds details of views, rules, defaults, triggers, CHECK constraints, and DEFAULT constraints.

It is possible to interrogate these data. By looking for rows with a P in the sysobjects table, we can obtain all the stored procedures. From that, we can find out when the stored procedure was created, and also move to the syscomments table by using the ID to retrieve detailed information about the procedure itself, like, if it is encrypted or not.

These tables are safe only for interrogation, although details within them can always change between SQL Server releases. One of the best methods to ensure that the code stored in your source control system matches that within your database is to check if the dates and times match or are within a few seconds of each other.

**!** **Although we have mentioned these tables, we strongly advise that you should never alter any information in these tables directly.**

**10**

## *Performance Consideration*

When a stored procedure is created, it passes through several steps. First of all, the T-SQL is parsed and resolved, saved to the disk, and stored in SQL Server. The first time the procedure is executed, the procedure is retrieved and optimized, on the basis of any data queries and values passed through parameters. SQL Server will inspect the code and try to use the best indexes on the tables, which are referenced by checking the statistics that are held for those tables.

The query plan is then cached within SQL Server, ready for any further executions. SQL Server will always use this plan, providing it doesn't retire the plan. Thus, the performance gain of stored procedures comes from compiled cached plans.

## *Network Consideration*

You may consider passing T-SQL statements to insert a row into a table, with very few characters. However, creating a stored procedure and passing only the name of the stored procedure, parameters, and their values reduces the characters needed. We can see the extra overhead imposed by the T-SQL statements on our network by multiplying this difference by the number of calls being made. This can be a significant issue, especially if we are using it over the Internet.

Compare the next two statements with each other:

```
INSERT INTO EmployeeTerritories (EmployeeID, TerritoryID)
VALUES (3,12345)
```

```
Ins_EmployeeTerritories @empId=3,@terrId=12345
```

The first statement has 74 characters, while the second has 46 characters, differing by a mere 28 characters. However, if this was a more column-intensive insert, with 10,000 of these in a day, for example, this amounts to almost 280k of wasted bandwidth! What if an image data type was being uploaded or downloaded? Anything that is of binary data type, such as images or sounds, and so on, is sent as binary values. These are converted to character strings, and this will double the size of the ad-hoc query that we are sending, when using T-SQL inline.

# Why Use Stored Procedures?

By using stored procedures, we can reduce the time a process can take, as stored procedures are compiled.

Another gain from using stored procedures is that they are much simpler to maintain, as compared to raw T-SQL code. Since the stored procedure is held centrally within the database, any required bug fix, upgrade, or modification can be completed centrally, thus reducing the downtime. If the code is embedded within a program, as in VB.NET, we have to not only change the code in one central place but also distribute it to every client running the software. Modification of web sites also brings in its own set of problems, and rolling out a new ASP.NET client can prove problematic. This can be settled by using stored procedures.

The code in a stored procedure is executed in a single batch of work. This means that it is not necessary to include a GO command while writing code for procedures. SQL Server will take any of those statements and implicitly execute them, as a batch.

Perhaps, the greatest reason to create a stored procedure rather than use inline T-SQL, is security. As we will discuss in *Chapter 8*, we have several security options at our fingertips while using a stored procedure. Along with other security measures, it helps to ensure that we can lock down our database from prying eyes.

> *Stored procedures are rarely used for creating other database objects with the exception of temporary tables, which are special tables created to complete a task within a stored procedure. There is more on temporary tables in Chapter 4.*

# Replication

Stored procedures can also be used to work with databases involved in replication. By creating a specialized custom stored procedure, which is placed on each publishing database, it is possible to resolve any row UPDATE conflicts that may occur. Stored procedures can aid in replication processing, and also ensure that a replicated database is optimized. We won't be teaching you about replication in this book, but we bring up the subject to ensure that you are aware of potential problems that can arise with stored procedures in a replication scenario.

Consider a scenario where either a stored procedure or T-SQL updates or deletes a large number of rows. We can't really put a deterministic figure on this, as there are a large number of factors, such as connection between the databases, network traffic, network size, and data type content of each row, defining this level.

For example, the publisher places each update into the log reader for publication to each subscriber of the database. The Distribution Agent takes one row at a time, distributes them to the subscriber, and updates the subscriber database. If there is more than one subscriber, or if there is a delay due to connection speed or network traffic, the subscriber can lag behind, if there is no break in processing at the publisher's side.

In a real life scenario, at one installation, we had a very fast publisher and subscriber link (between London and New York). Traffic on one table was relatively light, but due to stock market conditions an update had to take place. The developer in question didn't realise that they had to update 100,000 rows, so off they went, and altered the data. The publisher updated fairly quickly, but the subscriber took 3 hours to catch up.

How does replication, and problems like this fit into this book? In the above example, if the developer had placed the updates in a stored procedure and made it a **procedure execution article**, then SQL Server would have replicated the execution of the stored procedure and not the updates that took place.

**!** **You have to be 100% sure that the data in the publisher and the subscriber databases are consistent. If not, you can have a failure on one of the databases, but a success on another, thus compounding the data inconsistency. This can come about as a result of other transactions and data modifications being successful on the publisher, but not yet applied by the log reader on the subscriber.**

It's preferable to have the stored procedure set up as a **serializable procedure execution article**. By setting the isolation level to SERIALIZABLE within the stored procedure, we can make a stored procedure into this form. We'll see more information on isolation levels in Chapter 3.

If we have an isolation level that can allow dirty reads, then we can insert data into a table before a previous modification has been committed.

# Designing Good Stored Procedures

Before we go any further, let's look at some general principles for designing good stored procedures. You will find these ideas reinforced as you move through the book.

1.  As with any other programming language – keep it simple. Don't make your procedure complex to read and understand if it is only going to save a few microseconds of processing time. If a stored procedure is complex to understand, then applying bug fixes or upgrading will need a formidable effort.

2.  Document your code, especially if you have to create a complex section of code. Throughout the stored procedure, place comments with a description of the stored procedure and any changes made at the top. This is even more crucial if the source control system that you are using doesn't have this ability.

3.  At processing time, T-SQL works well with a set. Therefore, avoid cursors wherever possible; even if it means using two or three steps or maybe even a temporary table. This rule will be covered in detail in *Chapter 3*.

    Don't rule out cursors totally, though. There will be times, although relatively rare, when they will be more beneficial to the overall processing.

4.  If you pass parameters, then ensure that the values are within an acceptable range, especially if the parameter is optional and a value of NULL is permissible. If this is the case, then keep results in mind when this parameter forms part of a WHERE filter or a JOIN criterion.

5.  Always clean up. If you have used a cursor, close and deallocate it, so that memory and resources are freed up. Similarly, if you are using temporary tables, ensure that you explicitly drop them. A temporary table defined within a stored procedure can exist only for the lifetime of that process. However, if the stored procedure has been called from a parent process, and if it is an iterative process, then the temporary table may exist beyond the lifetime of the process.

    By dropping the temporary table explicitly, even if the code is moved from the stored procedure and run as standalone code within Query Analyzer, it will ensure that the table is cleared up. If you do not do this, then the temporary table will remain until the Query Analyzer session is closed, the temporary table is dropped through T-SQL code from within that Query Analyzer session, or SQL Server is recycled.

6.  When a stored procedure is complete either through an error or a successful process, ensure that you return a value. This is a simple method of checking that the stored procedure has terminated as you were expecting, and if not, then you can then deal with the problem within the calling procedure.

# Data integrity

Within a database, there are three different levels of integrity – **domain**, **entity**, and **referential**.

❑   **Domain integrity**
    Domain integrity ensures that the values for a specific column are valid and meet the relevant business rules. This is enforced through CHECK constraints, DEFAULT values, and FOREIGN KEY constraints.

❑   **Entity integrity**
    Entity integrity ensures that every row within a table is unique. This integrity is enforced through UNIQUE constraints and PRIMARY KEYS.

❑ **Referential integrity**
Referential integrity ensures that relationships between tables are maintained.
It can be enforced through FOREIGN KEYS as well as **cascading updates**.
This is the only type of integrity that is enforced by stored procedures.

*When a deletion or modification is performed on the parent table, SQL Server
also deletes or modifies all children of any table referenced by a foreign key.
This is known as cascading updates, and is set up at table creation.*

We will examine data integrity in *Chapter 7*, when we look at triggers, which are ideal
to ensure referential integrity.

# *Database Integrity Checks*

Even SQL Server can suffer from an odd glitch, whereby the database or the data in a
table may get corrupted. For example, there may be a fault with the network card or the
network router, which may result in generation of packets that corrupt the database. This
is rare but it can happen through no fault of the SQL Server, but we still need to be
aware of it, and have checks in place for recovering quickly from such a scenario.

Every night on our production server, once the overnight processing and backups have
been done, special stored procedures execute T-SQL commands to check if everything
is in order. These are mainly **DBCC (Database Console Commands)** statements, which
run when system usage is low (as they can be quite CPU and process-intensive).

The system procedures, which run these commands, are usually placed in jobs. If an
error occurs, these procedures will fail, and hence the job fails too. It will then produce
a page or e-mail, so that DBAs can check and fix the error manually. These DBCC
commands are usually run to list errors, but it is also possible to set them up to
automatically correct the errors. This needs extreme care, however.

We can also expand this by building stored procedures to be executed when SQL
Server starts up, known as **recycled procedures**, which can be used for checking the
integrity of the database. For example, we can set up auto reboot when the server
gives the 'blue screen of death', so that when the server reboots, SQL Server also
reboots, and is available for use again. By building a stored procedure that checks the
tables and data, or maybe even automatically fixes problems found, so that we are
back to a stable scenario after the crash.

If you meet the 'blue screen of death', it is advisable to carry lots of checks on the data
as well as the transaction log. Many corporations include their overnight checks as part
of the startup check. Thus, you can really gain by having stored procedures that run
when the SQL Server automatically starts up.

By executing the following system stored procedure, it's possible to check if this option
is set for the database:

```
sp_configure 'scan for startup procs'
```

If you receive the following message, the configuration option 'scan for startup procs' does not exist:

*Server: Msg 15123, Level 16, State 1, Procedure sp_configure, Line 78*

Then you need to run the following. This message indicates that advanced options are not set to be displayed, and the advanced option setting is:

```
EXEC sp_configure 'show advanced option',1
GO
RECONFIGURE
```

Valid configuration options are:

| | name | minimum | maximum | config_value | run_value |
|---|---|---|---|---|---|
| 1 | scan for startup procs | 0 | 1 | 0 | 0 |

The first column is the name of the option, the next two are the minimum and maximum values that the option can have, config_value is what the option is currently set to by sp_configure, whereas run_value is the setting when the option is actually used by SQL Server.

If a value of 1 is returned, then you can create and set up procedures to run automatically. To set this option you will execute:

```
sp_configure 'scan for startup procs',1
```

If we wanted a stored procedure to run when SQL Server starts up, we can do this through the sp_procoption system stored procedure. I won't give a specific example, as stored procedures designed to run at startup need a great deal of consideration. However, once you have your procedure, the syntax is demonstrated here:

```
sp_procoption @ProcName = 'ut_startsproc', @OptionName = 'startup',
@OptionValue = 'true'
```

> *Note the case on the parameters. On most installations this is not vital, but if you use a collation that is case sensitive you will need to use the above case.*

**!** **If SQL Server refuses to start and the problem can be an auto start procedure, then you can start SQL Server from a DOS prompt with minimal configuration to allow you to remove any problem, by using the -f option as shown below**

```
>sqlservr -c -f
```

*Stored procedures are certainly not replacements for functionality that already exists within the SQL Server, such as CHECK constraints. Procedures, such as triggers, can supplement these. If the CHECK constraint is more complex, it can be achieved with the CHECK constraint code. Stored procedures are also not meant for processes that run only once. The only exception to this rule will be if the procedure were a part of the setup process for building a new database or something similar.*

# Calling a Stored Procedure

Many people tend to miss a performance enhancement related to executing or calling a stored procedure. For example, if you wanted to call the [Ten Most Expensive Products] stored procedure in the northwind database, you can simply do it as:

```
[Ten Most Expensive Products]
```

You can skip EXEC(UTE), but you will need it if you run one stored procedure within another.

However, this is not the most efficient way to call a stored procedure. When such a command is processed, SQL Server has a hierarchical method of finding a stored procedure and executing it. First of all, it will take the login ID of the user who wants to execute the procedure and see if a stored procedure of that name exists. If it doesn't, then SQL Server will look for the stored procedure under the DBO login. Hence, always fully qualify your stored procedure with the owner.

# Rules for Stored Procedures

The biggest mistake anyone can make in naming stored procedures is to prefix them with sp_. This generally happens with developers who come from VB or VC background, where they get used to prefixing objects with their type.

*You will find stored procedures within SQL Server that start with sp_ but these are reserved for system stored procedures. We will look at them in Chapter 6.*

So how do we name our stored procedures? There are different naming standards and methods that we can employ. However, a commonly followed one is to prefix the stored procedure with what it does. If a stored procedure inserts data, then it will be prefixed with ins_, if it's returning rows of data then we will use sel_, and so on. This naming convention is for main stored procedures that are used as part of the system. When it comes to writing procedures to be used for supporting the system, then we may prefix the procedure with util_ for utility, or sup_ for support. Note that following this convention, triggers would be prefixed with tr_, and user defined functions with fn_.

If you are using a common database for several applications, then prefix stored procedures for common functionality with the name of the database, and ones specific to a separate system with a pseudonym for that system. For example, if `northwind` has a procedure that accesses `pubs`, then we will name it as `pub_sel_Authors`.

> *This naming convention is needed only when cross-database or cross-system functionality is included.*

Other rules include not using spaces in the name, or any 'specialized' characters such as %, &, and so on. Underscores, _, are allowed, and are the preferred method of naming tables and columns rather than using spaces. If you do wish to use a space instead, then while working with the object you will need to surround the name with square brackets.

Most procedures have parameters passed to them. It is vital that every parameter is tested to ensure that its value is within a valid range, especially in stored procedures for updation, where a parameter is used as part of the `WHERE` row filter criteria, if an invalid value is submitted we can end up updating every row in the table. Of course, it is impossible to check for a wrong value that unfortunately fits in the range.

One of the problems with stored procedures is the lack of comments within them. Even the simplest of stored procedures should have comments. Every stored procedure should also contain a quick description of itself, at the top. A more complex code should be properly commented throughout and the comments should be up to date.

When developing a stored procedure, we should keep a record of it in some source control system, like **Microsoft Visual SourceSafe**. The latest version will always be within our database, but what happens if we release the latest version and there is a problem? How can we rollback quickly to a previous version of the code? You may also develop an enhancement to the system, but may have to fix a bug also. Source control can help us here, as it allows us to easily access the production version of the stored procedure, make the change, document it, and perhaps even branch the code, so that the whole process of bug fixing while developing is completed in a secure environment.

> *If you use the source control software, ensure that it resides on a drive that is backed up nightly.*

The source control system may also be capable of automatically updating comments defining the version, the date and time of the last check-in. This can prevent rogue updates to the stored procedure code, which hasn't gone through the source control system, but it is not foolproof. It is possible to create a system stored procedure capable of checking this comment value, with a value entered within a system table when the stored procedure was created.

# Modifying Stored Procedures

If we drop a stored procedure and then use CREATE PROCEDURE to create it again, we would have to reassign the execute permissions that existed on the stored procedure before. If the permissions are to be retained, then we can use the ALTER PROCEDURE statement. The downside is that the creation date is not altered, so if you do have tools to check what procedures have changed since a specific date, then ALTER PROCEDURE will not pick this up.

The ALTER PROCEDURE statement will also reset the QUOTED_IDENTIFIER and ANSI_NULL parameters, just as a DROP and CREATE will, so take care to maintain the same settings, as there were before, when working on a stored procedure.

> *It is best to have these as company standards so that problems don't exist upon any alteration.*

It is also possible to rename a stored procedure in T-SQL by using sp_rename. If you rename a stored procedure, run sp_depends, which will give a list of all the dependencies on the procedure. Any other stored procedures listed will also have to be modified, otherwise they will not be able to find this procedure.

> *The system stored procedure sp_depends will list all the objects dependent on the object name that is passed to it.*

## Recompiling

When a stored procedure is created and placed in SQL Server, it will sit in the database until it is executed for the first time. At that point, SQL Server compiles the procedure optimising it based on current statistics on the tables used. If it is a subsequent execution, then there are two possible scenarios:

❑ **The stored procedure is no longer in the procedure cache**
This means that SQL Server has aged the plan out of memory. At this point the stored procedure is recompiled back into the cache and then executed.

❑ **The stored procedure is still in the procedure cache**
Then, the execution plan is taken from the cache and executed.

If an index or even columns are added to a table, and if they are likely to alter the query plan that has been built up for the set of tables used, then we should recompile all the dependent stored procedures, otherwise our stored procedure may not utilize the best method for accessing the data.

It is possible to set up a stored procedure to recompile every time it is executed, for example, when the stored procedure is run weekly to gather information about what has happened to the data over the week. Here, you may build a stored procedure that takes a look at share price movements and volumes of shares traded at that price to produce information for a graph depicting how a stock market has reacted to different types of movements. Another example can be when you have a database that holds archived data, and, every weekend the expired production data is placed in the archive database and a process is run to calculate stats on the historical data. Another scenario will be when a parameter coming into a stored procedure alters the basis of a join or a filter, which in turn, alters the execution plan wildly.

In all these situations, performance gains can be obtained if the stored procedure was recompiled before each execution. Keep in mind that these are stored procedures that process a heavy workload, but run very infrequently.

The syntax for adding WITH RECOMPILE is:

```
CREATE PROCEDURE name @parameters datatype(datalength) WITH RECOMPILE
```

> **Use this option with care and only if it totally necessary for your solution. Using this option will slow down the execution of the stored procedure, as there will be a recompilation with each execution.**

You can also manually recompile a stored procedure using the sp_recompile command. You will use this if you alter indexes on a table and do not expect a SQL Server recycle prior to the stored procedure being used. More on this subject will be covered in Chapter 2.

# Parameter Usage

Data will be passed in and out of a stored procedure, even when the purpose of the procedure is not to return information. All variables defined as parameters have to be prefixed with an @ sign. The normal practice is to define input parameters before any output parameters.

As with any column in a database, use the data type that is most appropriate for the parameter and if the parameter has to match with a column in the table, then ensure that both the data types match exactly.

If the parameter does not match a column but will be still used, for example, as a join condition or a filter condition, then use a data type and size appropriate to the type of data, rather than have everything as character data type. Also, wherever possible, use varchar or nvarchar rather than char, just as you will in your inline T-SQL, which will avoid unnecessary spaces being passed across networks.

# Flow control

This section will deal with ensuring that our stored procedure flows correctly. Although we will cover some T-SQL statements here, as we have indicated earlier, it is not within the scope of the book to teach you how these statements should be coded.

## Code Blocks/ BEGIN...END

When working with decisions, functions, or loops, there will be many instances when we have to execute more than one line of code. SQL Server has to know when a block of code starts and ends. In programming languages, we will find END IF statements or LOOP . . . UNTIL structures where there are keywords for defining the beginning and end of the block. This is not the case within SQL Server, which uses a BEGIN . . . END structure instead.

In the following snippet, we have two similar stored procedures. The difference is in the use of the BEGIN . . . END code block. Executing the first one will execute the second PRINT statement, as the IF statement will take only the first line as part of the decision:

```
CREATE PROCEDURE ut_NoBeginEnd
AS
BEGIN
    DECLARE @var1 int, @var2 int
    SET @var1 = 1
    SET @var2 = 2
    IF @var1 = @var2
       PRINT @var1
    PRINT @var2
END
```

Compare it with the following snippet. Here, neither of the PRINT statements will be executed:

```
CREATE PROCEDURE ut_BeginEnd
AS
BEGIN

    DECLARE @var1 int, @var2 int
    SET @var1 = 1
    SET @var2 = 2
    IF @var1 = @var2
```

```
    BEGIN
       PRINT @var1
       PRINT @var2
    END
  END
```

Now that we know how to demarcate blocks in our code, we can look at the IF statement in more detail.

# *Decisions*

There are two main ways to make decision in SQL Server. The first one makes decisions throughout our code, whereas the second one bases decisions on data returned in specific columns from the returned rows. There are other statements, such as NULLIF, which will return a NULL value if two expressions are similar, but this isn't decision processing and is more of a comparison. Let's start with the first IF statement.

## IF...ELSE

This is a simple Boolean decision processing strategy, where a statement is evaluated as either TRUE or FALSE. If the statement is TRUE, it will process the statements immediately following the IF. If the statement is FALSE, then it will process the statements following the ELSE statement, if there is one defined. If there is no ELSE statement, then processing will continue after the END of that statement block.

It is possible to evaluate more than a simple a = b type of statement; we can even include SELECT statements under the IF. However, you may find that having a SELECT statement within an IF, rather than placing the value into a variable and then testing it, is not as cost-effective. If we look at the execution plans of the following two statements, we can see the huge difference it makes while processing.

The first statement works faster, as a simple SELECT statement takes the table and processes the data.

```
DECLARE @AvgFound Money

SELECT @AvgFound = AVG(UnitPrice) FROM [Order Details]

IF @AvgFound < 10
   Print 'Less than 10'
ELSE
   Print 'More than 10'
```

Here's the execution plan of the above (we will have a more detailed explanation of the execution plan in the next chapter):

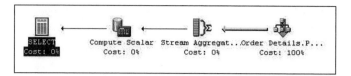

Here's the second code snippet:

```
IF (SELECT AVG(UnitPrice) FROM [Order Details]) < 10
   Print 'Less than 10'
ELSE
   Print 'More than 10'
```

The execution plan for the second statement is more complex:

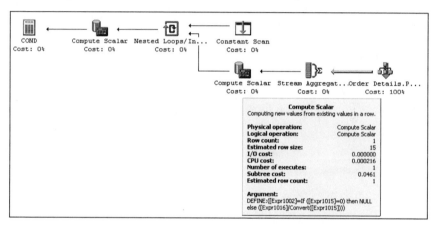

By letting the cursor hover over some of the details, you can see the underlying processing.

# CASE

Unlike the IF statement that is placed in code as part of a decision-making process, CASE can be found within any of the SELECT, UPDATE, and INSERT T-SQL data statements.

CASE statements won't work for DELETEs. To implement the CASE statement, two different methods can be employed. The first method is known as the simple CASE function. Here, an expression, which is to be tested, is the same throughout the possible options available. Let's look at its syntax:

```
CASE input_expression
   WHEN when_expression THEN result_expression
     [...n]
   [
     ELSE else_result_expression
   ]
END [AS column_alias]
```

This will be used, for example, when we have a column containing several values and we want to translate this value into something more meaningful, such as the output in the column. We can also include other SELECT statements. We can see this in action in the following code:

```
CREATE PROCEDURE ut_CASE_with_SELECT
AS
BEGIN

SELECT OrderId, Discount,
CASE Discount
WHEN 0 THEN 'No Discount'
WHEN (SELECT MAX(Discount) FROM [Order Details]) THEN 'Top Discount'
ELSE 'Average'
END AS Disc
FROM [order details]

END
```

There is a problem concerning the NULL values. In the following T-SQL, the Fax column contains either a fax number or NULL. Here, we test the column to check whether it's equal to another value however, we can't do this for NULL, where the test is ignored:

```
CREATE PROCEDURE ut_CASE_NULL_NotWorking
AS
BEGIN

SELECT CompanyName, Phone,
CASE Fax
WHEN NULL THEN 'No Fax'
ELSE Fax
END AS Fax
FROM Customers

END
```

However, by using the second type of CASE statement, we can search for NULL values. Again, let's begin by looking at its syntax:

```
CASE
WHEN Boolean_expression THEN true_result_expression
[...n]
[ELSE else_result_expression]
END
```

To solve the problem in our previous example, we can code the example as:

```
CREATE PROCEDURE ut_CASE_With_Null
AS
BEGIN

SELECT CompanyName, Phone,
```

```
CASE
WHEN FAX Is NULL THEN 'No Fax'
ELSE Fax
END AS Fax
FROM Customers

END
```

## GOTO label

As with programming languages, labels are frowned on and it is better to avoid using them. However, there is one exception – it is advisable to use them when you are branching to the end of a procedure for doing some cleanup or error coding. At times, even this can get messy, as you may have to code a GOTO around a GOTO label to avoid error processing. To clarify this, let's examine the following code:

```
IF @@ERROR > 0
  GOTO Error
  ...

GOTO ProcEnd
Error:
  ...

ProcEnd:
  RETURN
```

It is necessary to use GOTO ProcEnd for avoiding normal processing from slipping into the Error: labelled routine. In this instance it is not too confusing, but it can be, in complex stored procedures.

Now that we know how to make decisions, we can move on to processing information iteratively.

# Loops

At this point, we will not look at looping through a cursor, as cursors are covered in Chapter 3, which leaves us with one method for looping around a set of code.

## The WHILE Loop

To repeat a block of code, SQL Server gives us the WHILE statement. This will continue executing the block and forming the loop, until either the Boolean expression returns FALSE or we BREAK out of the code. The syntax is:

```
WHILE Boolean_expression
   { sql_statement | statement_block }
   [ BREAK ]
   { sql_statement | statement_block }
   [ CONTINUE ]
```

BREAK breaks the loop and passes the control to the statements outside the code block, while the CONTINUE statement will resume processing from the beginning of the loop.

We can see this in the following stored procedure:

```
CREATE PROCEDURE ut_WhileLoop
AS
BEGIN
   DECLARE @var1 int, @var2 int

   SET @var1 = 1
   SET @var2 = 1
   WHILE @var1 < 10
   BEGIN
     IF @var2 > 100
       BREAK
     SET @var2 = @var2 + @var2
     SET @var1 = @var1 + 1
   END
   PRINT 'Var1=' + CONVERT(CHAR(3),@var1) + ' and Var2=' +
   CONVERT(CHAR(3),@var2)

END
```

As with the IF statement, its common to see a WHILE statement working with a SELECT criterion.

## *Pausing and Halting execution*

The WAITFOR function can be used to pause a stored procedure for a certain amount of time. Pausing for a specific time will allow a stored procedure to run at the same time every single day. If you want the procedure to run only on certain days of the week, you can surround the code by a check to ensure that you are on a valid day.

There is a more efficient and controlled method to achieve this and also make the environment more secure, and that is to use **SQL Server Agent** and create a job. Here, you can provide various functionalities, such as e-mail notification of any failures, a more controlled start and end timings, as well as logging of the success or failure of the task. You can pause a stored procedure in multiples of a minute within a job in SQL Server Agent.

**Be extremely careful in your use of WAITFOR(). It will stop the processing of any stored procedure containing this statement until the time is reached or until the delay as expired. Any locks in this stored procedure will obviously stop any other stored procedure until the locks in the WAITFOR() procedure are released. Although it's a useful command, you can easily put your system in trouble if you get it wrong, for example, when you get the delay calculation wrong.**

# Nesting in Stored Procedures

Recursion is a scenario where a procedure calls itself. You will rarely come across these, and try to avoid them wherever possible as they can create problems. At times, a simple error in the code, such as an unexpected input data parameter, can cause your server to hang due to tempdb filling up. You may come across this when working with interest calculations in bank transactions.

SQL Server puts a limit of 32 on the number of times that a stored procedure can be called by itself. However, things can go wrong even in that time frame, so it's always advisable to have a good 'drop out' scenario. One method is to check the recursion level that we are at by using the @@NESTLEVEL system configuration function. To demonstrate nesting levels through recursion, check the following system function that we have to add to SQL Server. This example calculates the factorial of a number:

```
CREATE PROCEDURE ut_Factorial @ValIn bigint, @ValOut bigint output
AS
BEGIN
  IF @ValIn > 20
  BEGIN
    PRINT 'Invalid starting point. Has to be <= 20'
    RETURN -99
  END

  DECLARE @WorkValIn bigint, @WorkValOut bigint

  IF @ValIn != 1
    BEGIN
      SET @WorkValIn = @ValIn - 1
      PRINT @@NESTLEVEL
      EXEC ut_Factorial @WorkValIn, @WorkValOut OUTPUT
      SET @ValOut = @WorkValOut * @ValIn
    END
  ELSE
    SET @ValOut = 1

END
```

As the query optimizer tries to resolve the execution of ut_Factorial, which of course, doesn't exist until the stored procedure is placed into SQL Server, you will get the following error when you execute the above code.

Cannot add rows to sysdepends for the current stored procedure because it depends on the missing object 'ut_Factorial'. The stored procedure will still be created.

We know that the maximum nesting level will be the first value passed through @ValIn, as it reduces by one on each call to the procedure. We also have to check that we do not have more than a 20 level recursion invoked by the test at the top of the procedure.

We can see this in action with the following T-SQL code. The first digits listed will be the PRINT statement on the @@NESTLEVEL, which will show our current nesting level. We have to drop out here, if we have nested too many times:

```
DECLARE @FactIn int, @FactOut int
SET @FactIn = 8
EXEC Factorial @FactIn, @FactOut OUTPUT

PRINT 'Factorial of ' + CONVERT(varchar(3),@FactIn) + ' is ' +
CONVERT(varchar(20),@FactOut)
```

*If you execute a stored procedure that calls another stored procedure, the called stored procedure can access all objects created by the first stored procedure, including temporary tables, but cannot access values in the variables defined in the first procedure. Variable scope is local to that 'call'.*

Recursion of stored procedures should be avoided wherever possible, as it can cause more problems than it solves. This is true especially when we are not certain that the data will never cause a problem. Also, try to avoid creating temporary tables because if you attempt to recreate the table on the second or subsequent calls, it will already exist and the procedure will fail. In this scenario, we would create the temporary table if the @@NESTLEVEL is 1, and ignore that statement at any other call level.

# Returning Values

In most of our stored procedures, we will either modify or return a set of data. You may also wish to return some value that signifies a successful or failure. In the remaining stored procedures, we will perform some business functionality, where we may return values calculated during that time.

There are different ways to return this sort of information and it depends on the number of values we wish to return and also how we wish to handle these within either other stored procedures or calling programs. Let's look at each method now.

## *RETURN*

This is either implicit or explicit within a stored procedure, and will execute as the last statement of a stored procedure. This statement terminates the stored procedure immediately, with no further statements executing after this statement.

If RETURN is specified, then a value of 0 is returned, however, we can also return our own integer value. The normal practice is that a negative number returned indicates that an error has occurred. A positive number indicates some other reason, but it is often used to return the number of rows that have been returned or modified within a statement.

To demonstrate this, let's create a procedure that runs against the `Categories` table in `northwind` and returns the rows from the table and the number of rows found.

```
CREATE PROCEDURE sel_Categories
AS
BEGIN
  DECLARE @Rc INT
  SELECT CategoryName, Description
  FROM Categories

  SET @Rc = @@ROWCOUNT

  RETURN @Rc
  -- Any statement here will not execute
END
GO
```

If you are wish to execute this statement in the Query Analyzer, then you need to define it as:

```
DECLARE @RcRet INT
EXEC @RcRet = sel_Categories
SELECT @RcRet "No. Rows"
```

It is necessary to have a local variable defined for the return value to be placed at the end of the calling procedure. The final line simply prints out the return value.

> *If you return the value from a local variable, the setting of that local variable cannot be NULL, and has to be a valid integer number.*

The next section examines returning more than one value or non-integer values.

## OUTPUT

Even if a RETURN statement is defined, we can supplement or replace this by output parameters. There is a limit of 2,100 to the number of parameters we can define. When we come close to this number, we should review what we are doing.

Defining an output parameter is similar to an input parameter – define the name of the variable prefixed with an @ sign, the data type, and the precision, where necessary, and then finally, the keyword OUTPUT.

After taking the stored procedure above and altering it slightly, we can see:

```
CREATE PROCEDURE sel_CategoriesWithOutput @Rcnt INT OUTPUT
AS
BEGIN
  SELECT CategoryName, Description
  FROM Categories

  SET @Rcnt = @@ROWCOUNT
```

```
       RETURN 1
       -- Any statement here will not execute
    END
    GO
```

As we can see, we are still returning a value as well as the number of rows found in a parameter. To execute this stored procedure, we define the return code variable, as we did in the previous example, but also define the output parameter with the OUTPUT keyword:

```
    DECLARE @OutParm INT, @RetVal INT
    EXEC @RetVal = sel_CategoriesWithOutput @OutParm OUTPUT
    SELECT @OutParm "Output Parm", @RetVal "Return Value"
```

Now we will look at the last method of retrieving information from a stored procedure.

## Single Row of Data

Ignoring the fact that stored procedures will return data from a SELECT statement listing information that meets a specified set of criteria, it is also possible to return either a second set of records or a single row rowset that is the only information returned, neither of which can be attributed directly to a table. This is an unusual scenario and will only come about if you felt that the number of output parameters is excessive or if you are returning a set of information that will be simpler to use in the calling object as a tabular set of information rather than a set of values. A good example of this would be if the stored procedure was called as part of an Excel spreadsheet.

## When an Error Occurs

Working with errors brings up several other considerations besides simply returning a value, which we will examine in detail in the next chapter.

## Other Issues with Returning Values

It is possible to return a table as a data type from a stored procedure. A **table data type** is a special data type, and is simply a method to hold a temporary table in a variable rather than tempdb or your own database.

This data type should not be passed as the output parameter of a stored procedure, since the calling routine may not be able to handle that data type. If you want to return a rowset, it will be better to simply do that using the SELECT statement.

Ensure that the data types you are retrieving from a data source such as a table match the data types of the input and output parameters – there will definitely be problems when the data types don't match. For instance, a data type definition of CHAR(4) will always be 4 characters long. So if you placed 'TX' into a variable it will be 'TX  ' (two spaces appended). However, it will always be stored as 'TX' with no spaces in a VARCHAR. Here you will only be sending two extra characters with CHAR, but if you are doing this many thousands of times, it becomes evident that VARCHAR be a better option.

Use VARCHAR wherever you can, and INT instead of BIGINT, to reduce the overhead of passing unnecessary data. Also send at least the minimum number of characters so that potential errors with a data type that is too small are not created.

# Restoring the Example Databases to their Default Condition

We'll make much use of the pubs and Northwind databases for our examples in this book. Here's a tip for restoring them to their default condition. First, login as SA in Query Analyzer. Then, go to your SQL Server installation directory and browse to the INSTALL subdirectory under it. From this directory, run either the INSTPUBS.SQL or INSTNWND.SQL script in Query Analyzer to refresh the pubs or Northwind database, respectively. If your server is only in integrated mode, run the scripts, and then run the following script in the Query Analyzer:

```
USE dbname
GO
EXEC sp_changedbowner 'domain\userID'
GO
EXEC sp_changedbowner sa
GO
```

Here, dbname is either pubs or Northwind, and domain\userID will be your domain name and the user ID that you are logged in as while running the scripts. Note, that the quotes are necessary because of the backslash (\) in the string. This script will restore your pubs or Northwind database to the default condition. Note it will also put the guest account back into both databases – we'll talk more about the security issues raised by this account in Chapter 8.

# Summary

In this chapter, we covered several issues concerning stored procedures and have set the scene for the forthcoming chapters of this book. We have looked at what a stored procedure is, how to create one, and how stored procedures can ensure your development runs at its optimum. Even when a database is being replicated, stored procedures can and do improve performance.

Don't just forget your stored procedures once they are created, just as you will never forget your indexes. When a new index is added to a table, or any sort of modification is done to any dependent objects, the whole query tree requires compilation.

Finally, don't make stored procedures what they are not. Don't replace SQL Server functionality such as CHECK constraints with a stored procedure unless the CHECK constraint doesn't offer enough functionality

We shall return to these ideas in more detail as we progress though the book.

# SQL Server 2000

**Stored Procedures**

## Handbook

**2**

# 2

# Optimizing and Debugging

In this chapter, we will be discussing optimizing SQL Server's stored procedures. Here, our focus will not be on optimizing the SQL statements themselves, but instead, how SQL statements can be optimized within the context of a stored procedure.

In this chapter, we will also discuss error handling, signaling error conditions, and debugging stored procedures.

# Optimizing Stored Procedures

The performance of a stored procedure is largely dependent on the nature of the T-SQL code within it; however, there are a few things you can do to improve the overall performance of the stored procedure. As we mentioned, in this section, we won't specifically look at optimizing T-SQL code; instead, we will look at the general optimization techniques that we can apply to any stored procedure.

Let's now take a look at these general optimization techniques.

## SET NOCOUNT ON

SET NOCOUNT ON is probably the most important optimization setting for stored procedures. By using it, we can greatly reduce the time and network bandwidth used for executing stored procedures, especially the complex ones.

When a T-SQL DML statement (SELECT, INSERT, UPDATE, or DELETE) is executed, statistics relating to the number of rows affected by those statements are passed back to the client for interpretation. For example, suppose we execute the following statement in Query Analyzer:

```
SELECT *
FROM dbo.Customers
WHERE CustomerID LIKE 'AN%'
```

After execution, we will receive a rowset, and the statistic about the number of rows affected, such as:

```
(2 row(s) affected)
```

This is not particularly bothersome, and at times, can be even useful when executing a single command in an adhoc fashion. Now, consider the following example of a stored procedure:

```
CREATE PROCEDURE TestDataGenerator
AS

    DECLARE @count INT

    IF OBJECT_ID('dbo.TestDataTable') IS NULL
    BEGIN
      CREATE TABLE dbo.TestDataTable
      (
        IDCOL INT PRIMARY KEY,
        VarCharCol  VARCHAR(255)
      )
    END

    SELECT @count=1

    WHILE @count<100
    BEGIN
      INSERT TestDataTable(IDCOL, VarCharCol)
      SELECT  @count,
        REPLICATE(CHAR((@count%26)+65),@count%255)
      SELECT @count=@count+1
    END
```

This procedure creates a test table (if it doesn't already exist) and adds 100 rows to the test table; perhaps, not the most practical of stored procedures, but it demonstrates the point. Now execute this stored procedure by using the following command:

```
EXEC TestDataGenerator
```

We don't receive any rowsets back, as this is not the purpose of this particular procedure. However, we will receive 100 messages, 1 message for every INSERT operation, telling us that a row has been inserted:

```
(1 row(s) affected)

(1 row(s) affected)

(1 row(s) affected)
...
```

Each one of these messages consumes network bandwidth, which is simply a waste. Imagine the impact if we were inserting, for example, 1000 rows. A far more efficient approach would be to use the SET NOCOUNT command to disable the sending of these messages within the scope of the stored procedure. For example:

```
ALTER PROCEDURE TestDataGenerator
AS

SET NOCOUNT ON

    DECLARE @count INT
...
```

Now, if we execute the stored procedure, the 100 rows are still inserted, as before; however, no unnecessary messages are sent to our client application for each INSERT, thereby reducing network usage.

**NOCOUNT is limited to the scope of the procedure where it is set. This means that when the procedure where NOCOUNT ON is SET has completed execution NOCOUNT will return to its default value of OFF. Therefore, you need to set this explicitly within every procedure.**

# RECOMPILE

The RECOMPILE option forces the recompilation of a stored procedure's **execution plan** every time it is run. An execution plan can be thought of as a series of steps that SQL Server must follow internally to achieve the outcome that you have requested. It has the following syntax:

```
CREATE PROCEDURE procedure_name
WITH RECOMPILE
...
```

One of the benefits of using stored procedures is that the execution plan is compiled the first time the procedure is run, and from then on, the cached plan is used, which saves precious processing time. Depending on the complexity of the stored procedure, the query optimizer (the part of SQL Server that determines the execution plan) may consider many different plans before selecting the most appropriate one. At times, this consideration can be time-consuming, sometimes as long or longer than the actual execution of the stored procedure itself. Therefore, it is usually desirable to have SQL Server determine an execution plan for a stored procedure on its first execution, and then reuse that execution plan for subsequent executions.

So, when should we use the option of forcing the generation of a new execution plan, every time? This is appropriate only when every execution of the stored procedure differs in dynamics (the number of rows affected, indexes used, and so on) so substantially that the previous execution plan is not suitable. Causing the execution plan to recompile every time would ensure that the most appropriate plan is used. But this carries a real performance cost, as depending on the amount of code and complexity of code within the stored procedure, generating the execution plan for a stored procedure can increase the execution time of the stored procedure significantly (sometimes more than 100%).

If this were the case one would have to question the suitability of the stored procedure for the tasks that it has been assigned to do. To improve performance, in this situation, it may be more suitable to create multiple stored procedures that match all the dynamics of the various execution scenarios and call the appropriate procedure from within our client application. This would allow each procedure to retain its execution plan, thereby reducing execution time, as the procedure plan would not need to be generated each time it was run. It would still result in optimal performance of each execution, by allowing the user to select the most appropriate procedure (and therefore the most appropriate plan) for the type of execution requested.

Rather than embedding the RECOMPILE option into the stored procedure we can specify this as part of the execution statement, for example:

```
EXEC procedure_name parameters WITH RECOMPILE
```

While this has the same result as embedding the RECOMPILE option within the stored procedure, using this method gives us the ability to selectively choose when the execution plan is recompiled, rather than just recompiling by default on every execution.

# The Execution Plan

Whenever a T-SQL statement is executed, an execution plan is either newly generated, or the existing one is reused. However, for stored procedures the T-SQL statements are compiled into a single plan that is cached and reused as appropriate.

For example, take the following T-SQL statement:

```
SELECT Sum(od.UnitPrice)
FROM Orders o
INNER JOIN [Order Details] od ON o.OrderID = od.OrderID
WHERE o.Freight > 1000
```

Conceptually, the execution plan that SQL Server needs to follow to satisfy this request is:

1. Retrieve all rows from the Orders table where Freight is greater than 1000

2. Retrieve all rows from Order Details that have an OrderID in the set identified above

3. Join the two sets above together based on the OrderID column

4. Total the UnitPrice column for this set

5. Present the result

# Why Bother About the Execution Plan?

As a developer, why do you need to understand what's going on behind the scenes in SQL Server, and not simply execute your stored procedures without having to worry about how SQL Server chooses to carry out the request? From a performance perspective, being able to understand the execution plan and to look for obvious performance impacts is a valuable skill.

For every T-SQL statement there isn't just one potential execution plan, there may be many alternatives, and it is the job of the query optimizer to choose the most efficient one. What is determined as the most efficient one is based on a number of factors, including things like available indexes, data distributions, table sizes and so on.

If you view and understand the execution plan, you can see where the query consumes time and large amount of resources. This knowledge can help you to improve the performance, either by modifying your query to function in a more efficient manner, or by creating appropriate indexes to help reduce excessive resource usage.

# Viewing the Execution Plan

There are two views of the execution plan available from Query Analyzer: a graphical view and a textual view.

## Graphical View of the Execution Plan

Due to the ease of using the graphical execution plan, most people prefer this option, unless they explicitly want to capture the execution plan with script, for example. This option can be selected from the Query menu of the Query Analyzer or by clicking on the appropriate button in the toolbar.

If you select the Show Execution Plan option from the Query menu the execution plan is displayed only after the stored procedure has been executed. However, if you don't want to execute the stored procedure you can choose the Display Estimated Execution Plan option. When you select this option SQL Server goes through the motions of deciding on the execution plan it would use without actually executing the T-SQL statements.

This is a handy way of viewing the execution plan while developing the procedure, as it doesn't make any changes to our database.

To view the estimated execution plan click on the following button within Query Analyzer, shown circled in the figure below:

If we examine the Execution Plan tab, which is included with the usual Grids and Messages tabs along the bottom of our results window, we will see that it contains a graphical representation of our query execution plan:

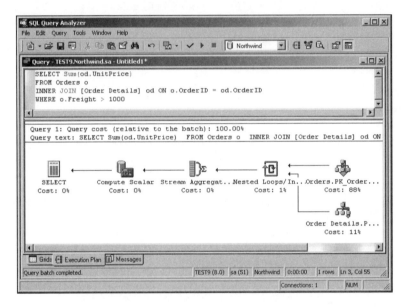

! **This graphical information is not produced directly by SQL Server but is instead created by Query Analyzer from the information provided by SQL Server regarding the execution plan it has chosen to use. Therefore, the execution plan cannot be seen visually, unless we are using the Query Analyzer tool.**

## Textual View of the Execution Plan

The execution plan can also be displayed in text format by using the following command:

```
SET SHOWPLAN_TEXT {ON | OFF}
```

As we mentioned earlier, most people will find the graphical execution plan easier to understand. However, if you need to retain the execution plan for an automated task or future analysis then the text option will be more suitable, as there is currently no in-built method for saving the graphical execution plan.

To view the execution plan as text, first SET SHOWPLAN_TEXT must be executed as the only command within a batch. Now when the query is executed, we receive the textual representation of the execution plan within our results pane:

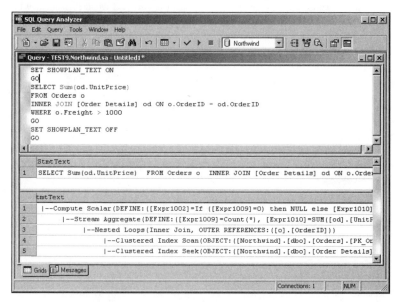

If we expand the results of this statement to make viewing this a little easier, we see that the first rowset contains a copy of our original query, whereas the second rowset contains the actual query execution plan that was followed by the SQL Server:

```
|--Compute Scalar(DEFINE:([Expr1002]=If ([Expr1009]=0) then NULL
      else [Expr1010]))

   |--Stream Aggregate(DEFINE:([Expr1009]=Count(*),
      [Expr1010]=SUM([od].[UnitPrice])))

      |--Nested Loops(Inner Join, OUTER REFERENCES:([o].[OrderID]))

         |--Clustered Index Scan(OBJECT:([Northwind].[dbo].
            [Orders].[PK_Orders] AS [o]),
            WHERE:([o].[Freight]>1000.00))

            |--Clustered Index Seek(OBJECT:([Northwind].[dbo].
               [Order Details].[PK_Order_Details] AS [od]),
               SEEK:([od].[OrderID]=[o].[OrderID]) ORDERED FORWARD)
```

Although not immediately obvious, this is the same execution plan that was represented visually in our previous example (the one relating to the graphical execution plan).

## The Execution Plan and Stored Procedures

For the sake of simplicity, so far we have been demonstrating execution plans using simple T-SQL statements. However, as this book is on stored procedures, it would be wise to address the issue of what happens to the execution plan when the statements are contained within a stored procedure. This is really quite easy, as the basic steps needed to resolve the query remain the same.

For example, let's convert the above example into a stored procedure:

```
CREATE PROCEDURE SumOfPriceForHighFreight
AS
    SELECT Sum(od.UnitPrice)
    FROM Orders o
    INNER JOIN [Order Details] od ON o.OrderID = od.OrderID
    WHERE o.Freight > 1000
```

On executing this stored procedure in the Query Analyzer (with Show Execution Plan turned on), we can see that the resulting execution plan remains the same as in the previous example:

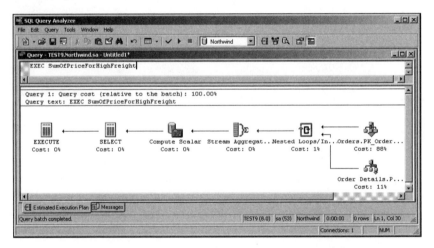

When optimizing a stored procedure, examining the execution plan is indispensable. It shows us the resource (such as time, CPU, and disk) utilization that the stored procedure is consuming, as a whole, allocated proportionally to each of the SQL statements within that procedure. This allows us to focus our attention on the SQL statements that have the potential for making the maximum impact.

If you need to optimize stored procedures frequently, you should learn to make the most out of the execution plan. Quite often, developers attempt to optimize a stored procedure without using the execution plan and end up being misguided. They spend a lot of time optimizing a SQL statement that is consuming a very low percentage of the total stored procedure resources, and thus miss out on optimizing the offending statements completely.

## Multiple Statements within the Stored Procedure

When multiple statements are executed within a batch or within a stored procedure, a single execution path is created for each query in the batch or stored procedure. However, each query's execution path is contained within one execution plan. For example, consider the following stored procedure:

```
CREATE PROCEDURE SomeOrderInformation
AS
    SELECT Count(*)
    FROM Orders o
    INNER JOIN [Order Details] od ON o.OrderID=od.OrderID
    WHERE od.UnitPrice > 50

    SELECT COUNT(*)
    FROM Orders o
    WHERE o.Freight < 1000
```

When we execute this stored procedure in the Query Analyzer (remember to turn on the display of the execution plan), we can see that an execution path is returned for each statement. However, as the statements within the stored procedure are treated as a single unit, each of these execution paths are compiled into one execution plan that is retained for the stored procedure:

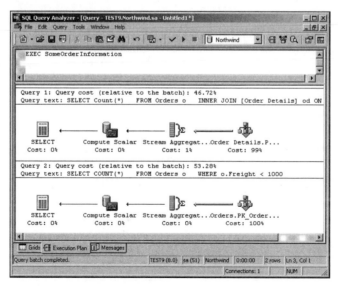

# Understanding the Execution Plan

Execution plans can be complicated, and you can spend a long time learning the functions of each operator in the execution plan. Once you have mastered the execution plan, you will be able to understand how SQL Server decides the execution plan for a query. Understanding the execution plan and then diagnosing performance issues is a scientific way of optimizing queries, unlike the usual approach of making a change and seeing if it runs quicker.

Due to the sheer number of operators (around 50), it's not possible for us to explain each one of them individually. Instead, we will offer pointers that will help you get started; for getting more detailed information you can refer to SQL Server Books Online, select the Index tab, and enter `operators (symbols)`, as the keyword.

## Cost

Understanding **cost** is the first step in understanding the execution plan from a performance perspective. To interpret the execution plan of a stored procedure, there are two costs that we need to be aware of:

❑   Query cost (relative to batch)

❑   Operator cost (relative to query)

Each of these differences, in application of cost, is explained next. However, the definition of cost remains the same for both situations. Cost is a metric used by the SQL Server for determining the impact of one operation in relation to another. In other words it is a measure of computing resources and takes into consideration things such as CPU, I/O, execution time needed, and so on.

### Query Cost (relative to the batch)

When multiple SQL statements are contained within a stored procedure, the cost relative to the batch is expressed as a percentage. This percentage shows the relationship between the cost of each individual SQL statement, and the combined total of all SQL statements within the stored procedure:

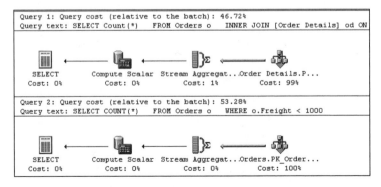

If we use our previous stored procedure, and examine the cost information within the execution plan, we can see that the cost of the first statement is 46.72% of the total cost, and the cost of the second statement is 53.28% of the total cost of the execution of the stored procedure. This shows that our second statement has a higher cost, or in other words, is slightly more resource-intensive than the first statement within this stored procedure.

**!** **The actual cost results that you receive when executing these examples may vary, as it is related to the resource availability (CPU, IO, Memory, etc.) on your system.**

### Operator Cost (relative to query)

The operator cost, on the other hand, is local in scope to a given statement. This expresses the cost (resource usage) of a single operator, as a percentage of the entire resource usage of the single SQL statement:

If we examine the operator cost of the first SQL statement of our SomeOrderInformation example, we will see that each operator has an associated cost. For this example, we can see that 99% of the cost of the first statement is consumed by the operator on the right (which is, in fact, the operation of pulling the rows out of the table). For more information on operators, please refer to SQL Server Books Online.

### The Thick Arrows

Before we get into this section we need to create the following tables and populate them with the data that we need for this example. To do this, run the following script:

```
SET NOCOUNT ON

CREATE TABLE ReallyReallyBig
    (
    IDCol INT NOT NULL,
    VarCharCol VARCHAR (255) NOT NULL
    )

CREATE TABLE ReallyReallyLittle
    (
    IDCol INT NOT NULL ,
    VarCharCol VARCHAR (255) NOT NULL
    )
```

```
DECLARE @Count INT
SELECT @Count=1

WHILE @Count<=10000
BEGIN
   -- Insert a row with some nonsensical character data
   INSERT ReallyReallyBig(IDCol, VarCharCol)
   VALUES(@Count,REPLICATE(CHAR((@Count % 26)+64),@Count % 255))
   SELECT @Count=@Count+1
END

INSERT ReallyReallyLittle(IDCol, VarCharCol)
VALUES(9999,'ABC')
```

The arrows that connect operators within the execution plan represent the passing of rowsets from one operator to another. Although users of SQL Server don't see this happening, conceptually this is what happens within SQL Server during the execution of the query.

In addition to showing the passing of rowsets, the thickness of the line is also a quick indicator of the number of rows passed from one operator to another. This is another easy way of identifying potential performance issues. For example, consider the following query:

```
SELECT *
FROM ReallyReallyBig rrb
INNER JOIN ReallyReallyLittle rrl on rrb.IDCol = rrl.IDCol
```

Let's assume for the moment that the ReallyReallyBig table contains 10,000 rows, and the ReallyReallyLittle table contains only a single row. At the moment, these tables have no indexes, and so when we run this query it takes a while. Sure, in this example we can probably guess that creating an index on the ReallyReallyBig.IDCol column will improve performance.

Now let's, look at the execution plan for this example:

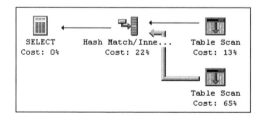

We can see a couple of things happening. As there are no indexes, *table scans* are used to retrieve the rows from our tables. The top table scan (the one having a cost of 13%) is taking place on the ReallyReallySmall table, but this is not a problem in itself, as it produces only one row. However, the bottom table scan takes place on the ReallyReallyBig table, and we can tell by the width of the connecting line that a large number or rows, in this case 10,000, are being passed from the table scan operator to the hash match operator. Within the hash match operator, both rowsets are joined, producing a single row, as output. Therefore, while our query only produces a single row as output, internally SQL Server has to pass around and join together 10,000 rows, which is what is taking all the time.

Armed with this knowledge, we can mitigate this situation by creating a single index on our ReallyReallyBig table:

```
CREATE NONCLUSTERED INDEX ix_ReallyReallyBig_idcol
ON ReallyReallyBig(IDCol)
```

When we reissue the query, we can see that the table scan on our ReallyReallyBig table has been replaced with a more efficient Index Seek operator, and hence, SQL Server isn't passing around 10,000 rows internally anymore. Instead, each of the retrieve operators only produces a single row making the whole query significantly more efficient:

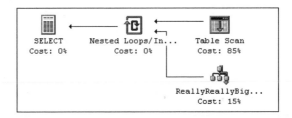

So, what caused such a major saving of resource? When the index for the ReallyReallyBig table was absent, every row from that table had to be pulled off the disk, in the form of a table scan, as SQL Server did not know in advance which rows to join to our ReallyReallySmall table. These rows (10,000 of them) then had to be passed to the hash match operator that compared the values of the join column in the ReallyReallyBig table with all the values of the join column in the ReallyReallySmall table. The matching rows are kept; the others discarded. In this example, only one row matched while the other 9999, from our ReallyReallyBig table are thrown away.

## Benefits of Understanding Cost

Once you understand the application of cost, optimization becomes a more scientific process. For example, if you have a complex stored procedure that contains many SQL statements the obvious way to approach this problem would be to:

1. Execute the stored procedure with the Show Execution Plan option turned on

2. Examine the query cost (relative to the batch) figures to see which queries are taking most of the resources

3. Examine the operator cost to see which operator(s) within that query are consuming the most resources

4. Optimize the query to reduce the operator cost

5. Repeat steps 1 through 4 for the other queries having high costs

This simple understanding of cost can help to save us many hours in optimization time that could possibly occur if we are unnecessarily attempting to optimize low-cost SQL statements.

# Common Mistakes

Before we look at error handling, let's examine some common causes of errors and misconceptions.

## *Batches and GO*

**!** **The GO keyword is NOT a T-SQL command. It is actually a command terminator that is interpreted by Query Analyzer (and isql.exe) to indicate the end of a command batch.**

For example, consider the following T-SQL batch:

```
SELECT * FROM Employees e
SELECT * FROM Customers c
GO

SELECT * FROM Orders o
GO
```

The SQL statements between the GO keyword are separate batches. They are sent to SQL Server together, as a group of commands, and the results of these commands are sent back from SQL Server together, as a group of results.

Using the previous batch example, we can highlight the non-command nature of the GO statement. For this, perform the following steps:

1.  Connect to SQL Server using Query Analyzer.

2.  Click **Tools | Options** to bring up the **Options** window, and then click the **Connections** tab.

3.  Change the **Batch separator** option to something other than **GO**, such as **APRESS**.

The screen will look like:

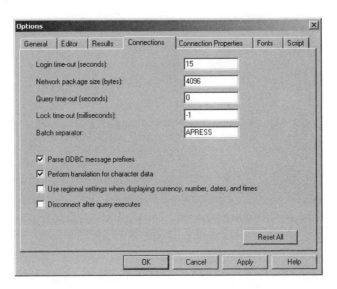

Now, when executing the previous batch query, if we leave the GO statements within the SQL code we will receive an error. If you change this to the value APRESS (that we set above) the batches should execute without any problem:

```
SELECT * FROM Employees e
SELECT * FROM Customers c
APRESS

SELECT * FROM Orders o
APRESS
```

The **Batch separator** is never sent to the SQL Server; rather, Query Analyzer uses it to end a batch and then strips it out of the SQL code before sending it to the SQL Server, for processing. Therefore, we cannot include **Batch separator** within stored procedures. If we do, Query Analyzer will interpret it as being the end of the procedure, and will not include any code after the GO keyword within the stored procedure.

# Dynamic SQL in Procedures

In SQL Server, we can use dynamic SQL, which is essentially a collection of SQL statements that we construct at runtime rather than at design time, for example:

```
USE Northwind
GO

CREATE PROCEDURE SelectAllFromTable
  @TableName  VARCHAR(255)
AS
  SET NOCOUNT ON
  DECLARE @SQLString VARCHAR(8000)
  SELECT @SQLString='SELECT * FROM ' + @TableName

  EXEC(@SQLString)
```

We will run the following statement to execute this procedure, and therefore the dynamic SQL command contained within it:

```
EXEC SelectAllFromTable 'Orders'
```

This approach appears nice and easy, as it allows us to create generic stored procedures that can query any table, at run time. However, this approach is poor for the following reasons:

❑ **Security**

Dynamic SQL breaks the stored procedure's security model; generally, stored procedures are used to prevent direct access to the base tables and this is enforced with permissions. However, if you choose to use dynamic SQL within your stored procedures, the users must have access to the base tables used within the dynamic statement. This makes stored procedures pointless for security purposes.

The security model of stored procedures is discussed in detail in Chapter 8.

❑ **Debugging**

It's difficult to debug code that doesn't exist during design time. Commands built dynamically at run time are a common source of bugs and identifying the cause of such bugs can be complex and time-consuming.

❑ **Optimization**

The execution plan of the dynamic command is not compiled during the first execution of the stored procedure; instead it is generated at run time, and will have to be compiled for every unique occurrence of the dynamic statement.

Contrary to other program languages, such as object-oriented languages like C# and Java, using stored procedures to create generic reusable objects is not considered a good approach. They exist to help you get the best performance and security from your database, and using them in the manner described above doesn't help you achieve this. Instead, a better approach for creating a generic stored procedure is to create many specific (although similar) stored procedures. While this ultimately results in increased code, the end result is more efficient, secure, and easier to debug.

## *Security*

As we mentioned in the previous section, people commonly use stored procedures to protect base tables from direct user interaction. The assumption is that only valid information will be passed to the stored procedure. However, this assumption is flawed. We will have to use some form of validation within the stored procedure to realize this assumption. For example, consider the following stored procedures:

```
CREATE PROCEDURE AddNewSale
    @CustomerID  INT,
    @ItemID VARCHAR(255),
    @Quantity INT,
    @RATE Money
AS
SET NOCOUNT ON

    INSERT dbo.Sales(Customer, Item, Quantity, Rate)
    VALUES(@Customer, @ItemID, @Quantity, @Rate)
```

This procedure in its current format offers no protection to the information contained within the base table, as it will allow any user to modify the underlying data. If this approach is to be useful as a security measure we could include some form of validation within the procedure to check the integrity of the change. For example let us assume our business logic allows anyone in an organisation to enter a sale. However, only sales that have been entered by sales managers get entered directly into the Sales table. Any sales entered by other people get placed into a PendingSales table where they are held until a sales manager approves (at which point it is entered as a sale):

```
CREATE PROCEDURE AddNewSale
    @CustomerID    INT,
    @ItemID VARCHAR(255),
    @Quantity INT,
    @RATE Money
AS
SET NOCOUNT ON

    IF IS_MEMBER('CheckIfSalesManager') =1
    BEGIN
```

```
        INSERT dbo.Sales(IDCol,VarCharCol)
        VALUES(@IDValue, @VarCharValue)

END
ELSE
BEGIN

        INSERT dbo.PendingSales(IDCol,VarCharCol)
        VALUES(@IDValue, @VarCharValue)

END
```

Now, this procedure uses the IS_MEMBER system function to check if the current user issuing the INSERT request is a member of the Sales Manager database role. If they are, then it allows them to INSERT the new row directly into the sales table, otherwise the INSERT is placed within the PendingSales table.

**!** **Data validation rules, such as length, NULL values, lists of possible values, and range checking should be applied directly to a column within the table by using CHECK constraints. If you intend to use stored procedures as a security measure in your application, rules checking the validity of the values passed as parameters should be contained within the stored procedures.**

# Error Handling

Error handling is a simple, yet often overlooked, component of good stored procedures. Effective error handling allows us, as the database developer, to inform the client tools of any failure in the application or database logic. Notice the difference between these two types of logic:

❑   **Application logic**
    The logic is mainly associated with our business/application rules that we explicitly check within the code.

❑   **Database logic**
    The logic is associated with the retrieval and modification of rows within the database tables. We may not explicitly check the database logic, however we should respond to error conditions raised by SQL Server.

The Table1_INSERT example we used in the previous section follows application logic, as this relates to the business rules surrounding our application. It could be modified as:

```
CREATE PROCEDURE Table1_INSERT
...
    INSERT dbo.Table1(IDCol,VarCharCol)
    VALUES(@IDValue, @VarCharValue)

END
ELSE
BEGIN

    -- Some form of application error is generated
    -- to inform the end user that the INSERT
    -- request failed.

END
```

Failure of database logic is a somewhat easier to handle, for example an attempt to insert rows with duplicate primary keys is a failure of database logic:

```
CREATE TABLE #PK_Test
(
    IDCOL int PRIMARY KEY
)

INSERT #PK_TEST VALUES(1)
INSERT #PK_TEST VALUES(1)

DROP TABLE #PK_Test
```

Even through an error is generated in the INSERT statement above the code continues to run and the table is dropped with the next statement. This is because the violation of a constraint does not generate an error severe enough to halt code execution.

Not all database logic errors require checking. Only those which can be thought of as "soft errors", or errors that occur at run time and do not halt the execution of code, require checking. Other errors generated by SQL Server which result in the execution of code being halted will inform the calling application of the error condition automatically. These errors cannot be trapped or handled from within a stored procedure, as SQL Server does not support exception handling from within T-SQL.

The way we check for these soft errors is by using the @@ERROR global variable.

# @@ERROR

@@ERROR gives the error condition of the last SQL command. If the last command was successful this will be 0; otherwise, this will be a non-zero value. Using @@ERROR we can determine the error number of the error that occurred when the last command was executed, but not the severity number of that error.

There are a couple of approaches to using @@ERROR; the most common one is to check and handle the error condition immediately after the statement that generated the error. An alternative is to handle the error in a stored procedure "catch all" error logic routine.

For example, if you handle the @@ERROR value after each statement, you would use error handling code like:

```
CREATE PROCEDURE ErrorDemo

    @Key1     INT,
    @Key2     INT,
    @Key3     INT,
    @Value1   VARCHAR(255),
    @Value2   VARCHAR(255),
    @Value3   VARCHAR(255)

AS
SET NOCOUNT ON

UPDATE Table1 Set Col2=@Value1 WHERE Col1=@Key1

IF @@ERROR<>0
BEGIN
  PRINT 'Handle error here'
END

UPDATE Table2 Set Col2=@Value2 WHERE Col1=@Key2

IF @@ERROR<>0
BEGIN
  PRINT 'Handle error here'
END

UPDATE Table3 Set Col2=@Value3 WHERE Col1=@Key3

IF @@ERROR<>0
BEGIN
  PRINT 'Handle error here'
END
```

To handle the error more generically, we could rewrite this procedure as:

```
ALTER PROCEDURE ErrorDemo

    @Key1     INT,
    @Key2     INT,
    @Key3     INT,
    @Value1   VARCHAR(255),
    @Value2   VARCHAR(255),
    @Value3   VARCHAR(255)
```

```
AS
SET NOCOUNT ON

DECLARE @ErrorValue INT

UPDATE Table1 Set Col2=@Value1 WHERE Col1=@Key1

IF @@ERROR<>0
  SELECT @ErrorValue=@@ERROR

UPDATE Table2 Set Col2=@Value2 WHERE Col1=@Key2

IF @@ERROR<>0
  SELECT @ErrorValue=@@ERROR

UPDATE Table3 Set Col2=@Value3 WHERE Col1=@Key3

IF @@ERROR<>0
  SELECT @ErrorValue=@@ERROR

IF @ErrorValue<>0
BEGIN
  PRINT 'Generically handle error'
END
```

The difference between these procedures is that the first one requires more code to handle errors, but we can check each statement for an error and raise a specific error message for our client application. One the other hand, the second method requires less code; however, if one or more errors took place and we do not know which statement caused the error, we can only raise a generic error message in our client application.

The command we use to raise error messages in our client applications is RAISERROR (note the missing E between RAISE and ERROR).

## RAISERROR & Return Parameters

RAISERROR, manually, throws an error condition back to the client application that is executing commands against SQL Server. It is has the following syntax:

```
RAISERROR ( { msg_id | msg_str } { , severity , state } , argument )
```

While there are other ways of passing errors back to our client application, such as the return parameter of our stored procedure, RAISERROR is more convenient. It usually causes the client application's error handler to be invoked to deal with the situation (for example, causing an exception to be thrown in the .NET Framework). RAISERROR is used to throw an error condition back to our client application for an unexpected situation, and it includes as much information as possible to help the user or the application in determining the cause of the problem.

Return parameters on stored procedures are another way of passing a failure indication back to our client application, but these really serve a different purpose. They don't cause the client application's error handler to be invoked. They are usually used to indicate the success or failure of a stored procedure based on a set of known or expected conditions – usually 0 for success, and 1 and above for "expected" failure situations that can be interpreted by client applications.

**!** **RAISERROR and return parameters are not mutually exclusive. Normally, RAISERROR is used to indicate that an unexpected error has occurred and return parameters are used to indicate an expected failure condition.**

The following is an example of using RAISERROR within a stored procedure:

```
CREATE PROCEDURE RAISERRORTest
   @IDCol   int

AS
   DECLARE @ErrorString VARCHAR(8000),
           @ErrorValue INT

   IF OBJECT_ID('dbo.RAISERRORTestTable') IS NULL
   BEGIN
     CREATE TABLE dbo.RAISERRORTestTable
       (
          IDCOL   int PRIMARY KEY
       )
   END

   INSERT dbo.RAISERRORTestTable(IDCol) VALUES(@IDCol)
   SELECT @ErrorValue = @@ERROR

   IF @ErrorValue<>0
   BEGIN
     SELECT @ErrorString='The following error has occured: ' +
                         CAST(@ErrorValue AS VARCHAR(8))
     RAISERROR( @ErrorString,16,1)
   END
```

Now, execute the following statements:

```
EXEC RAISERRORTest 1

EXEC RAISERRORTest 1
```

The first statement executes successfully, while the second one causes a primary key violation. This violation generates an informational message, which appears within our Query Analyzer window:

```
Server: Msg 2627, Level 14, State 1, Procedure RAISERRORTest, Line 16
Violation of PRIMARY KEY constraint 'PK__RAISERRORTestTab__5BE2A6F2'.
Cannot insert duplicate key in object 'RAISERRORTestTable'.
```

However, as code execution continues the manual error is also raised, which can be caught within the application's error handling routines because of its higher severity:

```
Server: Msg 50000, Level 16, State 1, Procedure RAISERRORTest, Line 19
The following error has occured: 2627
```

# SQL Server Debugger

The SQL Server debugger, released with SQL Sever 2000, is an improved and easier-to-use tool, as compared to its earlier versions. Prior to SQL Server 2000, while the debugger existed, it required a relatively complicated setup procedure that most developers didn't bother to do. Now, this is a much more integrated solution, with the functionality being built directly into Query Analyzer.

**!** **Visual Studio .NET also includes the ability to debug stored procedures. While we don't discuss Visual Studio .NET here, if you use it for your development you should check the documentation included with it for more details.**

Before we start to explain the SQL Server Debugger, let's take a quick look at its user interface.

## *Finding the Debugger*

As we mentioned, the debugger is integrated into Query Analyzer. The following screenshot shows a typical debugging session:

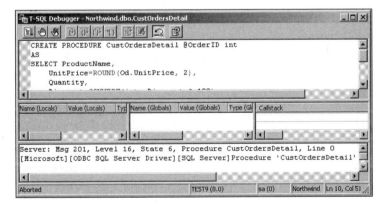

To start the debugging tool we need to locate a stored procedure by using the Object Browser of Query Analyzer. Then, right-click on the stored procedure and select Debug from the context menu; alternatively select Debug from the Window menu.

! If you receive the following error message, it means that the SQL Server service is currently running under the Local System security context. You need to change the service to run under a local machine user account or a domain user account before debugging will work. See SQL Server Books Online for more information on how to do this.

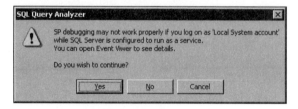

## Using the Debugger

In this section, we will look at using the debugger for debugging a stored procedure. First, let's create the stored procedure to debug, which we will store in and run against the Northwind database.

```
CREATE PROCEDURE DebugMePlease
  @NoOfCustomers  INT
AS
SET NOCOUNT ON

DECLARE @CustomerCount INT

SELECT @CustomerCount=Count(*)
FROM Customers

IF @CustomerCount>@NoOfCustomers
BEGIN
  SELECT *
  FROM Orders O
  INNER JOIN [Order Deals] od ON o.Orderid=od.Orderid
END
```

Now, let's try executing this procedure:

```
EXEC DebugMePlease 10
```

It will give us the following error message:

```
Server: Msg 208, Level 16, State 1, Procedure DebugMePlease, Line 14
Invalid object name 'Order Deals'.
```

As this was a simple stored procedure, we can quickly step through and identify the offending row. However, for the purposes of our discussion let's assume that this is a complicated process. So, instead of searching through it, we will debug it by using the debugger.

To do this we locate our stored procedure in the Object Browser (press *F8* if it isn't visible) and then navigate into the Northwind database's stored procedures, until we find one called DebugMePlease. Right-click on it and select **Debug**.

You will be presented with a window, where we need to enter a value for our NoOfCustomers parameter. For now enter 10 and click **Execute**:

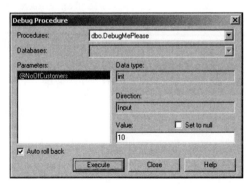

Within the Debug window we have the following choices:

| Icon | Name | Description |
|------|------|-------------|
| | Go | Run the code within the debugger window either to the next breakpoint or the end of the procedure. |
| | Toggle Breakpoint | Place a breakpoint immediately preceding the current command. Clicking again removes a previously placed breakpoint. |
| | Remove All Breakpoints | Remove all breakpoints from the current debugger window. |
| | Step Into | Execute one statement at time. If the current statement is a call to another stored procedure, then that procedure will be opened within the debugger window for debugging. |
| | Step Over | Execute one statement at time. If the current statement is a call to another stored procedure, then that procedure will be executed as a single command without being opened within the debugger window. |
| | Step Out | If you are currently within a stored procedure that was called by a parent stored procedure, which is being debugged (because you stepped into it), this will execute the code to the end of the child procedure and step back out to the parent procedure. |
| | Run to Cursor | Executes all statements from the current position to the statement where the cursor is currently located. |
| | Restart | End the current execution and starts the stored procedure execution again from the beginning. |
| | Stop Debugging | Stops the current execution that is taking place within the debugger. |
| | Auto Rollback | When auto rollback is turned on, any changes made by statements that are executed during the debugging session are undone. When this is turned off, the changes made are retained; be careful while using this. |

For our simple example, we will use the Step Into button to step through our code.

> **If you hover the mouse pointer over the debugger buttons their equivalent key shortcuts will be displayed. It is often faster to step through code by using the shortcut key, for example pressing *F11* will start the Step Into feature.**

Notice that, as we step through the code, the current value of our local variables is displayed within the middle portion of the debugger window.

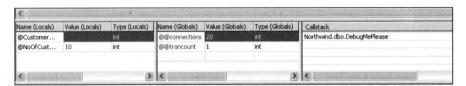

| Name (Locals) | Value (Locals) | Type (Locals) | Name (Globals) | Value (Globals) | Type (Globals) | Callstack |
|---|---|---|---|---|---|---|
| @Customer... | | int | @@connections | 20 | int | Northwind.dbo.DebugMePlease |
| @NoOfCust... | 10 | int | @@trancount | 1 | int | |

If we continue stepping through our simple procedure, we can quickly identify the T-SQL command that is the source of our error, which of course is this command:

```
SELECT *
FROM Orders O
INNER JOIN [Order Deals] od ON o.Orderid=od.Orderid
```

Now armed with this knowledge, we can fix our procedure by fixing the offending statement as shown below:

```
ALTER PROCEDURE DebugMePlease
   @NoOfCustomers  INT
AS
SET NOCOUNT ON

DECLARE @CustomerCount INT

SELECT @CustomerCount=Count(*)
FROM Customers

IF @CustomerCount>@NoOfCustomers
BEGIN
   SELECT *
   FROM Orders O
   INNER JOIN [Order Details] od ON o.Orderid=od.Orderid
END
```

An now when we execute this procedure:

```
EXEC DebugMePlease 10
```

We get the desired output:

| | OrderID | CustomerID | EmployeeID | OrderDate | RequiredDate |
|---|---|---|---|---|---|
| 1 | 10248 | VINET | 5 | 1996-07-04 00:00:00.000 | 1996-08-01 00:00:0 |
| 2 | 10248 | VINET | 5 | 1996-07-04 00:00:00.000 | 1996-08-01 00:00:0 |
| 3 | 10248 | VINET | 5 | 1996-07-04 00:00:00.000 | 1996-08-01 00:00:0 |
| 4 | 10249 | TOMSP | 6 | 1996-07-05 00:00:00.000 | 1996-08-16 00:00:0 |
| 5 | 10249 | TOMSP | 6 | 1996-07-05 00:00:00.000 | 1996-08-16 00:00:0 |
| 6 | 10250 | HANAR | 4 | 1996-07-08 00:00:00.000 | 1996-08-05 00:00:0 |
| 7 | 10250 | HANAR | 4 | 1996-07-08 00:00:00.000 | 1996-08-05 00:00:0 |
| 8 | 10250 | HANAR | 4 | 1996-07-08 00:00:00.000 | 1996-08-05 00:00:0 |
| 9 | 10251 | VICTE | 3 | 1996-07-08 00:00:00.000 | 1996-08-05 00:00:0 |
| 10 | 10251 | VICTE | 3 | 1996-07-08 00:00:00.000 | 1996-08-05 00:00:0 |

# Summary

Optimization and debugging is a wide topic; here in this chapter we focused on optimizing stored procedures. Briefly speaking, the performance of a stored procedure is the result of the collective performance of all the statements that make up that procedure. However, as we discussed, from an optimization point of view, we can make the process of identifying the cause of performance issues easier by being able to understand the execution plan generated when running a stored procedure.

Then we looked at error handling, and we also discussed throwing errors. Then we went on to discuss the debugger in SQL Server. It makes isolating bugs within stored procedures much easier than having to simply wade through lines of code for finding the problematic line. This is even more relevant when working with procedures that call other procedures or functions as the offending line would be much more difficult to isolate without the assistance of the debugger.

# SQL Server 2000

## Stored Procedures

# Handbook

# 3

# 3

# Concurrency, Cursors, and Transactions

In this chapter, we will cover cursors, transactions, and concurrency:

❑ **Cursors**
These are mechanisms to code non-set-based operations into T-SQL statements. In general, their use is considered bad practice, but can be useful when building stored procedures if used properly.

❑ **Transactions**
Transactions are used to group together similar operations into one atomic logical operation. Transactions are important, as it can be dangerous to write stored procedures that modify data, without using transactions. Transactions allow us to construct stored procedures in the 'either all or nothing' manner, where if one part fails, any changes that have already been applied will be undone.

❑ **Concurrency**
Concurrency is related to multi tasking of operations. In databases, we are concerned with the number of queries that can be executed at the same time, especially making use of the same resources and data. Under concurrency, we will look at locks, which are the markers used by SQL Server to decide whether the commands can be executed concurrently or not. We will also discuss methods to maximize concurrency by using some programming schemes to limit SQL locking between read-only and read-write sessions.

Initially, these topics might seem unrelated; however, upon deeper discussion, we will discover that they are related. Now, let's examine each in detail.

# Cursors

Operations in relational database systems, like SQL Server, are all centered on set-based operations, which means that we can operate on more than one row at a time. All the classic SQL statements, such as SELECT, INSERT, UPDATE, and DELETE, are set-based, as they operate on sets of data. A set of data may be one row, a couple of rows, or even millions of rows. SQL Server is optimized for these kinds of operations. Almost all programming in T-SQL should be done using set-based operations.

However, there are some occasions when we cannot perform actions in a set-based manner. For such occasions, we have cursors. The real problem with cursors lies in understanding when and where to use them. If used improperly (where set-based operations will suffice), they can heavily degrade the system. Cursors perform operations at a record level; they do not benefit from the efficiencies of a database technology and so use more system resources (memory and processor cycles), than necessary.

Prior to SQL Server 2000, cursors were frequently employed, as there were only a few operations that could be done without using cursors; even operations like a moderately complex string manipulation, had to use cursors. However, SQL Server 2000 introduced user defined functions (for details, refer to Chapter 6), which can be used to package operations that cannot be done directly in an SQL statement. An example of this is a complex calculation that requires a lookup into multiple tables, like a sales tax calculation for instance, where you may need to take into consideration the type of item (food, medicine, and so on), the state the purchaser is in, and more. There may be fifty different ways to calculate it in fifty different locales. Previously, we may have encapsulated that logic into a stored procedure, but then have to cursor through the set row by row to calculate the sales tax for each item. With a function, this kind of operation is no longer needed; you simply change the stored procedure to a user defined function, and code it directly into the SQL DML statement.

In this section, we will discuss the basic syntax of cursors, and the best practices for their use. Do not confuse the T-SQL cursors with the cursors that we use to move data between the server and the client. They are closely related, but the issues involved in their use are different. Cursors are more necessary on the client.

## *Syntax*

There are two different styles for implementing cursors. The first is a special cursor syntax, while the other is a more typical syntax where the cursor is referred to by a variable. In this section, we will briefly look at the different syntaxes and what the settings mean.

The cursor syntax is a kind of heavy overkill in T-SQL coding, and you will find that you do not need many of the settings that are available, since many settings are heavily centered on modifying data in the cursor. This is because we use the same cursors in our client applications and will declare and start these server-side cursors to work through a set of data for client consumption. However, we seldom need to do such things in our stored procedure code, because unlike client-side operations, we know which row we want to modify, and how we want to modify it.

The Query Analyzer tool has several cursor templates that can be used to automate writing the coding of cursors. They can be accessed via the Edit | Insert Template menu, in the Using Cursors folder (assuming you have not made any modifications to your template directories, that is). The templates are useful for getting started, though you will need to modify them for best practices, in most cases.

## Special Cursor Syntax

Let's now look at the basic syntax for cursors:

```
DECLARE cursor_name CURSOR [LOCAL | GLOBAL]
    [FORWARD_ONLY | SCROLL]
    [STATIC | KEYSET | DYNAMIC | FAST_FORWARD]
    [READ_ONLY | SCROLL_LOCKS | OPTIMISTIC]
    [TYPE_WARNING]
FOR <selectStatement>
[FOR UPDATE[OF column_name[ ,...n]]]
```

The cursor_name value must be a value conforming to the rules for naming identifiers.

### Cursor Scoping

```
[LOCAL | GLOBAL]
```

From a coding standpoint, this is the most important part of the declaration. If we declare the cursor as LOCAL, it will be scoped to the stored procedure (or batch) that we are working with. Therefore, it will be automatically destroyed when the procedure finishes executing. If it is GLOBAL, it is scoped to the connection, and even after the procedure is finished, the cursor is still active until destroyed. Unless you have some valid reason to use your cursor after the procedure is complete (for example, in your client code or in a different procedure that your code will execute), it is best to declare it as LOCAL. This guarantees that your cursor is only accessible to the authorized code, and will be destroyed when your code finishes executing, even if something occurs to interrupt the code being executed (like an unhandled, unexpected error), and your deallocation code never gets the chance to execute.

If you do not specify either LOCAL or GLOBAL, the type of cursor will be governed by the CURSOR_DEFAULT database setting. It is set using the SET clause of the ALTER DATABASE command:

```
ALTER DATABASE <databaseName>
    SET CURSOR_DEFAULT LOCAL --or GLOBAL
```

The current value of this setting can be checked by using the
DATABASEPROPERTYEX() function:

```
SELECT DATABASEPROPERTYEX(db_name(), 'IsLocalCursorsDefault')
```

If it returns 1, then LOCAL is the default, otherwise GLOBAL is the default.

### Direction

```
[FORWARD_ONLY | SCROLL]
```

It is usually best to use a FORWARD_ONLY cursor, which is the faster of the two, since
we seldom need to SCROLL back and forth in a cursor in a stored procedure. This
setting is commonly left blank, since we cannot specify these if we have specified
FAST_FORWARD (see below), which is usually the best in stored procedures, and
FORWARD_ONLY is the default, unless you specify STATIC, KEYSET, or DYNAMIC type
cursor, covered in the next sub section.

### Type

```
[STATIC | KEYSET | DYNAMIC | FAST_FORWARD]
```

STATIC cursor types fetch all rows resulting from the SELECT statement, and copy
them to a temporary table.

KEYSET cursor types fetch all keys from the SELECT statement, and copies them into a
temporary table. This obviously requires some unique key to be identified by SQL Server.

DYNAMIC fetches the data as you request it, so unlike the previous types, the actual row
that will be fetched is not known until you fetch it. FAST_FORWARD is an optimized static,
read-only, forward-only cursor type, which should be used in most cases.

### Updateability

```
[READ_ONLY | SCROLL_LOCKS | OPTIMISTIC]
```

READ_ONLY specifies that we do not intend to modify the data in the cursor. Without
this setting, we can make changes to the data using the UPDATE...WHERE CURRENT OF
CURSOR syntax to make changes to the current row to which the cursor is pointing.
This is usually a bad idea, because it makes code quite difficult to deal with, and as
such, it is generally not a good practice to use the CURRENT OF CURSOR syntax. It does
not mean that we cannot update the data that the cursor was built from, using an
UPDATE statement via a key of the data in the cursor.

SCROLL_LOCKS tells SQL Server to hold locks on the rows in the cursor, so that if we fetch a row, we know that we have it to ourselves, and can modify it. OPTIMISTIC uses an optimistic locking mechanism to make sure that the data fetched remains unmodified in the database table. This is done by using a column with a TIMESTAMP data type, and comparing the timestamp of the physical table to the timestamp in the cursor, or with a checksum of the fields in the table and cursor. It is similar to the type of optimistic locking schemes that we will implement in the *Concurrency* section of this chapter.

### Warnings

```
[TYPE_WARNING]
```

No matter what type we specify, depending on the requirements of the settings, SQL Server may have to change the type of cursor that is being implemented. For example, if we choose a KEYSET cursor, and SQL Server cannot determine a key, it will probably downgrade to a STATIC cursor type. By including the KEYSET setting, a warning message will be raised to the client telling them that the type has been changed. It is generally used to tell dynamic clients what is going on, so they can adjust their features accordingly. The client can then interrogate SQL Server to see what kind of cursor is being used. For more information, check the sp_cursor_list, sp_describe_cursor, sp_describe_cursor_columns, and sp_describe_cursor_tables topics in SQL Server Books Online.

In case of the conversion from KEYSET to STATIC, the users will no longer be able to modify the data in the cursor. As always, ensure that your client can respond to a warning message.

### Cursor Source

```
FOR <selectStatement>
```

This can be any SELECT statement, but you cannot include the keywords COMPUTE, COMPUTE BY, FOR BROWSE, and INTO. The SELECT statement used for the cursor will determine whether the query can meet the cursor options chosen, or not. For example, if your SELECT statement has no discernable unique columns, you will not be able to choose a KEYSET cursor type, since no key will be found.

### Data Updateability

```
[FOR UPDATE [OF column_name[ ,...n]]]
```

This option is included for completeness. If you set this, it allows you to update the data in the cursor, and let it modify the data in the table. If you list the column names, then only these columns can be updated, but if you omit all the column names, all the columns will be updateable. This does not make sense for stored procedures, as it makes the code messy. It is a far better practice to update rows of data using a key in the cursor columns. It makes your intentions clearer, and is easier to test. For more details, you can refer to the UPDATE topic in **SQL Server Books Online**.

## Alternate Cursor Syntax

There is another form of the declaration that is more natural in stored procedures. It is based on using cursors named as variables:

```
DECLARE @cursorVariable CURSOR
SET    @cursorVariable = CURSOR <options> FOR <selectStatement>…
```

The same options exist for the cursor except for LOCAL and GLOBAL. All variable-based cursors are local cursors, making them better, but we also have a method to use them in subordinate objects. In the original syntax, we mentioned that if you wanted to use the cursor in a subordinate procedure, you had to declare it as GLOBAL.

When dealing with cursors as variables, using cursors in subordinate procedures is more natural. If you need to use a variable cursor in a subordinate procedure, you can pass it as a parameter rather than creating it as GLOBAL (assuming that it has been created) when you call another procedure. It may seem like more work to require declaration of the parameter, but it specifically documents that we intend to use a cursor built elsewhere. There is no performance gain while using variable-based cursors, and so their use is a matter of coding conventions only.

# Accessing Cursors from Code

Now that we have created the cursor, let's look at how to reference it from our code.

## Opening Cursors

Once we have declared the cursor, we need to open it. The following statement does this:

```
OPEN <cursorName>
```

## FETCH Statement

Once we have opened the cursor, it creates the set and is ready to use. Now we can use the FETCH statement to move back and forth through the set. The syntax for FETCH is:

```
FETCH
   [[FIRST | NEXT | PRIOR | LAST
      | ABSOLUTE { n | @nvar }
      | RELATIVE { n | @nvar }
   ]
   FROM
   ]
{{ [GLOBAL] cursor_name } | @cursor_variable_name}
[INTO @<variable>, @<variable2>, ... , @<variableN>]
```

There are two parts to the FETCH statement that we need to discuss – FETCH and INTO. We use FETCH to position the internal pointer on a given row in the set, while INTO is used to extract the values from FETCH into variables for use. Omitting the INTO clause in stored procedures is highly discouraged, since you cannot programmatically determine the data in the current row of the cursor while using T-SQL. Besides, it will return a result set for each FETCH statement, which is seldom desired when building procedures. The common goal for stored procedures is to either do something to a group of rows, or to build a single result set. This functionality should be used in the cursors between client and server, and not in stored procedures.

```
FETCH <position> INTO <Variables>
```

This is used to position the cursor pointer on a row in the set. You have the following options for <position>:

❏ FIRST
It gets the first row from the set.

❏ NEXT
It selects the row after the currently selected row.

❏ PRIOR
It selects the row before the currently selected row.

❏ LAST
It gets the last row in the set.

❏ ABSOLUTE <*number of row*>
It returns the *n*th row in the set. It can be a variable value.

❏ RELATIVE <*number of row*>
It returns the *n*th row from the current row. It can be negative, and may be a variable.

❏ No position information
If the position information is missing, it re-fetches the current row.

```
FROM {{[ GLOBAL ] <cursor name >} | @<cursor variable name>}
```

This is where you choose the cursor that you are going to use for the FETCH statement. GLOBAL is used to refer to a cursor that was not declared within the scope of your procedure. Otherwise, an error will be raised by SQL Server, saying that it does not know the cursor you are referring to. When the actual call is made, the cursor you are referring to must have been declared as GLOBAL, and may not be a variable-based cursor. The proper way to handle this is to pass the cursor as a variable to a stored procedure.

```
[INTO @<variable>, @<variable2>, ... , @<variableN>]
```

INTO is used to take the values from the SELECT statement, and place them into the variables for use. For example, if the cursor was declared as:

```
DECLARE @cursorVar CURSOR
SET @cursorVar = CURSOR FAST_FORWARD FOR
  SELECT orderId, customerId
  FROM northwind..orders
--open the cursor
OPEN @cursorVar
```

Then, you will have to fashion your FETCH with INTO in the following manner:

```
DECLARE @orderId INT, @customerId CHAR(5)

--fetches the current row, which is the first
FETCH FROM @cursorVar INTO @orderId, @customerId

SELECT @orderId, @customerId
```

The SELECT statement will return:

```
10248   VINET
```

Finally, there are some other syntactical elements we need to look at – statements to check the status of the FETCH statement, and statements to close the cursor.

## @@FETCH_STATUS

@@FETCH_STATUS is a global integer variable that holds the status of the last cursor FETCH statement issued against any cursor currently opened by the connection. It can have the following values:

| Value | Description |
|-------|-------------|
| 0 | The value that you fetched was there and the FETCH statement was successful. |
| -1 | The FETCH statement failed – the most common reason for this is that the row was beyond the result set. |
| -2 | The row that you were fetching no longer exists; for example, it may have been deleted by another user. |

Be careful to check the value of @@FETCH_STATUS immediately after fetching from the cursor, as this value is global for all cursors that might exist in your connection so if you call a subordinate procedure that uses a cursor, it can reset the value of @@FETCH_STATUS.

## Closing Cursors

Finally, we need to close our cursor with the CLOSE and DEALLOCATE statements:

```
CLOSE {{[GLOBAL] cursor_name} | cursor_variable_name}
```

```
DEALLOCATE {{[GLOBAL] cursor_name} | @cursor_variable_name}
```

CLOSE is used to close the cursor, although you can reopen it. Deallocating the cursor removes it from memory. This is especially important for global cursors, since the cursor is scoped to the entire connection, and will not be automatically destroyed when the procedure ends.

Now, let's look at the various uses of cursors.

# Uses of Cursors

In this section, we will look at some cases that involve the use of cursors:

❑ **Formatting a Result Set**
   This may be needed when we cannot formulate a result set by using the set-based operations in T-SQL, but we can use cursors to step through the set to build another set.

❑ **Batch Operations**
   Frequently, we may need to loop through a set of data and run some operation that needs to do multiple operations per row. Cursors are ideal for this situation.

Let's look at these scenarios in detail.

## Formatting a Result Set

When formatting a result set, there are two possibilities:

❑ Formatting fields in a result set, or

❑ Building a complex result set that cannot be made in the current version of T-SQL

### Formatting Fields in a Result Set

In this case, we take a query, place the results in a temporary table, and then loop through each row in the temporary table, updating fields in the result set. We might adopt this method to perform some complex calculation that does not fit into standard SQL. For example, let's look at the following cursor code based on the Northwind database. Note that, to keep the example manageable, we have simplified it:

The code will give us all orders, the customer, and the total of each order

First, we create a temporary table for our output:

```
--first create our temp table
CREATE TABLE #holdOutput
   (
       orderId INT PRIMARY KEY NONCLUSTERED,
       companyName NVARCHAR(40),
       orderTotal  MONEY NULL
   )
```

Then, we load the temporary table with all of the orders, with the name of the company that the order was made for:

```
--then go and fetch rows from database, with
--only the columns that do not need formatting
INSERT INTO #holdOutput (orderId, companyName)
SELECT Orders.OrderId, Customers.CompanyName
FROM Orders
   JOIN Customers
   ON Orders.CustomerId = Customers.CustomerId
```

Then we declare the cursor of the FAST_FORWARD type, from SELECT statement of all rows in the temporary table.

```
--DECLARE our cursor which will contain the keys of #holdOutput table
DECLARE @outputCursor CURSOR
SET @outputCursor = CURSOR FAST_FORWARD FOR
   SELECT orderId
   FROM #holdOutput
```

Next, we open the cursor and build a variable for holding the key of the cursor.

```
--open the cursor
OPEN @outputCursor

--variable to fetch into
DECLARE @orderId INT
```

Now, we fetch the first row (which we are already on) from the @outputCursor, and check the @@FETCH_STATUS.

```
--fetch the first row from our cursor
FETCH FROM @outputCursor INTO @orderId
WHILE @@fetch_status = 0
--loop until a fetch is invalid, in this
--case past end of table
   BEGIN
```

Then, we update our temporary table from the key to our unitPrice from all of the
Order Details table values. Note that we use the northwind database by default in
all code snippets in this chapter.

```
--update the total field
UPDATE #holdOutput
SET orderTotal = (SELECT sum(unitPrice * quantity)
                  FROM [order details]
                  WHERE orderId = @orderId)
WHERE orderId = @orderId
```

Now, we fetch the next row from the cursor:

```
--get the next row
FETCH NEXT FROM @outputCursor INTO @orderId
END
```

Once the @@fetch_status is not equal to 0, we exit the WHILE loop and output all
the rows of our temporary table:

```
--get the output
SELECT *
FROM #holdOutput
```

Finally, clean up and exit.

```
CLOSE @outputCursor
DEALLOCATE @outputCursor

DROP TABLE #holdOutput
```

Prior to SQL Server 2000, this was a common operation. In a real life situation, this will
represent a complex query, which might include complex calculations that could not
be represented in a sub-query. However, in SQL Server 2000, we have user defined
functions (UDFs) to cover this situation, which we will see more of in Chapter 6.

In the previous example, we updated a field called orderTotal. Using a UDF, the
same example can be written as:

```
CREATE FUNCTION order$returnTotal
   (
     @orderId INt
   ) RETURNS money
AS
  BEGIN
    RETURN (SELECT sum(unitPrice * quantity)
            FROM [order details]
            WHERE orderId = @orderId
            )
  END
```

Then, our query will look like:

```
SELECT orders.orderId, customers.companyName,
  dbo.order$returnTotal(orders.orderId)
FROM orders
  JOIN customers
  ON orders.customerId = customers.customerId
```

This query, included in the downloadable sample code, returns exactly the same data more efficiently, and with lesser code. Even for this small set, you will notice an appreciable difference in performance between the previous example and this function. Essentially, both perform the same operations, but the latter is optimized, faster, and certainly easier to read and manage. Chapter 6 will cover UDFs in detail.

### Building a Complex Result Set

Generally, you can formulate any result set that you need; however, in some cases it is not possible. For example, let's consider the case where we want to build a random set of data. This kind of operation is useful if you have millions or even billions of rows of data (like logging data from a web site). In our case, we are going to randomly pick employees for some study, such as doing a sample blood test, or filling out a questionnaire.

For our example code, we will use the RAND function from T-SQL to choose approximately half the employees. We will do this by executing the following code snippet:

```
ROUND(RAND(),0)
```

RAND returns a floating-point number between 0 and 1. We then round it off to either 0 or 1. I included test code that will sum this 100 times in the sample code, and the totals were consistently, about 50 on average – sometimes high thirties, and sometimes low sixties, but decently random.

Sadly, we cannot do this in a simple SELECT statement, because the RAND function executes only once for the entire statement:

```
SELECT ROUND(RAND(),0) AS rand, employeeId
FROM employees
```

This will return:

```
rand    employeeId
-----   ------------
0.0        3
0.0        4
0.0        8
```

| | |
|-----|---|
| 0.0 | 1 |
| 0.0 | 2 |
| 0.0 | 6 |
| 0.0 | 7 |
| 0.0 | 5 |
| 0.0 | 9 |

Note that it might return the same result with all 1s instead of the 0s. Since we get this result, we cannot build a WHERE clause around WHERE 1 = ROUND(RAND(),0). Therefore, we have to build a temporary table to hold the employees IDs, and then execute a RAND function for each row:

```
CREATE TABLE #holdEmployees
  (
    employeeId INT
  )

DECLARE @outputCursor cursor
SET @outputCursor = CURSOR FAST_FORWARD FOR
  SELECT employeeId
  FROM employees

--open the cursor
OPEN @outputCursor

--variable to fetch into
DECLARE @employeeId INT

--fetch the first row from our cursor
FETCH FROM @outputCursor INTO @employeeId

WHILE @@fetch_status = 0
--loop until a fetch is invalid, in this
--case past end of table
  BEGIN
    INSERT INTO #holdEmployees (employeeId)
    SELECT @employeeId
    WHERE 1 = ROUND (RAND(),0)

    FETCH NEXT FROM @outputCursor INTO @employeeId
  END
```

Once we have built the set, we run the SELECT query:

```
SELECT *
FROM employees
  JOIN #holdEmployees
  ON employees.employeeId = #holdEmployees.employeeId

DROP TABLE #holdEmployees
DROP TABLE #holdOutput
```

When you execute this code, you can observe that it gives us a good random sampling in this small set. This kind of logic could be used for several purposes, like selecting a percentage of customers for sending promotion mails, questionnaires, and so on.

## Batch Operations

Even today, many businesses rely upon batch operation for processing their information. For example, an online retailer might take the order, mark a product as being committed, and verify the payment method while the user is sitting at his web browser waiting for the Thank you for your order message to come up. Later, a process might go through all of the day's orders, post the money to accounts, schedule the order, and perform the other housekeeping tasks.

The other classic example is that of an accounting system. It is also what our example code will implement. Take the case of a donation system. All day, money is received by different processes, through multiple channels (phone, mail, online, and so on). Each donation will have several different outcomes, such as sending a 'Thank you' card, a product, and certainly a receipt. It might also add the donor to a list for being contacted later, for follow-ups. We will also want to move the money received to the accounts receivable system, possibly debiting the account from where the money will be used, and crediting the cash accounts.

For our example code, however, we will assume that all of the various activities have been coded into a stored procedure called donation$processNew:

```
CREATE PROCEDURE donation$processNew
(
  @donationId  INT
) AS
BEGIN
  UPDATE #donation
  SET  processedFlag = 1
  WHERE  donationId = @donationId
END
```

This simply flips the processedFlag bit on our #donation table. Obviously in reality processing donations will be a far more intensive process, but the overall manner of processing a batch of them could be similar to the following code.

First, we create a temporary table, in place of a permanent donation table.

```
CREATE TABLE #donation
  (
    donationId INT identity PRIMARY KEY,
    donorId INT,   --fkey to a donor table
    amount MONEY,
    DATE SMALLDATETIME,
    processedFlag BIT DEFAULT 0
  )
```

**78**

In the sample code, we will load the table with some simple data. Next, we declare our cursor for looping through our donation records, and open the cursor.

```
--DECLARE our cursor, which will contain the keys
--of the #holdOutput table
DECLARE @donorCursor cursor
SET @donorCursor = CURSOR FAST_FORWARD FOR
  SELECT donationId
  FROM #donation
  WHERE processedFlag = 0

--open the cursor
OPEN @donorCursor
```

Then we declare our variables, and fetch the first row of the cursor:

```
--variable to fetch into
DECLARE @donationId INT, @returnValue INT, @message VARCHAR(1000)

FETCH @donorCursor INTO @donationId
```

The loop steps through each of the rows in the cursor, and runs the donation$processNew() function. We check the error status and then return value, just in case our subordinate procedure causes any unexpected errors:

```
WHILE @@fetch_status = 0
  BEGIN
  BEGIN TRANSACTION

    EXECUTE @returnValue = donation$processNew @donationId

    IF @@error <> 0 OR @returnValue < 0
      BEGIN
        ROLLBACK TRANSACTION
        SET @message = 'Donation ' + cast(@donationId as varchar(10)) +
          ' failed.'
        RAISERROR 50001 @message
      END
    ELSE
      BEGIN
        COMMIT TRANSACTION
      END

    FETCH  NEXT FROM @donorCursor INTO @donationId
  END
```

Finally, we clean up:

```
CLOSE @donorCursor
DEALLOCATE @donorCursor
DROP TABLE #donation
```

In some cases, it is actually better to write code that runs outside the SQL Server, and simply calls the stored procedures. The SQL Agent is quite similar to this as it is written external to the T-SQL kernel. This method enables us to take advantage of multi-threading, by using multiple SQL connections. We will discuss the factors enabling us to run more than one SQL process concurrently in the *Concurrency* section.

# Best Practices

The best practice is to avoid cursors, but the truth is best stated as – whenever possible, avoid cursors. The problem with cursors is that they are seldom needed, and typically used unnecessarily. Earlier, in the *Formatting Fields in a Result Set* section we looked at an example where we used a cursor needlessly, as it was possible to use a user-defined function. However, in the other cases, since there were no methods in T-SQL to perform the task we needed, our use of cursors was justified.

The following are good practices while using cursors, which will help you to write faster code when cursors are needed.

❑   **Use read-only, fast forward-only cursors whenever possible**
When writing stored procedure code that employs cursors, we rarely need to modify the data in the cursor, nor will we need to move back and forth through the data. In such cases, we can use fast forward-only cursors, as they have optimizations that make them the fastest cursors.

❑   **It can be faster to build cursors on temporary tables**
It may be better to build a cursor on a set of data in a local temporary table (with a single # in front of the name), especially when we need to hold the cursor for a long time, or even through a transaction. There will be no concurrency issues while locking tables that the other users may need, as the temporary table is scoped (to us).

❑   **Close and deallocate cursors when you are finished with them**
Be sure to close and deallocate cursors as soon as possible. Cursors use resources, which may be holding other resources. This, in turn, can slow down other processes.

❑   **Keep the data set in the cursor as small as possible**
When building the data set for the cursor, make the WHERE clause as specific as possible. It can be tempting to include the WHERE clause in the cursor loop, but avoid this, as the smaller the data set, the faster the cursor, as it will use fewer resources on the server to maintain state.

❑ **Use local cursors**

This is not a performance requirement, but is a good coding practice. Using local cursors (either referenced as a variable, or declared as LOCAL) will help us to prevent issues arising from name clashes, where two procedures have the same cursor names and one calls the other. The preferred method of using cursors declared in one procedure in another one is to pass cursors as parameters.

Cursors are great tools, which give us a lot of control in dealing with data. As we mentioned earlier, it is important to use them only when needed, since they are not the optimal way to deal with data in SQL Server. The best practice is to always comment your cursor code (as well as all your other code) with an explanation of why you are using a cursor, and if it is necessarily needed).

# Transactions

When it comes to writing stored procedures, transactions are an important topic. Most of the procedures we write, for modifying data in any SQL Server database table, will require transactions. In this section, we will briefly define what a transaction is, and cover the basics of the syntax.

Transactions are used to keep the data that we write to and read from tables consistent. A transaction guarantees that one or more statements either complete successfully or fail totally. Every statement that is executed in SQL Server is run within the control of a transaction. This includes INSERT, UPDATE, DELETE, and even SELECT statements. For modification statements, like INSERT, UPDATE, and DELETE, locks are placed, and all changes are recorded in the transaction log. If any operation fails, or if the user asks for an undo operation, the transaction log is used to undo the operations already performed.

We have said that we log whenever we modify data in the database. Since **every** modification operation is logged, we have to be aware of this when considering how large to make our transaction log. How long this change log is stored is based on the recovery model that your database is operating under.

There are three models:

❑ **Simple**: The log is maintained only until your operation is executed.

❑ **Full**: The log is maintained until you explicitly clear out the log.

❑ **Bulk-Logged**: It keeps a log much like the full mode, but does not log some operations, like SELECT INTO, bulk-loads, index creations, or text operations.

Even in simple mode, we have to be careful about log space, since if we make large numbers of changes we have to hold the log rows until we commit our transaction. This is just a taste of transaction log management; for a more full explanation, please see *SQL Server 2000 Programming* by Robert Viera, ISBN: 1-86100-448-6.

There is a common acronym which explains the purpose of transactions. This acronym is **ACID**, and it stands for:

❑ **Atomicity**
Every operation within a transaction is treated as a singular operation; either all of its data modifications are performed, or none of them.

❑ **Consistency**
Once the transaction is completed, the system must be left in a consistent state.

❑ **Isolation**
This means that the operations within a transaction must be suitably isolated from other transactions. In other words, no other transactions should see data in the intermediate state within the transaction until it is finalized. This is done by using locks (for details on locks refer to the *Concurrency Controls* section).

❑ **Durability**
Once a transaction is complete, all changes must be persisted, as requested. The modifications should persist even in the event of a system failure.

The key is that, when we write statements to modify data by using one or more SQL statements, we need to make use of transactions to ensure that data is written securely. A typical problem with procedures and operations in T-SQL code using transactions is that when unexpected errors (like security problems, constraint failures, and so on) occur in code, we end up leaving orphaned data.

# Syntax

The syntax for transactions is simple. There are three variants that we will need to look at: simple transactions, savepoints, and distributed transactions.

## Simple Transactions

In the simplest form, there are three commands that are required: BEGIN TRANSACTION (to start the transaction), COMMIT TRANSACTION (to save the data), or ROLLBACK TRANSACTION (to undo the changes that were made).

For example, consider the case where we are building a stored procedure to modify two tables. Let's call these tables table1 and table2. We will modify table1, check the error status, and then modify table2:

```
BEGIN TRANSACTION

UPDATE table1
--Code for updating table1
...
```

```
--check error status
if @@error <> 0
  ROLLBACK TRANSACTION
  RETURN -100

UPDATE table2
--Code for updating table1
...

if @@error <> 0
  ROLLBACK TRANSACTION
  RETURN -100

COMMIT TRANSACTION
```

Now, in case some unforeseen error occurs while updating either table1 or table2, we will not be stranded. Be careful not to forget to close the transaction (either commit it, or roll it back) because it can cause many problems. The biggest is that you can freeze resources that other users may wish to use (covered in detail in the *Concurrency* section of this chapter), and nearly as bad is that, if you forget to close the transaction, the status of the changes made will be in limbo.

You can extend the functionality of transactions by adding a transaction name, as shown:

```
BEGIN TRANSACTION <tranName> OR <@tranvariable> WITH MARK
```

This will make a mark in the transaction log, which we can use as a placeholder when restoring a transaction log. A good example of its use might be to build a process that marks the transaction log every day before some daily batch process, especially where we put the database in a single-user mode. We mark the transaction log, run the process, and if there are any troubles, we can restore the database to the mark in the log, no matter when the process was executed.

WITH MARK is optional, but without it, the code gets complicated. It allows us to match our BEGIN TRANSACTION to a ROLLBACK TRANSACTION, for example:

```
BEGIN TRANSACTION one
ROLLBACK TRANSACTION one
```

Note that only the first mark is registered, so the following code will return an error:

```
BEGIN TRANSACTION one
BEGIN TRANSACTION two
ROLLBACK TRANSACTION two
```

The error message will be:

Server: Msg 6401, Level 16, State 1, Line 3
Cannot roll back two. No transaction or savepoint of that name was found.

This will leave the transaction open, and so named transactions are seldom used in our stored procedure transaction code.

### Nesting Transactions

While coding transactions, we can nest them. Note that we will have to execute the same number of COMMIT TRANSACTION commands as BEGIN TRANSACTION commands. We can tell how many BEGIN TRANSACTION commands have been executed without being committed by using the @@TRANCOUNT global variable, which gives the number of BEGIN TRANSACTIONs. When @@TRANCOUNT equals zero, we are not in a transaction.

There does not seem to be any functional limit to the number of transactions that can be nested. Testing ten million nest levels on my 1.8 GHz laptop test machine with 512MB of RAM took fifty seconds, which is clearly more than any transaction will ever need.

As an example, execute the following:

```
SELECT @@TRANCOUNT AS zeroDeep
BEGIN TRANSACTION
SELECT @@TRANCOUNT AS oneDeep
```

It returns:

```
zeroDeep
-----------
0

oneDeep
-----------
1
```

Then, we can nest another transaction, and check @@TRANCOUNT to see whether it has incremented. Afterwards, we commit that transaction and check @@TRANCOUNT again:

```
BEGIN TRANSACTION
SELECT @@TRANCOUNT AS twoDeep
COMMIT TRANSACTION
SELECT @@TRANCOUNT AS oneDeep
```

This returns:

```
twoDeep
-----------
2
```

```
oneDeep
-----------
1
```

Finally, we close the final transaction:

```
COMMIT TRANSACTION
SELECT @@TRANCOUNT AS zeroDeep
```

It returns:

```
zeroDeep
-----------
0
```

One additional feature of transactions is that it only takes one ROLLBACK
TRANSACTION command to rollback as many transactions as you have nested.
Therefore, if you have nested 100 transactions, and you issue one rollback transaction,
all transactions are rolled back. For example:

```
BEGIN TRANSACTION
BEGIN TRANSACTION
BEGIN TRANSACTION
BEGIN TRANSACTION
BEGIN TRANSACTION
BEGIN TRANSACTION
BEGIN TRANSACTION

SELECT @@trancount AS InTran

ROLLBACK TRANSACTION

SELECT @@trancount AS OutTran
```

will return:

```
InTran
-----------
7
```

```
OutTran
-----------
0
```

This is the trickiest part of using transactions in our code. We cannot issue ROLLBACK TRANSACTION command without being aware of what its influence will be on the code.

In the above example, had we issued an UPDATE statement immediately after the rollback command, it would not have been executed within an explicit transaction. If we issue a COMMIT TRANSACTION, after the rollback command, we will get the following error:

```
Server: Msg 3902, Level 16, State 1, Line 12
The COMMIT TRANSACTION request has no corresponding BEGIN TRANSACTION.
```

## Savepoints

A tool is available to rollback only certain parts of a transaction:

```
SAVE TRANSACTION <savePointName>
```

For example:

```
CREATE TABLE performer
  (
    performerId INT identity,
    name VARCHAR(100)
  )

BEGIN TRANSACTION

INSERT INTO performer(name) VALUES ('Simple Minds')

SAVE TRANSACTION savePoint

INSERT INTO performer(name) VALUES ('Air Supply')

ROLLBACK TRANSACTION savePoint

COMMIT TRANSACTION

SELECT * FROM performer
```

The output of this listing is:

```
performerId   name
-----------   ---------------
1             Simple Minds
```

In the code, we have two INSERT statements within our transaction, but there is only one row in the output! Obviously, the row that we rolled back in the savepoint was not persisted.

Note that you do not have to commit a savepoint; it will not harm anything if not used. It simply places a mark in the transaction log, if the user asks for a rollback to the savepoint, it tells where to rollback to. Note also that the rest of the operations in the overall transaction are not affected. Savepoints give us the power to reflect changes on only a part of the transaction, giving us more control of what to do if we are handling a large number of operations.

Savepoints do not affect the value of @@TRANCOUNT, nor do they release any locks that might have been held by the operations that are rolled back.

## Distributed Transactions

Occasionally, we may need to update data on a server different from the one on which our code resides. **Microsoft Distributed Transaction Co-ordinator service (MSDTC)** gives us this ability.

If our server is running the MSDTC service, we can use the BEGIN DISTRIBUTED TRANSACTION command to start a transaction that covers the code residing on our server, as well as the remote server, for example:

```
BEGIN DISTRIBUTED TRANSACTION

--remote server
UPDATE remoteServer.pubs.dbo.authors
SET phone = '555 555-5555'
WHERE au_id = '267-41-2394'

If @@error <> 0
  BEGIN
    ROLLBACK TRANSACTION
    RETURN 0
  END

--local server
UPDATE pubs.dbo.authors
SET phone = '555 555-5555'
WHERE au_id = '267-41-2394'

IF @@error <> 0
  BEGIN
    ROLLBACK TRANSACTION
    RETURN 0
  END

COMMIT TRANSACTION
```

The distributed transaction syntax also covers the local transaction. There is a configuration option, REMOTE PROC TRANS, which will automatically upgrade a BEGIN TRANSACTION command to a BEGIN DISTRIBUTED TRANSACTION command. This is useful if you frequently use distributed transactions.

## Explicit versus Implicit Transactions

Before we finish our discussion on transactions, we should cover one further thing. We have alluded to the fact that every single statement is executed in a transaction. This is an important point, which we should understand when writing code. Internally, SQL Server starts a transaction every time we execute any SQL statement. Therefore, even if we do not explicitly start a transaction, SQL Server automatically starts a new transaction whenever a statement starts, and commits or rolls it back depending on whether or not any errors occur. Just as we can code nested transactions, SQL Server can also nest these transactions.

There is a setting that SQL Server provides us to changes this behavior – SET IMPLICIT_TRANSACTION. When this setting is turned on, and we are not already within an explicitly executed BEGIN TRANSACTION, then a BEGIN TRANSACTION is automatically executed when any of ALTER TABLE, FETCH, REVOKE, CREATE, GRANT, SELECT, DELETE, INSERT, TRUNCATE TABLE, DROP, OPEN, or UPDATE are executed.

Note that, in such a scenario, we will have to explicitly execute a COMMIT TRANSACTION or ROLLBACK TRANSACTION command to end the transaction, otherwise if the connection terminates, all data will be lost.

It is not a typical setting used by SQL Server programmers, but is worth mentioning because if you set ANSI_DEFAULTS ON, IMPLICIT_TRANSACTION will be enabled.

Because every SELECT statement is executed within a transaction, the rows are moved from the server to the client inside a transaction; the SELECT statement is not finished until the entire result set is exhausted, and the transaction has not ended. Bear this in mind while studying the *Concurrency* section, as we will discuss all of the resources and settings for managing concurrent SQL operations.

## Compiled SQL Server Code

Now that we have discussed the basics of transactions, we need to discuss the slight differences involved in using them in our compiled code. It is nearly the same, but there are some subtle differences. We cannot use transactions in user defined functions, but we can use them in stored procedures and triggers.

### Stored Procedures

Stored procedures, being simply compiled batches of code, use transactions just like we discussed. We cannot affect the transaction nesting level within a procedure. In other words, if we start a transaction, we must also commit the transaction.

It is better not to execute a rollback transaction in a stored procedure, so that there is no chance that we will rollback to a transaction count different from that at the beginning of the procedure, protecting us from the situation where our code is executed in another transaction. Rather, it is always better to start a transaction, and then follow it by a savepoint. Later, if we need to rollback the transaction, we can rollback to the savepoint, and finally commit the transaction. It is then up to the stored procedure to signal any caller that it has failed.

As an example, let's build the following simple procedure that does nothing but execute a BEGIN TRANSACTION and a ROLLBACK TRANSACTION:

```
CREATE PROCEDURE tranTest
AS
BEGIN
   SELECT @@TRANCOUNT AS trancount
   BEGIN TRANSACTION
   ROLLBACK TRANSACTION
END
```

If we execute this procedure outside a transaction, it returns a single row with a 0 value. However,

```
BEGIN TRANSACTION
EXECUTE tranTest
COMMIT TRANSACTION
```

However, if we execute this, it returns:

Server: Msg 266, Level 16, State 2, Procedure tranTest, Line 5
Transaction count after EXECUTE indicates that a COMMIT or ROLLBACK TRANSACTION statement is missing. Previous count = 1, current count = 0.

Server: Msg 3902, Level 16, State 1, Line 3
The COMMIT TRANSACTION request has no corresponding BEGIN TRANSACTION.

The errors occur as we affect the transaction depth when we roll back the transaction inside the procedure.

We can recode our procedure as the following:

```
CREATE PROCEDURE tranTest
AS
BEGIN
   DECLARE @savepoint VARCHAR(30)
   SET @savepoint = cast(object_name(@@procId) AS VARCHAR(27)) +
                    cast(@@nestlevel AS VARCHAR(3))
```

```
   SELECT @savepoint AS savepointName, @@TRANCOUNT AS trancount
   BEGIN TRANSACTION
     SAVE TRANSACTION @savepoint
   ROLLBACK TRANSACTION @savepoint
   COMMIT TRANSACTION
END
```

Now, we can execute it from within any number of transactions, and it will never fail. Since we are able to call our procedures from other procedures (even recursively from the same procedure), or even external programs, it is important that we take these precautions to make sure that our code is safe under any calling circumstances.

In addition, naming of savepoints is important. As savepoints are not scoped to a procedure, we need to ensure that they are always unique. I tend to use the procedure name (retrieved here by using the object_name function called for the @@procId, but you could just enter it textually) and the current transaction nesting level. This guarantees that I can never have the same savepoint active. It will be also possible to use @@nestLevel, as it will be always unique in the calling chain, for a given connection.

### Triggers

Triggers are part of a special transaction that is started and completed for every data modification operation. We discussed this in the *Implicit and Explicit Transactions* section. As we mentioned, every operation is done within a transaction, and the trigger is implicitly part of that transaction.

Just as in stored procedures, we can start transactions, set savepoints, and rollback to a savepoint. However, if you execute a rollback transaction, instead of an error, the entire batch is cancelled. This is a common practice and SQL Server does this to protect our data. For more details on triggers, please refer to *Chapter 7.*

## Best Practices

Transactions are an extremely valuable tool for maintaining the consistency of our database. Any place where we need to modify data is a likely candidate for a transaction. They give us a great deal of control over what goes in our database and how.

Consider the following best practices when using transactions in your stored procedure code:

❑ **Don't call rollback transaction without a savepoint name in a procedure**
Since you aren't allowed to change the transaction nesting level (@@TRANCOUNT), in cases where you need to call the code from a different procedure this practice will prevent us from causing problems.

❑ **Use transactions as liberally as needed**
It is very important to protect our data, one hundred percent of the time. Each time you modify the data, you need to enclose it in a transaction. This gives you a chance to check the status, the number of rows modified, and so on; and, even rollback the modification if you want to.

Best practices (or actually worst practices) for transactions are highly tied to the concepts that we will cover while discussing concurrency. Quite often, they are painted as bad things, due to some of the problems involved with bloating of the transaction log, and blocking of other users – a topic that will be covered in detail in the next section. For now, we will keep our focus narrow, and say that transactions are a positive thing, as they protect our data from spurious problems arising from partial sets of data being entered.

# Concurrency

If you have studied queuing theory, or you have ever stood in a line waiting to purchase your favorite flavor of ice-cream behind a hundred other patrons in the only active line, as there was a single cashier at the counter, you will understand the basics of concurrency. Concurrency is all about multi-tasking, or being able to do more than one thing at a time.

The answer to concurrency problems in the ice-cream store is easy – get more cashiers to operate the other registers. If there are 100 patrons and 10 lines rather than 1, things will speed up by a factor of 10. If all the users of the database did not access the same resources; database system design would be as simple as this. However, in building database solutions, there is always more to it.

When users are working on different areas of the database, it is not a big problem (though there are issues involved in using the same hardware subsystems). However, this is not always the case, and we certainly do not want our users to make wrong decisions based on the data we show them. Sometimes, users will use our database for storing time-sensitive data. For example, if we are writing a shipping program, we certainly do not want to accidentally ship the same item to multiple customers because two users happened to use the same data at the same time. It is possible to write triggers that cover such situations, but we still have concurrency issues that allow data anomalies to slip through, caused by multiple users modifying our data at the same time. Therefore, what if a user checks to see if a situation is correct, then does some other action, like checking a balance and then making a withdrawal? Another user might have done the same thing at the same time, and then both withdraw the total amount from the same account, with the final balance ending up below zero. Whether this is acceptable depends on the individual situation.

In the rest of this section, we will look at some of the different issues surrounding concurrency in SQL Server applications:

❏ **OS and Hardware Issues**
We will briefly discuss various issues that are out of the control of SQL code

❏ **SQL Server Concurrency Controls**
Here, we will explain locks and isolation levels

❏ **Balancing Safety and Concurrency**
Here, we will discuss ways of protecting our data from users, simultaneously making changes to data, and placing our data into less-than-adequate situations, while also maximizing concurrency

# OS and Hardware Issues

SQL Server is designed to run on a variety of hardware. The same code will run on a low-end PC and even on a clustered array of servers that rival some supercomputers. There is even a version running on a handheld running Pocket PC (though in its current version, it will not support stored procedures). Every machine running a version of SQL Server, from Personal to Enterprise edition, can have a vastly different concurrency profile. In this section, we will briefly touch on some of the issues governing concurrency which our stored procedures do not need to concern themselves with.

We execute the stored procedure code in a single thread. In other words, we cannot spawn additional threads from our procedure code. However, SQL Server and the OS are balancing all the requests from multiple users, in terms of executing code to support requests for memory (both RAM and disk), networking, video, running all of the operating system functionality, including all the services loaded on our server, and even executing our stored procedure code.

It is beyond the scope of this book to delve deeply into these details, but it is important to mention that concurrency is heavily tied to our hardware architecture. The number of CPUs, disk channels and disk drives, network cards, and the amount of RAM we have, will all affect concurrency. However, for the rest of this chapter, we will ignore these types of issues, and leave them to hardware-oriented books, such as Kalen Delaney's *Inside SQL Server 2000*, from Microsoft Press.

We will focus only on software-related issues pertaining to, how SQL Server manages concurrency between SQL Server processes. We will also look at ways and means of maximizing concurrency in our SQL code.

# Concurrency Controls

In this section, we will look at the different controls used internally by SQL Server, as well as those programmed by us in our stored procedure code, to manage issues of concurrency.

# SQL Server

To get a reasonable understanding of how SQL Server manages concurrency, we need to cover:

- **Locks**

  These are holds puts by SQL Server on objects for access by a single user only.

- **Isolation Levels**

  These are settings used to control the length of time for which SQL Server holds on to the locks.

## Locks

Locks are tokens laid down by the SQL Server processes to "stake their claim" to the different resources available, to prevent another process, and causing inconsistencies. They are like the 'Diver Down' markers that deep-sea divers place on top of the water when working below the water. They do this to alert other divers, pleasure boaters, fishermen, and others, that they are underwater. Every SQL Server process applies a lock to almost everything it does, to ensure that no other user can affect the operation that it is doing.

A lock has two parts – the type of lock and the mode of lock. In the following table, we have listed the different types and modes of locks and a brief explanation of each.

Much is made of the fact that SQL Server uses row-based locks, but there are five different types of locks that SQL Server can use to lock varying portions of the database, with the row being the finest, and full database lock being the coarsest. They are used to protect our processes in various manners. The granularities of locks are:

| Type of Lock | Granularity |
|---|---|
| Row | A single row in a table |
| Key or Key-Range | A single value or range of values |
| Page | A eight kilobyte index or data page |
| Extent | A group of eight 8K pages (64K); this is only used when allocating new space to the database |
| Table | An entire table, including all rows and indexes |
| Database | The entire database |

At the point of request, SQL Server determines approximately how much of the database will be needed to satisfy the request. This is calculated on the basis of several factors (the details of which are undocumented), some of which include the cost of acquiring the lock, the amount of resources needed, and how long the locks will be held, which we will be discussing in the next section. It is also possible for the query processor to upgrade the lock if it is taking up unexpectedly large quantities of resources.

For example, if large parts of a table are locked with row locks, it might switch to a table lock to finish out the process. Or, if you are adding large numbers of rows into a clustered table in sequential order, you might use a page lock on the new pages that are being added.

The granularity of the lock defines only how much of the database we will lock. The second part of the lock is the mode of the lock. It refers to how strict the lock is, when dealing with other locks. These available modes are:

| Mode | Description |
| --- | --- |
| Shared | This is used generally when you want to look at the data. Multiple processes can have a shared lock on the same resource. However, it prevents other processes from modifying the locked data. |
| Exclusive | As the name implies, this gives exclusive access to a resource. Only one process may have an active exclusive lock on a resource. |
| Update | This is used to inform other processes that we are planning to modify the data, but are not quite ready to do so. While we are still preparing to do the modification, other connections may also issue shared locks, but not update or exclusive locks. Update locks are used to prevent deadlocks (we cover them later in this section) by marking rows that will possibly be updated by a statement, rather than upgrading from shared directly to an exclusive lock. |
| Intent | This communicates with other objects that we are planning to take one of the previously listed modes. You might see **intent share**, **intent exclusive**, or **shared with intent exclusive**. |
| Schema | This is used to lock the structure of an object when it is in use, so that you cannot alter a table when a user is reading data from it. |

Each of these modes, coupled with the granularity, describes a locking situation. For example, an exclusive table lock will mean that no other user can access any data in the table. An update row lock will say that other users could look at the data in the row, but any statement that might modify data in the table will have to wait until after this process has been completed.

As far as concurrency is considered, locks are not desirable. Whenever a resource is locked in a way that another process cannot use it to complete its processing, concurrency is lowered, as the process must wait for the other to complete before it can continue. This is generally referred to as **blocking**. Of course we must have locks, and we must have blocking to maintain our data integrity. In the next section, we will discuss isolation levels that determine how long locks are held. Executing the stored procedure sp_who2 will give you a list of all processes, with a column BlkBy that will tell you if any users are blocked, and which user is doing the blocking. Enterprise Manager also contains a node for seeing current activity, in the <serverName>\Management\Current Activity\Process Info node.

There is also a **bulk update** mode that is used to lock the table while inserting data in bulk into the table, and the TABLOCK hint is applied (covered in the next paragraph) here. It is analogous to an exclusive table lock for concurrency issues.

We can force SQL Server to use a different type of lock from what it might ordinarily choose by using locking hints on our queries. For individual tables in a FROM clause, we can set the type of lock to be used like this:

```
FROM  table1 WITH (<hintList>)
   JOIN table2 WITH (<hintList>)
```

Note that these hints will work on all query types. In the case of locking, we have five different hints we can use:

❑ **PAGLOCK**
   Forces the optimizer to choose page locks for the given table

❑ **NOLOCK**
   Leaves no locks, and honors no locks for the given table

❑ **ROWLOCK**
   Forces row-level locks to be used for the table

❑ **TABLOCK**
   Goes directly to table locks, rather than row locks or page locks, and can speed some operations, but seriously lowers concurrency

❑ **TABLOCKX**
   Same as TABLOCK, but uses exclusive locks, rather than the more common shared locks, and forces single threaded use of the table, rather than NOLOCK access

Note that SQL Server can override our hints if it is necessary, for example the case where we choose NoLock, but then modify the table in the query. Exclusive locks will still be held on the table for the rows that are modified, though not on rows that are simply looked at.

**Deadlocks**

One term that is frequently bandied about is **deadlocks**. A deadlock is a circumstance where two processes are trying to use the same objects, but neither will ever be able to complete because it is blocked by the other connection. For example, consider that we have two processes (processes 1 and 2), and two resources (resources A and B). Then the following steps will lead to a deadlock:

❑ Process 1 takes a lock on Resource A, and at the same time, Process 2 takes a lock on Resource B.

❑ Then Process 1 tries to get access to Resource B. As it is locked by Process 2, Process 1 will go into a wait state.

❑ Then Process 2 tries to get access to Resource A, but since it is locked by Process 1, Process 2 will go into a wait state.

At this point, there is no way to resolve this issue, without ending one of the processes. Therefore, SQL Server will arbitrarily kill one of the processes (unless one of the processes has voluntarily raised the likelihood of it being the killed process by using SET DEADLOCK_PRIORITY LOW, and the other process has not). SQL Server raises the following error to the client to tell it that their process was stopped:

Server: Msg 1205, Level 13, State 1, Line 4
Transaction (Process ID 55) was deadlocked on lock resources with another process and has been chosen as the deadlock victim. Rerun the transaction.

At this point, we should be able to resubmit the very same request. This assumes that we are working within a transaction for multiple data modifications, and know what was rolled back.

### Isolation Levels

In the previous section on locks, we mentioned that every SQL Server process applies a lock to almost anything it does, to ensure that no other users can affect the operation that it is performing. Locks are placed to make sure that, while SQL Server is actually using the resource, the resource is protected. However, exactly how long SQL Server holds locks, or whether locks prevent other processes from looking at the data that we have locked, is controlled by what level of isolation we have set up in a given connection or process.

Depending on how safe we need our transactions to be, and how concurrent we need our processes to be, we can use several different models of isolation. To illustrate this point, consider that the safest method will be to put an exclusive lock on the entire database, do our operations, and release the lock. While this was common in early file-based systems, it is not really a viable idea when you need to support a large number of concurrent users, no matter how beefy your hardware platform may be.

From inside a transaction, locks can be held for a variable amount of time to protect the data we are working with. For example, consider the following hypothetical code snippet:

```
BEGIN TRANSACTION
SAVE TRANSACTION savePoint

IF EXISTS ( SELECT * FROM tableA WHERE tableAId = 'value' )
BEGIN
  UPDATE tableB
  SET status = 'UPDATED'
  WHERE tableAId = 'value'
```

```
    IF @@error <> 0
    BEGIN
        RAISERROR 50001 'Error updating tableB'
        ROLLBACK TRANSACTION savePoint
    END
END

COMMIT TRANSACTION
```

First, we check to see if a key-value exists in tableA, and if it does, we update a value in tableB. On first glance, this seems very secure – if a record exists when we check in tableA, it will exist when we update tableB. However, the security of this transaction is based solely on how long the locks are held on the SELECT from tableA. While the row may exist when we run the IF EXISTS block, what happens if an exclusive table lock exists on tableB when we execute the update on tableB, and we are blocked waiting for the lock to be cleared? During this period, when we are waiting for the table lock on tableB to be cleared, the row we have been told existed could be deleted from tableA, if we do not maintain our lock on the row until our transaction is complete.

What is interesting is the fact that under the default isolation level that SQL Server connections operate in, no lock will have been kept on tableA, leaving a hole in our data integrity.

Before we define the isolation levels, there are two concepts that we need to mention briefly. These are **repeatable reads** and **phantom rows**. Suppose that we execute a statement such as:

```
SELECT * FROM table
```

and the rows returned are:

```
ColumnName
-----------
row1
row2
```

For this SELECT statement to be considered as a repeatable read, we must be able to execute the statement multiple times and get back at least the same results. However, we may get back an extra row, like:

```
ColumnName
-----------
row1
row2
row3
```

This still passes the test for repeatable read, which can seem confusing since the results of the read were not really repeatable, but that is how it is defined. The value row3 is a phantom row.

Let's look at the four isolation levels to see what is allowed:

| Isolation Level | Description |
| --- | --- |
| READUNCOMMITTED | Ignore all locks, and do not issue locks. We can see any data that has been saved to the table, regardless of whether or not it is part of a transaction that has not been committed (hence the name). However, it will leave exclusive locks if you do modify data, to keep other users from changing data that you have not committed. Primarily valuable for reporting when you can accept a margin of error that this will allow. |
| READCOMMITTED | The default isolation level, does not allow us to see uncommitted data. All shared and update locks are released, as soon as we have finished using the resource. Exclusive locks are held until the end of the transaction. Here, we do not have protection for repeatable reads or phantoms. |
| REPEATABLEREAD | This includes protection from data being deleted from under our operation. Shared locks are now held during the entire transaction, to prevent other users from modifying the data we have touched. |
| SERIALIZABLE | This takes everything from repeatable read, and adds in phantom protection, by taking not only locks on existing data that we have read, but also key locks on any ranges of data that could match any SQL statement executed. |

The syntax for setting the isolation level is:

```
SET TRANSACTION ISOLATION LEVEL <level>
```

Here, <level> can be any of the four settings in the table above. The default isolation level is read committed, and is generally the best balance between concurrency and integrity.

Note that it is not always the proper setting. If we refer to our previous example code block, where we check if a value exists in one table, and then modify another, it is important to remember that the isolation level we use will depend on the types of tables that tableA and tableB represent. For example, if we are implementing a medical sales system that allows the user to ship a critical product to a customer, we will perform the following checks (in pseudo-code):

```
BEGIN TRANSACTION
IF (product in inventory) > (amount requested)
BEGIN
   Decrement inventory
   PRINT Bill Of Lading
END
   COMMIT TRANSACTION
```

We will probably want to use the REPEATABLEREAD isolation level, since we will not want to accidentally print two bills for the same product for two users, regardless of how small the probability is. In read committed, multiple users may block on the step to decrement inventory, after the check to see if the decrementing was valid.

> *Note that locks are held not just for operations that you directly execute, but also for any constraints that fire to check existence in other tables, and any code executed in trigger code. The isolation level in effect controls the duration for which these locks are held.*

It is extremely important that, while considering solutions, we keep in mind the locking and isolation levels. As we build more and more critical solutions with SQL Server, it is imperative that we make sure that we protect data to a level that is commensurate with the value of the data. If we are building procedures to support a system on a space shuttle, or a life support system, this becomes more important than in the case of a sales system, or a pediatrician's schedule. In the next section, we will look at coding schemes aimed at improving the concurrency of our stored procedures.

We can apply an isolation level to only a given table in a query in a query hint, rather than an entire query. These hints are READ UNCOMMITTED, READ COMMITTED, REPEATABLE READ, and SERIALIZABLE, and behave as their corresponding isolation levels do. Note again that these hints may be overridden in cases were data is modified, especially in the case of READ UNCOMMITTED.

## Coding for Integrity and Concurrency

As we build database systems, we must consider the fact that multiple users will attempt to modify our data, at the same time. So far, in this chapter we have talked at length about the different mechanisms (like transactions, varying isolation levels, and so on), for protecting our data. Now, we need to discuss the different mechanisms to keep our users from stepping on one another's toes.

The general progression of events in most applications is the same. First, we fetch some data for a user or a process to look at, operate on it, make changes to it, or make some decision based on it. After the users have performed the operations, they will either commit the changes to the database, or possibly save data to a different table based on the decision. While the user has the data cached on their client, what happens if a different user wants the data, or wants to make a change to the same data? For this, we use one of these while coding our database application:

❑ **Pessimistic**
We assume it is likely that users will try to modify the same data, so we make the access to tables and data single-threaded.

❑ **Optimistic**
Instead of blocking access to tables, we assume that it is unlikely that users will try to modify the exact same row at the same time, so we will only verify that the data is the same as the data when we fetched it.

Using one or both of these schemes, it is usually possible to protect data in our multi-user system to an acceptable level of integrity and concurrency.

### Pessimistic Locking

A pessimistic locking scheme is very restrictive. Generally, the idea is straightforward – begin a transaction, most likely a serializable one, fetch the data, manipulate the data, modify the data, and finally commit the transaction. The goal is to serialize or single-thread all access to data we are interested in, to make sure that no other users can touch the data we are working on.

The only real problem here is that we will block all access to the row that we are working with. This sounds good, but the main issue is that any query to the tables where the data was locked might have to wait for the user to complete the access. Even if the row will not actually be involved in the answer to a query, there is a possibility that the query will be held up. For example, if one user has a single row locked in a table, and the next user executes a different query that requires a table scan on the same table, even if the results of this query do not need the same row in use, they will be blocked, as they might need that row. Soon, a chain of users will be waiting on one particular user.

All this might even be reasonable, but what if the user decides to take a break? All users will then have to wait until this user finishes the access to the data, and if the user has modified one piece of data with complex triggers, and still has more to go, all access to most of our data will be blocked because a user was forgetful and did not close the application.

We can relieve some of the long-term stress on our system by reducing the time we hold locks for, like releasing the lock when we are not actually modifying the data (refetch the data when the user makes a change to a field), and by setting time limits on how long a user can keep the data before rolling back the transaction. However, either way, we can block access to large quantities of data for a long period, considering that we will need to lock any domain tables that the user will rely on to choose values for the table, so no related data that we might use is changed. This is not optimum, so this type of locking is seldom, if ever, used.

**Optimistic Locking**

The opposite of pessimistic locking is optimistic locking. Here, we simply assume that the likelihood of users stepping on one another is very limited. Therefore, we choose to take locks only during actual data modification activities, since most of the time users just look around, and even if the data that we are looking at is slightly out of date, it will not really hurt anything. This is true of almost all applications, including banking ones. Consider the ATM machine, where you go to withdraw money. It will only allow you to withdraw as much money as it believes you have, but if your spouse has withdrawn money somewhere else simultaneously, the result is that more money is taken out than you have.

Optimistic locking schemes can be broken down into two types. In all cases, we only lock the data at the point where the user modifies the data. We protect the data in the server using constraints, triggers, and so on. We will choose the best isolation level depending upon how important perfection is, since, as seen before in the *Isolation Levels* subsection, the default of READ UNCOMMITTED is flawed because for some milliseconds, it leaves open the possibility that one user can change data on which our transaction depends. For the most part, it is considered appropriate to use the default, as it greatly enhances concurrency, and the probability of someone modifying data during your transaction is comparable to the chances of being hit by lightning ten sunny days in a row. It could happen, but it is very unlikely.

If we think back to the progression of events – user fetches data, modifies data, and finally commits data to the database – there can be a long interval between data fetch and actually committing the changes to the database. In fact, it is also possible that other users could have also fetched and modified the data during that period.

Instead of locking the data by using physical SQL Server locks, we will employ one of the following schemes:

❑ **Unchecked**
This is the most commonly employed scheme. If two users modify the same row in the database, then the last user wins. It is not really the best idea, as the first user may have had something important to say, and this method rejects their changes. We will not cover this any further because it is straightforward.

❑ **Row-based scheme**
We protect our data at the row level, by checking to see if the row we are modifying is the same as in the physical table. If not, we will refresh the data from the table, showing the user what was changed.

❑ **Logical unit of work**
A logical unit of work is used to group a parent record with all of its children data to allow a single optimistic lock to cover multiple tables, for example, an invoice, and the line items for that invoice. We treat modifications to the line items in the same manner as a modification to the invoice for locking purposes.

An important point to note about optimistic locking is that it is not enforced by the database, and must be coded into every procedure that is written against the tables. If we have an invalid optimistic lock value, the tables themselves will not deny access to the data; it is up to the programmers to follow the rules that the database architect lays down.

**Row-Based Scheme**

In a row-based scheme, we indicate that we will check on a row-by-row basis whether or not the data that the user has retrieved is still the same as the one that they fetched. Therefore, the order of events is now: fetch data, modify data, check to see that the rows of data are still the same as they were, and then commit the changes.

There are three common methods to implement row-based optimistic locking:

❑ **Check all fields in the table**
If you cannot modify the table, which the next two methods require, you can check that the data you had fetched is still the same, then modify the data. This method is the most difficult, since any procedure you write must contain parameters for the previous values of data, which is not a good idea, if you can help it. It is useful when building data-grid type applications, where we execute direct updates to the table. Since this book deals with stored procedures only, we will not cover this method.

❑ **Add a date-time column to the table**
We set this value when the table is inserted, and subsequently updated. Every procedure we write for modifying or deleting data from the table will need a column for the previous value of the timestamp. Every update to the table to modify the value in the table will be required to update the date-time column. Generally, it is best to use a trigger for keeping the date-time column up to date, and often we will include a column to tell which user modified the data last. Later, in this section, we will write a simple INSTEAD OF trigger to support this function.

❑ **Use a timestamp column**
In the previous method, we used a manually controlled value to manage the optimistic lock value. In this method, we will use the built-in control, using a column with a timestamp data type. The timestamp data type automatically gets a new value for every command used to modify a given row in a table.

As an example, let's look at a simple table, which is person with the structure:

```
CREATE TABLE person
(
    personId INT IDENTITY(1,1),
    firstName VARCHAR(60) NOT NULL,
    middleName VARCHAR(60) NOT NULL,
    lastName VARCHAR(60) NOT NULL,
```

```
        dateOfBirth DATETIME NOT NULL,
        rowLastModifyDate DATETIME NOT NULL default getdate(),
        rowModifiedByUserIdentifier NVARCHAR(128) NOT NULL
           DEFAULT suser_name(),
              CONSTRAINT XPKperson PRIMARY KEY (personId)
)
```

Note the two fields for our optimistic lock, named rowLastModifyDate and rowModifiedByUserIdentifier. We will use these to hold the last date and time of modification, and SQL Server's user identifier for the modifying user. For this, instead of triggers, we will use the following INSERT and UPDATE:

```
CREATE TRIGGER person$insteadOfUpdate ON person
INSTEAD OF UPDATE
AS

DECLARE @numRows INTEGER
SET     @numRows = @@rowcount

IF @numRows = 0 --no need to go into this trigger if no rows modified
    RETURN

SET NOCOUNT ON --must come after the @@rowcount setting

DECLARE @msg VARCHAR(8000) --holding for output message

UPDATE person
SET firstName = inserted.firstName,
    middleName = inserted.middleName,
    lastName = inserted.lastName,
    dateOfBirth = inserted.dateOfBirth,
    rowLastModifyDate = getdate(),
    rowModifiedByUserIdentifier = suser_name()
FROM inserted
    JOIN person
           ON person.personId = inserted.personId
IF @@error <> 0
  BEGIN
        SET  @msg = 'There was a problem in the instead of trigger
                     for the update of person record(s).'
        RAISERROR 50000 @msg
        ROLLBACK TRANSACTION
        RETURN
  END
END
```

The INSTEAD OF INSERT trigger is included in the code download. Since we have this in an INSTEAD OF trigger, the user or programmer cannot overwrite the values, even if they include it in the field list of an INSERT.

Next, we will include the checking code in our stored procedure, like the highlighted code in this procedure. The declaration for this procedure will include the key, all of the logically 'modifiable' fields, and the optimistic locking field:

```
CREATE PROCEDURE person$upd
(
    --primary key
    @r_personId int,
    --updateable fields
    @firstName VARCHAR(60)  ,
    @middleName VARCHAR(60)  ,
    @lastName VARCHAR(60)  ,
    @dateOfBirth DATETIME  ,

    --optimistic lock
    @rowModifiedByUserIdentifier NVARCHAR(128)   = NULL
)
AS
```

Then, we set up some of our basic variables and savepoint names, and finally start a transaction and set our savepoint:

```
--   Turns off the message returned at the end of each statement
--   that states how many rows were affected
SET NOCOUNT ON

BEGIN
    DECLARE   @rowcount INT,     --checks the rowcount returned
        @error    INT,           --used to hold the error code after a call
        @msg    VARCHAR(255),    --used to preformat error messages
            @retval    INT,      --general purpose var for return values
        @savepoint VARCHAR(30)   --holds the transaction name

    SET      @savepoint = CAST(object_name(@@procid) AS varchar(27))
                       + CAST(@@nestlevel AS varchar(3))
    BEGIN TRANSACTION
    SAVE TRANSACTION @savepoint
```

Then, we update the table, based on the key value passed in, and the optimistic locking value. This will not harm performance because it will do a primary key lookup:

```
UPDATE   person
    SET   firstName = @firstName ,
          middleName = @middleName ,
          lastName = @lastName ,
          dateOfBirth = @dateOfBirth
  WHERE   personId = @r_personId
    AND   rowModifiedByUserIdentifier = @rowModifiedByUserIdentifier
```

Next, we have our error-handling block. We check to see if an error has occurred:

```
--get the rowcount and error level for the error handling code
SELECT @rowcount = @@rowcount, @error = @@error

IF @error != 0  --an error occurred outside of this procedure
  BEGIN
     SELECT @msg = 'Problem occurred modifying the person record.'
     RAISERROR 50001 @msg
     ROLLBACK TRANSACTION @savepoint
     COMMIT TRANSACTION
     RETURN -100
  END
```

Then, check to see if the rowcount is 0, since it will mean that either the key value does not exist, or the row has been modified.

```
ELSE IF (@rowcount = 0 )
     BEGIN
             --check existance
             IF EXISTS ( SELECT *
                         FROM    person
                         WHERE   personId = @r_personId )
               BEGIN
                  SELECT @msg = 'The person record you tried to'+
                       'modify has been modified by another user.'
               END
             ELSE
               BEGIN
                  SELECT @msg = 'The person record you tried to'+
                                         'modify does not exist.'
               END

          RAISERROR 50001 @msg
          ROLLBACK TRANSACTION @savepoint
          COMMIT TRANSACTION
          RETURN -100
     END
```

Finally, we close the transaction and return a 0.

```
     COMMIT TRANSACTION
     RETURN 0
  END
```

If however, we were to define our table as:

```
CREATE TABLE person
(
     personId INT IDENTITY(1,1),
     firstName VARCHAR(60) NOT NULL,
     middleName VARCHAR(60) NOT NULL,
     lastName VARCHAR(60) NOT NULL,
     dateOfBirth DATETIME NOT NULL,
     autoTimestamp TIMESTAMP NOT NULL,
     constraint XPKperson PRIMARY KEY (personId)
)
```

With a `timestamp` datatype column, very little will change with our procedures, and we will not need the INSTEAD OF triggers. In the next block of code, this is all that will change. In the parameters:

```
CREATE PROCEDURE person$upd
(
     @r_personId INT,
     @firstName VARCHAR(60)   ,
     @middleName VARCHAR(60)   ,
     @lastName VARCHAR(60)   ,
     @dateOfBirth DATETIME   ,
     @autoTimestamp TIMESTAMP
)
AS
```

and in the UPDATE statement:

```
UPDATE  person
    SET  firstName = @firstName ,
         middleName = @middleName ,
         lastName = @lastName ,
         dateOfBirth = @dateOfBirth
  WHERE  personId = @r_personId
    AND  @autoTimestamp = autoTimestamp
```

It is much easier to implement, but lacks the documentation of who made the last change to the table, and when. The `timestamp` column is a VARBINARY(16), and is simply a value that is guaranteed to be unique within a database.

### Logical Unit of Work

While row-based optimistic locks are very helpful, they do have a drawback. In many cases, several tables together actually make one 'object'. A good example is an invoice and line items. The idea behind a logical unit of work is that instead of having a row based lock on the invoice and all of the line items, we might only have one on the invoice, and use the same value for the line items. Therefore, we expect that the user will always fetch not only the invoice, but also its line items into its cache when it is dealing with the invoice. Assuming we are using a timestamp column, we will use the same kind of logic as we have used previously on the invoice table. However, when the user wants to insert, update, or delete line items for the invoice, the procedure will require the @autoTimestamp parameter, and will check the value against the invoice, before UPDATE. Consider that we have two tables, minimally defined as:

**106**

```
--leaving off who invoice is for
CREATE TABLE invoice
(
     invoiceId INT IDENTITY(1,1),
     number VARCHAR(20) NOT NULL,
     autoTimestamp TIMESTAMP NOT NULL,

     CONSTRAINT XPKinvoice PRIMARY KEY (invoiceId)
)

--also forgetting what product that the line item is for
CREATE TABLE invoiceLineItem
(
     invoiceLineItemId int NOT NULL,
     invoiceId INT NULL,
     itemCount INT NOT NULL,
     cost INT NOT NULL,
     CONSTRAINT XPKinvoiceLineItem PRIMARY KEY (invoiceLineItemId)
)
```

For our delete procedure for invoiceLineItem, for the parameters we will have:

```
CREATE PROCEDURE invoiceLineItem$del
(
    @r_invoiceLineItemId INT,   -- just need the primary key

    --this will be the timestamp of the invoice table
    @autoTimestamp TIMESTAMP
)
```

Next, we use the following logic in the DELETE statement:

```
DELETE   invoiceLineItem
FROM     invoiceLineItem
JOIN invoice
ON invoice.invoiceId = invoiceLineItem.invoiceId
WHERE    invoiceLineItem.invoiceLineItemId = @r_invoiceLineItemId
   AND   @autoTimestamp = invoice.autoTimestamp
```

Instead of checking the timestamp on an invoiceLineItem row, we are now checking the timestamp on the invoice table. Additionally, we will need to update the timestamp value on the invoice table when we make our change.

The rest of the code will be similar to the code we used in the update procedure. Again, all code for the examples will be included in the download for the book.

# Best Practices

The most important goal of any SQL Server application is to maintain the integrity of the data that is to be stored. Whenever we work to increase the number of concurrent users that our system can handle, we must still make sure that the integrity of our data is still maintained.

The following is a brief list of suggestions to help maximize concurrency:

❑ **Recognize the difference between hardware limitations and SQL Server concurrency issues**
If the hardware usage is at its maximum (with excessive disk queuing, 90% CPU utilization, and so on), consider adding more hardware. However, if you were single-threading calls through your database, due to locking issues, you would have to add twenty processors and a terabyte of RAM to see a little improvement.

❑ **Keep transactions as short as possible**
The smaller the transaction, the less chance there is of it holding locks. Try not to declare variables, create temporary tables, etc. inside a transaction, unless it is necessary. Make sure that all table access within transactions is executed as atomic operations.

❑ **Fetch all rows from a query as fast as possible**
Depending on the isolation level and editability of the rows being returned, there can be locks held that would interfere with the other users' ability to modify or even read rows.

❑ **Minimize use of cursors**
Cursors require more resources (CPU if nothing else) than typical SQL statements. Use them when and if they are needed, and no more.

❑ **Make sure that all queries use good plans**
The better queries are, the faster they execute, and it follows that more code can be executed within the same resource framework.

❑ **Use some form of optimistic locking mechanism**
Preferably use a timestamp column, as it requires the smallest amount of coding, and is managed entirely by SQL Server. The only code that will be required when programming will be to validate the value in the timestamp column.

# Summary

In this chapter, we have covered quite a bit of ground in three somewhat connected areas of SQL Server stored procedure coding.

**Cursors** are tools for writing row-at-a-time logic in our stored procedures. We should minimize their use in T-SQL code. They are great tools if you need them, but most of the uses of cursors could easily be rewritten using user-defined functions and basic SQL code. SQL Server does a better job using these facilities than it does with cursors.

**Transactions** are used to give us the ability to group together multiple operations into one, in our stored procedures. When you have multiple calls, where one call must succeed for the previous calls to be valid, use a transaction. Without them, we tend to get orphaned rows in our databases that can cause the DBA a real headache.

**Concurrency** actually consists of a number of topics, but it boils down to managing the needs of the integrity of the data against the desire to have more than one user working on the server at one time. It is dependent on the hardware subsystems and OS, as well as SQL Server locks, and how we manage them with isolation levels. The primary thing is to keep operations short, only touching the data that is needed to solve the problem at hand.

# SQL Server 2000

## Stored Procedures

# Handbook

**4**

# Common Practices with Stored Procedures

In the previous chapters, we discussed the benefits, disadvantages, and the syntax of stored procedures. In this chapter, we will focus on the purposes of stored procedures within our applications. Here's an outline of what we intend to discuss:

❑ Typical purposes of stored procedures

❑ Points to avoid while using stored procedures

*This chapter assumes that you are familiar with the stored procedure creation syntax and T-SQL in general. If you want clarification regarding the syntax, please feel free to refer to the earlier chapters.*

# Typical Purposes

In Chapter 1, we discussed the uses of stored procedures, but in addition to these, stored procedures have many more purposes:

❑ Encapsulating logic

❑ Improving performance

❑ Easing administration

❑ Abstracting the underlying base tables away from developers

❑ Simplifying code updates

- ❏ Improving database security
- ❏ Improving data validation
- ❏ Executing code at SQL Server startup

Stored procedures help to separate SQL code from the client applications. They eliminate the embedded T-SQL statements (also known as Inline T-SQL) and the surrounding logic from the application written in a compiled language, such as VB or C#, by placing the T-SQL statements into stored procedures within the SQL Server. The T-SQL statements within the compiled application are replaced with calls to the stored procedures.

## Encapsulating Logic

Encapsulating logic is an important aspect of stored procedures. It refers to placing all the commands necessary to perform an activity together, and exposing that group of commands as a single executable unit. Some important points regarding encapsulating logic are:

- ❏ Values passed to it through predefined parameters
- ❏ The output is produced in a consistent predefined format
- ❏ Setting values or dependencies is not required in the calling routine
- ❏ The routine is callable from anywhere within the application
- ❏ The routine can be called from multiple applications

Stored procedures help in implementing encapsulated logic, such as routines of code that we execute from different areas of an application, for example, a routine to create an order.

First, we need to create a hypothetical table for invoices. This table contains information on the customer invoices and the data payments received for them.

```
CREATE TABLE dbo.apress_Invoice
(
    InvoiceID            CHAR(5) PRIMARY KEY,
    OrderID              INT REFERENCES Orders(OrderId) NOT NULL,
    InvoiceDate          DATETIME NOT NULL,
    DueDate              DATETIME NOT NULL,
    PaymentReceivedDate  DATETIME NULL
)
```

Next, we insert some data into this invoice table for our testing purposes. We insert dummy invoices that came several months before the current date, and the due date which is one month after the invoice date.

```
INSERT apress_Invoice
SELECT '00001', 10643, DATEADD(MM,-5,GETDATE()),
  DATEADD(MM,-4,GETDATE()),NULL

INSERT apress_Invoice
SELECT '00002', 10692, DATEADD(MM,-4,GETDATE()),
  DATEADD(MM,-3,GETDATE()),NULL

INSERT apress_Invoice
SELECT '00003', 10702, DATEADD(MM,-3,GETDATE()),
  DATEADD(MM,-2,GETDATE()),NULL
```

We can now create our procedure that encapsulates the logic surrounding the creation of orders for our application.

First, we specify what information is needed to create a new order. As we have not defaulted the parameters to NULL (using @EmployeeID INT = NULL), we stipulate that these parameters must always be passed to create a new order, excluding any that will cause an error.

```
CREATE PROCEDURE CreateNewOrder
    @CustomerID    NVARCHAR(5),
    @EmployeeID    INT,
    @RequiredDate  DATETIME
AS
 SET NOCOUNT ON
```

Next, we issue a SELECT statement that counts the number of records that exist in the invoice table for the specified customer with a due date of 2 months (or more) before the current date, and have no payment received date (the number of invoices where the payment is more than 2 months overdue).

```
DECLARE @UnpaidInvoices INT,
        @NewOrderID INT

SELECT @UnpaidInvoices = COUNT(*)
FROM apress_Invoice i
INNER JOIN Orders o ON i.OrderID = o.OrderID
WHERE DueDate <= DATEADD(MM,-2,GETDATE())
AND PaymentReceivedDate IS NULL
AND o.CustomerID = @CustomerID
```

Next, if the number of unpaid invoices is greater than 2, then instead of adding a new order, we pass an error back to our client application specifying that the order cannot be created, and the reason behind it.

```
IF @UnpaidInvoices > 2
 BEGIN

    RAISERROR('This order cannot proceed as the customer has too many
unpaid invoices',16,1)
    RETURN 1

 END
```

Otherwise, we create the order as requested, and return the newly created order information back to the client application.

```
INSERT Orders(CustomerID, EmployeeID, OrderDate, RequiredDate)
SELECT @CustomerID, @EmployeeID, GETDATE(), @RequiredDate

SELECT OrderID, CustomerID, EmployeeID,
       OrderDate, RequiredDate
FROM dbo.Orders
```

This procedure can be called from anywhere within our application, and we can be sure that the business rules surrounding the order creation process will be applied, no matter where we call it. For example, we request an invoice creation from within a client application by executing the stored procedure with the following parameters:

```
EXEC CreateNewOrder 'ANATR',6,'20030610'
```

We receive the new order information back, as expected:

11080  ANATR 6  2003-01-02 11:51:35.247 2003-06-10 00:00:00.000

This is because the business rules for this particular customer are met. However, now we execute the stored procedure with a different set of parameters for a different customer:

```
EXEC CreateNewOrder 'ALFKI',6,'20030610'
```

We get a very different result, as this particular customer violates the business rules specified within our stored procedure:

Server: Msg 50000, Level 16, State 1,Procedure CreateNewOrder, Line 21
This order cannot proceed as the customer has too many unpaid invoices

Encapsulation provides us with obvious benefits, such as one location to maintain the code and another to debug it when a problem is discovered. However, ideally, stored procedures should be specific to the function as our aim is not code minimization but performance. We will look at this in more detail in the *Generic Stored Procedure* section.

# Improving Performance

By moving individual SQL statements and the surrounding data logic into stored procedure, we can improve the performance of our application by reducing the data sent over the network. To do this, we need to examine the data needed by our application's front end for processing or displaying, and then move the process of obtaining this information into a stored procedure, which is executed on the SQL Server. This can reduce the number of network round trips involved, by keeping the conversations between the client application and SQL Server short.

For example, suppose we need to create some application code that shows our organizational structure with the CEO at the top, and all the direct reports shown underneath this position (with appropriate indenting). There are a couple of ways we can approach such a problem; as you will see the two methods we demonstrate are two rather different approaches for reaching the same result.

For example, we use the following table for storing the details of employees:

```
USE Northwind
GO

CREATE TABLE EmployeeHierarchy

    (
        EmployeeID INT PRIMARY KEY,
        FirstName VARCHAR(255),
        LastName VARCHAR(255),
        ManagerID INT REFERENCES Employees(EmployeeID)
    )
```

Before we go any further, let's populate this structure with some sample data for this example. We can use the data located within the Northwind database to fill our table.

```
INSERT EmployeeHierarchy
SELECT TOP 1
    EmployeeID,
    FirstName,
    LastName,
    NULL
FROM Employees e1
ORDER BY NEWID()

WHILE @@ROWCOUNT<>0
BEGIN
    INSERT EmployeeHierarchy
    SELECT   TOP 1
        EmployeeID,
        FirstName,
```

```
        LastName,
        (SELECT TOP 1 EmployeeID
    FROM dbo.EmployeeHierarchy e2
    WHERE e1.EmployeeID <> e2.EmployeeID
    ORDER BY NEWID())
  FROM Employees e1
  WHERE e1.EmployeeID NOT IN
      (SELECT EmployeeID FROM EmployeeHierarchy)
END
```

The first INSERT statement within this script inserts a random employee as our organization's boss (an employee who has a NULL in their ManagersID column). TOP 1 used in conjunction with ORDER BY NEWID() gives us a random row as every time this function is called a different value is generated, which gives us an unpredictable order (and TOP 1 picks off the first row from that unpredictable order).

```
INSERT EmployeeHierarchy
SELECT TOP 1
  EmployeeID,
  FirstName,
  LastName,
  NULL
FROM Employees e1
ORDER BY NEWID()
```

Next we loop around while there are rows being affected, and on each pass of the loop we INSERT an employee into our EmployeeHierarchy table with a random employee as their manager. This is done when the employee doesn't already exist within our EmployeeHierarchy table, and where the manager is not the same employee as the current employee being inserted.

```
WHILE @@ROWCOUNT<>0
BEGIN
  INSERT EmployeeHierarchy
  SELECT    TOP 1
    EmployeeID,
    FirstName,
    LastName,
    (SELECT TOP 1 EmployeeID
    FROM dbo.EmployeeHierarchy e2
    WHERE e1.EmployeeID <> e2.EmployeeID
    ORDER BY NEWID())
  FROM Employees e1
  WHERE e1.EmployeeID NOT IN
      (SELECT EmployeeID FROM EmployeeHierarchy)
END
```

Okay, now we have our test data let's assume that we also have a VB application for displaying this information. This application may carry out the following steps – in this example we'll actually be using VB.NET code.

Further, let's assume that we also have a VB.NET application for displaying these details:

Now, we examine what this piece of code does. First, we define the objects we need and define a connection string for connecting to our SQL Server using Integrated Security.

```
Private Sub ShowManagerID(ByVal ManagerID As Integer, _
                          ByVal Level As Integer)

Dim cnSQL As New SqlConnection("Server=.;Integrated Security=SSPI;"& _
                          "Database=HRExmaple")
Dim cmdSQL As New SqlCommand()
Dim drSQL As SqlDataReader
Dim CurrentID As Integer
```

Next, we define an SQLCommand object. The command associated with this command object is a SQL Query which will retrieve all the child rows for the specified ManagerID. Don't worry if you're not too familiar with the exact details of the code – the SELECT statement should give you a good idea of what's going on here.

```
With cmdSQL
   .Connection = cnSQL
   .CommandText = "SELECT EmployeeID, FirstName, LastName " & _
                  "FROM Employees WHERE ManagerID=" & ManagerID
   .CommandType = CommandType.Text
End With
```

Next, we open a connection and execute this query.

```
cnSQL.Open()
drSQL = cmdSQL.ExecuteReader
```

In a While loop, we loop around every employee who reports to the specified manager. We execute this again in a nested fashion to retrieve all employees who work for the current employee, and display the output with a suitable number of spaces:

```
While drSQL.Read
   Console.WriteLine( Space(Level) & _
                      drSQL("FirstName") & _
                      drSQL("LastName"))
   ShowManagerID(drSQL("EmployeeID"), Level + 1)
End While
End Sub
```

In this example, we can see that there may be many round trips. If the organization has 1000 employees, it would translate into 1000 round trips, not to mention the opening and closing of 1000 `DataReader` objects which will likely impact on our application performance.

> **You should use a tool like SQL Profiler to examine the volume of statements sent by the application to the SQL Server if you plan to deploy your application over a slow link, especially if the application is not using stored procedures.**

An alternative approach is to examine what the client application really wants. In our case, it's a structure from which it can display the employee chart, and then to push the logic involved in creating this structure back to the SQL Server.

For example, we can use the following stored procedure for creating the employee chart:

```
CREATE PROCEDURE GetOrgChart
AS
  SET NOCOUNT ON

  CREATE TABLE #OrgChart
    (
      EmployeeID INT,
      EmpLevel   INT,
      FirstName  VARCHAR(20),
      LastName   VARCHAR(20)
    )
  DECLARE @Level INT

  SELECT @Level=1

  -- Insert our Boss
  INSERT  #OrgChart
  SELECT TOP 1
          e.EmployeeID, @Level, e.FirstName, e.LastName
  FROM   EmployeeHierarchy e
  WHERE ManagerID IS NULL

  WHILE @@Rowcount>0
  BEGIN
    SELECT @Level=@Level+1

    INSERT  #OrgChart
    SELECT  e.EmployeeID, @Level, e.FirstName, e.LastName
    FROM   EmployeeHierarchy e
    INNER JOIN #OrgChart oc2
      ON e.ManagerID = oc2.EmployeeId
```

```
      LEFT OUTER JOIN #OrgChart oc
        ON e.EmployeeID = oc.EmployeeId
      WHERE oc.EmployeeId IS NULL
   END

   SELECT * FROM #OrgChart ORDER BY EmpLevel
```

This stored procedure retrieves all the employees from our Employee table and adds a Level value, which can be used by our client application to construct the employee chart. Therefore, within our client application, we can code the following to retrieve this data:

```
Private Sub ShowOrgChart()

Dim cnSQL As New SqlConnection("Server=.;Integrated Security=SSPI;"& _
                              "Database=Northwind")
Dim cmdSQL As New SqlCommand()
Dim drSQL As SqlDataReader

With cmdSQL
   .Connection = cnSQL
   .CommandText = "GetOrgChart"
   .CommandType = CommandType.StoredProcedure
End With

cnSQL.Open()
drSQL = cmdSQL.ExecuteReader

While drSQL.Read
   Console.WriteLine( Space(drSQL("EmpLevel")) & _
                      drSQL("FirstName") & _
                      drSQL("LastName"))

End While

drSQL.Close()
cnSQL.Close()

End Sub
```

This code executes our stored procedure once and loops through the result set. Only one request will be made to SQL Server irrespective of the number of employees in our organization.

All of this can be achieved in a number of different ways. However, it demonstrates how a simple change in the location of certain application logic can lead to significant increases in network efficiency.

> **Ensure that you use the SET NOCOUNT ON option within your stored procedure. This prevents SQL Server from sending status information to the client application after the execution of each statement in the stored procedure.**

# Easing Administration

If our application is deployed in a full-scale SQL Server production environment, then the DBA will look after the database component of the application and ensure that the performance of the database falls within acceptable benchmarks. The number, physical size, and distribution of rows in various tables change over a period, thus affecting the performance of queries, effectiveness of existing indexes, and the decisions made by SQL Server about the execution plan.

If the queries are located within the stored procedures, then the DBA can easily examine the existing queries and optimize indexing to support them by adding query hints or redesigning a query, which can be done independent of the compiled application code (the front end). However, if the SQL statements are embedded within our compiled application code, they cannot be improved unless the DBA accesses the application's source code, makes the changes, recompiles it, and then redeploys it at the user's end, using tools such as the SQL Profiler.

Thus, if the DBA is unable to access the code to solve the problem, then it will come back to the developer for resolution, and solving production performance issues can be complex and time consuming. So, make it easier for the DBA to inspect your SQL code.

*I roughly estimate, from experience, that 85% of database performance problems or more are caused by inappropriate database design or sub-optimal SQL code, and the other 15% relate to configuration issues. If you restrict your DBA to optimizing configuration issues, you will find that they have little ability to maintain the performance of the database environment.*

## Performance Tuning

Another important reason for allowing the DBA to access the SQL script is that performance tuning cannot be done effectively in the development environment. Performance tuning isn't about making the individual statements execute quicker but balancing resources to ensure that every critical activity meets response time requirements

It is easy to speed up individual SELECT statements by just creating a bunch of indexes that cover everything that the queries need. However, this will affect other operations on the database, namely data modification. In simple words, our development environment should match the production environment dynamics in terms of size, volume, load, and hardware, each of which is essential for effective performance tuning.

# Simplifying Code Deployment

As a developer, this approach also offers some deployment benefits, especially if we use client-server architecture. We may have deployed our application code to hundreds or thousands of users. Any change in the query or surrounding data logic will require recompilation of the application and redeployment to all user machines.

If the change in the application coincides with a structural change within the database, we will have to ensure that all users receive the update at the same time. This is necessary to avoid the existing copy of the application from 'breaking down' due to the change in the database. This can be a complex issue with a large numbers of users spanning multiple locations. However, we can reduce the need to redeploy the compiled application by coding the data logic into the stored procedures, which will enable handling structural changes by changing only the stored procedure, as all user applications share them.

> **The deployment issues discussed are relevant to client-server style applications. Many applications developed recently use n-tier architecture while locating application code on centralized servers in an organization. This also helps mitigate the deployment issue, as code has to be deployed only once to the application servers and all users will receive the updated version.**

## Improving Database Security

SQL Server allows us to select various granular levels of security at the schema level. This helps to ensure that only authorized users can SELECT, INSERT, UPDATE, or DELETE the information from a table (and execute other DDL commands).

While planning application security, many developers miss the fact that security within SQL Server is simply an authorization mechanism, and not a validation mechanism. In other words, when we apply security within SQL Server we simply grant or deny the user the ability to utilize a resource. We do not specify the valid use of a resource.

If we do not use stored procedures, and instead grant permissions to a user to modify rows within a given table, we cannot dictate how those permissions should be used by that user. For example, if we want a user to have the rights for adding, deleting, and modifying customer records, we can issue the following command:

```
GRANT SELECT, INSERT, UPDATE, DELETE ON Customers TO Fred
```

This allows our database user Fred the right to SELECT, INSERT, UPDATE, and DELETE rows within our Customers database. These permissions will be required when Fred works on the front-end application developed for our Customers database, but do not restrict Fred's ability to exploit those permissions. For example, Fred can connect to the database using a query tool and execute DELETE all customers from the database.

```
DELETE Customers
```

Therefore instead of granting permissions directly to our database users, building stored procedures on which the EXECUTE permission has been granted to our database users (owner of the stored procedure) will be a better approach. The stored procedures can thus ensure that our users do not accidentally do anything that will severely damage our database information by carrying out the normal database application tasks in a controlled manner.

Consider the following stored procedure:

```
CREATE PROCEDURE DeleteCustomer @CustomerID INT
AS
    SET NOCOUNT ON

    DELETE Customers
    WHERE CustomerID=@CustomerID
```

Fred can still accidentally delete customers by passing a customerID to this procedure. However, he cannot delete all our records with one statement, which he will have to do by passing every customerID individually to the stored procedure. Now, if this downside is also unacceptable to us, we can use a status flag to indicate a deleted record instead of physically deleting records from the database:

```
CREATE PROCEDURE DeleteCustomer @CustomerID INT
AS
    SET NOCOUNT ON

    UPDATE Customers
    SET Delete=1
    WHERE CustomerID=@CustomerID
```

This will allow us to undo accidental DELETEs. We can change this stored procedure without affecting our client application (as long as we ensure that the stored procedures retrieving customer information exclude the rows with Deleted = 1) as it is abstracted from our client application

## *Improving Data Validation*

Security and validation go hand in hand. Security refers to preventing users from gaining access to rows for executing statements, while validation is concerned with the interpretation of the logic contained in those statements.

If we assume that our users have been granted access to INSERT rows into an Order Details table, this permission alone does not restrict 'what' they can insert. For example, the following INSERT statement is valid:

```
INSERT [Order Details](CustomerID, ProductID, Quantity)
VALUES(2, 102, 1000)
```

However, this should not happen if there are only 25 widgets available, and we should be able to enter an order only if there is enough quantity.

Therefore, we can create an alternative stored procedure instead. First, a transaction begins and the stored procedure compares the available stock with the desired quantity. An update lock hint is used to ensure that no other process changes the quantity of this product, until our transaction is complete.

```
CREATE PROCEDURE AddNewOrder
  @CustomerID AS INT,
  @ProductID AS INT,
  @Quantity AS INT
AS
  SET NOCOUNT ON

BEGIN TRANSACTION

IF (SELECT StockOnHand FROM .Stock WITH (UPDLOCK)
    WHERE ProductID=@ProductID) >=@Quantity
BEGIN
```

If there is enough stock, then the order is created, the stock is reduced, and the transaction is committed.

```
INSERT ORDERS(CustomerID, ProductID, Quantity)
VALUES(@CustomerID, @ProductID, @Quantity)

UPDATE STOCK
  SET StockOnHand = StockOnHand - @Quantity
WHERE ProductID = @ProductID

COMMIT TRANSACTION
```

If there is not enough stock, an error is generated and the transaction is rolled back:

```
ELSE
BEGIN
  RAISERROR("There is not enough stock to add this order",16,1)
  ROLLBACK TRANSACTION
END
```

If our users add orders using this stored procedure and have the ability to INSERT into the Orders table, then we can be sure that orders will not be created when there is no stock available.

## Constraints

Constraints, such as CHECK and FOREIGN KEY, protect our data and hence should be used wherever possible. However, while these provide some protection at the lowest level, there are still some benefits of the validation logic in a stored procedure.

First, constraints are evaluated during the course of the modification transaction. A violation of a constraint causes the transaction to be aborted and rolled back. While this is not so much of a problem for short transactions, it can be a significant waste of resource for long ones. We can check to see if the parameters are valid before starting any costly modification activity by validating the parameters before commencing any data modification statement.

For example, if our inventory system requires the ability to reduce the cost of our products uniformly by a fixed amount, our SQL code will look like:

```
CREATE PROCEDURE UpdateAllPrices @PriceReduction money
AS
UPDATE Products
 SET UnitPrice=UnitPrice-@PriceReduction
```

Now, our Products table has the following CHECK constraint on the UnitPrice column:

```
CONSTRAINT [CK_Products_UnitPrice] CHECK ([UnitPrice] >= 0)
```

This check ensures that the UnitPrice is over or equal to zero. If we execute this procedure with a price reduction of $10 resulting in a UnitPrice of less than 0, we will receive the following error message:

```
Server: Msg 547, Level 16, State 1, Line 1
UPDATE statement conflicted with COLUMN CHECK constraint 'CK_Products_UnitPrice'. The
conflict occurred in database 'Northwind', table 'Products', column 'UnitPrice'.
The statement has been terminated.
```

Unfortunately, this error condition is determined only when the condition is encountered, before which hundreds or thousands of rows could have been changed. All the rows that have been correctly modified must be rolled back, as all this occurs within the context of a transaction (either an explicit or an implicit transaction is defined by SQL Server, as in this example).

Therefore, while it is important to have the CHECK constraint, we can improve performance by doing some validation beforehand. After making a slight modification to our code, we have a procedure that validates the change before starting the transaction:

```
ALTER PROCEDURE UpdateAllPrices @PriceReduction money
AS
IF (Select Count(*) FROM Products
    WHERE UnitPrice-@PriceReduction<=0) >0
  BEGIN
    RAISERROR('Price change will result in some free products',16,1)
  END
ELSE
  BEGIN
    UPDATE Products
    SET UnitPrice=UnitPrice-@PriceReduction
  END
```

This stops the transaction from starting if it is known to fail, and also has the added benefit of allowing us to define more friendly error messages for interpretation by the calling application:

Server: Msg 50000, Level 16, State 1, Line 8
Price change will result in some free products

## Why not Build Validation in the Front-End Application?

Building validation logic into the front-end application is a common approach and is often used for performance benefits. Obviously, the load on the database server is reduced if we check the data for validity based on rules built into the application, as the database server is touched only when the modification is known to succeed. The problem with this approach and is security.

We are leaving the database exposed by building the validation logic into the front-end application. Using these methods, there is nothing to stop our users from opening up a connection to SQL Server by using a tool other than our application, such as Query Analyzer, Microsoft Access, or something similar and then issuing the command:

```
DELETE Customers
```

As all the validation will be handled in the front-end application, this command will be executed and the Customers database will be deleted.

SQL Server has the ability to 'tie' the database to specific applications by using an application role. Application roles are assigned a secret password that the developers can compile into their executable code, and the password can be passed to SQL Server when the application runs, providing the assigned permissions to the specific connection opened from that application. This prevents users from using other applications for establishing a connection with all permissions. Therefore, using application roles in conjunction with front-end validation of data is an acceptable approach for single purpose databases. Refer to SQL Server Books Online for more information on application roles.

The ability to integrate applications is becoming increasingly desirable within an enterprise environment. Users are not expected to re key data into a number of different applications anymore as the back-end processes do this. Ideally, these related applications would share the same data source so that there would be no need to distribute data between multiple systems. However, this is a difficult task, especially when we deal with applications from different vendors.

In addition, integration becomes less robust if data validation is performed in the front-end application, as the application validation rules are unknown at the back end, which is where the integration engine clips in.

In large enterprise applications that use multi-tier architectures, it is common to use a 'middle ground' approach and provide an integration point with a set of APIs that external applications can use. These APIs contain the validation logic needed for integration and are exposed publicly, separate from the application front end.

## Triggers

Triggers are a special type of stored procedure that we can use to enforce validation and auditing. Note that we will discuss about triggers in detail in Chapter 7.

Triggers and stored procedures have a couple of major differences that we should consider while selecting the most appropriate method:

|  | Stored Procedures | Triggers |
|---|---|---|
| User access to the base table | Not required. | Required. |
| Passing in parameters | Parameters can be passed. | Parameters cannot be passed. |
| Transactions | Multiple statements that are executed within a stored procedure do not participate within a common transaction unless explicitly defined. This can be done with the BEGIN TRAN, COMMIT TRAN, and ROLLBACK TRAN statements. | All statements executed in a trigger occur within a common transaction. In addition, transaction performs the modification to the base table that caused the trigger to be fired. |
| Ability of a user to bypass the stored procedures or triggers while performing validation on a base table | Stored Procedures can be bypassed if the user has permissions to access the base table. | Triggers cannot be bypassed by normal users. Object owners can disable a trigger. |

Triggers have the advantage that we can be sure that their logic is not bypassed. They are great for auditing purposes, so that we can be sure that every change on a given table is audited by the trigger. This is especially important if we are not using stored procedures to make changes to the table, or if we have many stored procedures that make changes to a given table. A trigger ensures that no code that makes modifications is forgotten about, thereby bypassing auditing requirements.

However, if we are not allowing direct access to base tables and have a manageable number of stored procedures that make changes to a given table, we may find it beneficial to use stored procedures, rather than triggers, to validate application logic. This is because triggers are executed within the context of a user transaction. This impact may be significant for AFTER triggers (refer to Chapter 7 for details), as the logic is checked after the data modification is made. The transaction is rolled back and the changes are undone if any validation problem is found. This impact is less significant for BEFORE triggers, as the changes can be checked before the modification takes place.

> **Essentially, if you need users to be able to make changes directly to a base table (for example, when they are using a tool that doesn't support stored procedures), then you need to use triggers to provide validation over and above what you can achieve with constraints.**

# Executing Code at SQL Server Startup

You can use the master.dbo.sp_procoption system stored procedure to specify the name of a stored procedure that must be executed as soon as SQL Server starts up For example, if you run an auditing procedure from within T-SQL, which captures information to a trace file. We can ensure that the auditing routine is started every time SQL Server is started with the sp_procoption system procedure, so that we do not lose important auditing information just because we forgot to begin the auditing process after a system restart.

**! A procedure must exist within the master database for setting it to start up automatically.**

For example, assume that we have a stored procedure that audits logon and logoff events to the C:\AuditTrace.trc file. If we want to be sure that we captured all logons and logoffs that occur on our server, we need to set this procedure to execute automatically with the SQL Server startup.

```
CREATE PROCEDURE dbo.AuditAccess
AS
  SET NOCOUNT ON
  DECLARE  @TraceID INT,
           @maxfilesize BIGINT
  SET @maxfilesize = 5
  EXEC sp_trace_create @TraceID output, 0, N'C:\AuditTrace.trc',
           @maxfilesize, NULL
```

The details of the commands used in this procedure can be found in SQL Server Books Online. We create a trace file named c:\AuditTrace.trc in the first section of code, where user access to our server will be recorded.

Next, we add all the trace events that correspond to the activities that we wish to audit. Each event must be added using a separate call to the sp_trace_setevent stored procedure. See the definition of the sp_trace_setevent stored procedure in SQL Server Books Online to find the corresponding event definition for each parameter value.

```
DECLARE @on bit
SET @on = 1
EXEC sp_trace_SETevent @TraceID, 14, 1, @on
EXEC sp_trace_SETevent @TraceID, 14, 6, @on
. . .
EXEC sp_trace_SETevent @TraceID, 15, 1, @on
EXEC sp_trace_SETevent @TraceID, 15, 6, @on
. . .
```

When we have set all the events that we want to audit, we set the trace status to 1, which corresponds to starting the trace:

```
EXEC sp_trace_SETstatus @TraceID, 1
```

To set this procedure to start automatically, we issue the sp_procoption stored procedure specifying our stored procedure name, the startup option and either ON or OFF depending on whether we want it to execute on startup or not. For example:

```
EXEC sp_procoption 'dbo.AuditAccess','startup','ON'
```

As we are using this only as an example and do not really want an SQL Trace to start every time we restart our server (especially in a test environment), we should disable this option now using the following command:

```
EXEC sp_procoption 'dbo.AuditAccess','startup','OFF'
```

However, if you want to have a continuous audit running on your server, you can use this as a template and expand it to meet your own requirements.

# Points to Avoid While Using Stored Procedures

Avoid the following while using stored procedures:

- ❑ Stored procedure grouping/versioning
- ❑ Nesting
- ❑ Generic stored procedures
- ❑ Many parameters

Each of these, although technically valid, should be avoided for logistical or maintenance reasons. We will discuss these reasons in the following sections.

## Stored Procedure Grouping

Multiple stored procedures can be grouped together with a single name by specifying a group number at the time of creation, for example:

```
GO
CREATE PROCEDURE GroupProcedure;1
AS
   SELECT COUNT(*) FROM Employees
   GO
   CREATE PROCEDURE GroupProcedure;2
   AS
      SELECT COUNT(*) FROM Orders
      GO
      CREATE PROCEDURE GroupProcedure;3
      AS
         SELECT COUNT(*) FROM Customers
         GO
```

We simply specify the procedure name followed by its number in the group, or just the procedure name, to execute it.

For example, the command:

```
EXEC GroupProcedure
```

is equivalent to:

```
EXEC GroupProcedure;1
```

**129**

These commands will return a COUNT(*) from the Employees table

The command:

```
EXEC GroupProcedure;2
```

returns a COUNT(*) from Orders, while the command:

```
EXEC GroupProcedure;3 -- Returns a COUNT(*) from Customers
```

returns COUNT(*) from Customers.

We simply execute the DROP PROCEDURE statement followed by the procedure group name, to remove the entire group of stored procedures:

```
DROP PROCEDURE GroupProcedure
```

**! It is not possible to drop individual members of the procedure group.**

For example, the following command will result in error:

```
DROP PROCEDURE GroupProcedure;3
```

The error returned is:

```
Server: Msg 170, Level 15, State 1, Line 1
Line 1: Incorrect syntax near ';'.
```

A practical use for this functionality is yet unknown, as it adds unneeded complexity. In addition, if we have multiple procedures with multiple functions, it can be used to create individual procedures with specific names to identify the functions.

Even if the procedures are related, we can use a naming scheme that shows the procedures are related, but it still allows us to assign a name based on function. On the other hand, grouped procedures appear as a single procedure within tools, such as Query Analyzer's Object Browser. The developer must remember the arbitrary number corresponding to a particular function.

**! Advanced features of SQL Server, such as deferred name resolution and auto-recompilation, reduce the need to drop and recreate multiple procedures. Hence, it should be considered for backward compatibility only, unless you think of a practical use for this feature.**

## Nesting Stored Procedures

Stored procedures can be nested (one procedure calling another procedure, which in turn calls another procedure, and so on). However, there is a limit of 32 levels on the nesting depth. If you are writing stored procedures that drill into other procedures use the @@Nestlevel global variable to examine the levels that the current execution is in, allowing you to exit gracefully when you reach the limit of 32 levels.

For more information on nesting stored procedures, refer to Chapter 1.

## Generic Stored Procedures

We have discussed earlier that it is a good approach to create specific procedures to support application functions rather than generic procedures to minimize code to optimize the performance of stored procedures. For example, a stored procedure used to create an invoice is a specific function that can be optimized to provide acceptable performance in the context of the production environment.

Conceptually 'creation' procedures (procedures that update rows) can be generalized into a single procedure that accepts a bunch of parameters. One of these parameters will be the name of the table that the rows are to be updated. While this approach certainly reduces the amount of code to maintain, optimization may be difficult, as the SQL query and the indexes required to satisfy the query optimally may change between executions, depending on the combination of parameters used. In addition, logic outside the generic operation will need to be removed from the stored procedures and pushed back into the application tier, which may require additional network round trips for processing.

> **Creating generic stored procedures is a common approach used by developers, who are experienced with traditional application development environments. This is a valid approach depending on your application architecture, however you should be aware that performance optimization might be more difficult if you keep your stored procedures generic.**

## Stored Procedures with Many Parameters

Stored procedures having many parameters go hand-in-hand with the generic procedures that we discussed in the previous section. Having many parameters is an indication that we have actually combined the logic for several stored procedures into one generic procedure. For example:

```
CREATE PROCEDURE SelectProc
  @Option1 INT=NULL,
  @CustomerId INT=NULL,
  @Option2 INT=NULL,
  @OrderId INT=NULL,
  @Option3 INT=NULL,
  @EmployeeId INT=NULL
AS
  SET NOCOUNT ON
  IF @Option1 IS NOT NULL
  BEGIN
    SELECT *
    FROM dbo.Customers
    WHERE CustomerID=@CustomerID
  END

  IF @Option2 IS NOT NULL
  BEGIN
    SELECT *
    FROM dbo.Orders
    WHERE OrderID=@OrderID
  END

  IF @Option3 IS NOT NULL
  BEGIN
    SELECT *
    FROM dbo.Employees
    WHERE EmployeeID=@EmployeeID
  END
```

The client application must be aware of the type of information it requires to correctly set the parameters for calling this stored procedure correctly. If this is the case, it is much more desirable and maintainable to have separate stored procedures, each with specific parameters for the specific function of the procedure. For example:

```
CREATE PROCEDURE GetCustomers @CustomerId INT=NULL
AS
  SET NOCOUNT ON
  SELECT *
  FROM dbo.Customers
  WHERE CustomerID=@CustomerID

GO

CREATE PROCEDURE GetOrders @OrderId INT=NULL

AS
  SET NOCOUNT ON
  SELECT *
  FROM dbo.Orders
```

```
    WHERE OrderID=@OrderID
GO

CREATE PROCEDURE GetEmployees @EmployeeId INT=NULL
AS
    SET NOCOUNT ON
    SELECT *
    FROM dbo.Employees
    WHERE EmployeeID=@EmployeeID
    GO
```

The second approach may result in a slightly increased number of network round trips to retrieve the same information; however, we have the additional benefit of being able to alter, optimize, and maintain each stored procedure individually.

# Summary

In this chapter, we have looked at utilizing stored procedures for effectively maintaining, securing, and optimizing our database, independent of the client applications that use it. We have discussed how creating function-specific stored procedures allow the DBA to optimize each individual area of function in the context of the complete application. We have also looked at the increased performance and easier maintainability resulting from stored procedures.

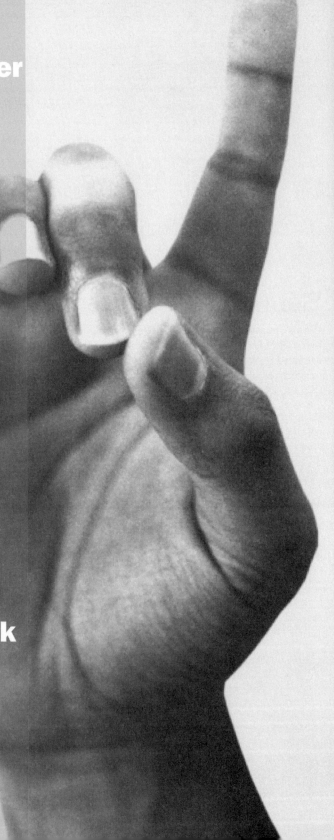

SQL Server
2000

Stored Procedures

Handbook

5

**5**

# System Stored Procedures

We could write a whole book only on system stored procedures. In fact someone already has; it's written by the Microsoft SQL Server team and is available under the *System Stored Procedures* section, which is included under the *Transact-SQL Reference* section of SQL Server Books Online. It covers over 250 system stored procedures that are documented in good detail. If you need information about a particular system stored procedure, this is the best place to begin with.

In this chapter, we will not repeat the material covered by SQL Server Books Online. Rather, we will be giving you an overview of system stored procedures, and their implementation by Microsoft. We will also look at some of the undocumented functionalities provided with SQL Server, which Microsoft uses to make their system stored procedures work. Along the way, we'll be giving you tips and tricks on when to use (and on avoiding) their quite useful, but obviously 'unsupported', undocumented functionalities.

Later, we will give our list of top 25 (in no particular order) documented system stored procedures. That said, if we get 1000 DBAs in a room and ask them to list their top 25 system stored procedures, we'll get 1000 (alright, maybe 999) different lists. So please don't quibble over our non-definitive list.

The actual number of system stored procedures can be found out by doing a query on the SYSOBJECTS table where type equals P (a stored procedure) or type equals X (an extended stored procedure). This would yield us a figure of over 1100 in SQL Server 2000 Service Pack 2. Using the same query on the msdb and distribution databases will give us over 350 more stored procedures which Microsoft had put in its build. However, the number of system stored procedures that have been actually documented by Microsoft is around 400.

Readers involved in managing SQL Servers, as a part of their day-to-day task, will find this chapter quite helpful. The section on Mining System Stored Procedures will be especially useful to those involved in T-SQL coding.

Let's now start our discussion with a brief overview of system stored procedures.

# System Stored Procedures

Traditionally, in a SQL Server, a system stored procedure is a stored procedure that exists in the master database and begins with the three characters sp_. System stored procedures are provided by Microsoft to keep users from having to directly access system tables, while performing administrative tasks. When DBAs talk about system stored procedures, you will often hear them pronounce it as *SP underscore* .

System stored procedures also include some extended stored procedures. There are a very small number of system stored procedures beginning with xp_ (pronounced as *XP underscore*). They replace the functionality provided by the earlier versions of system extended stored procedures, having the same name. Extended stored procedures are different from stored procedures in that while stored procedures execute T-SQL code, extended stored procedures execute C++ code in the SQL Server memory space. These extended stored procedures may begin with the prefix sp_ but often begin with the three characters xp_ as well.

As we can see, some system stored procedures begin with sp_, others with xp_. There is a reason behind this. Object types in the master database, including stored procedures and extended stored procedures, having a **global scope** are created with the sp_ prefix. Stored procedures created with the xp_ prefix do not have this global scope. By global scope, we mean that they can be called from any database, as if they were contained in that database. They don't need to be fully qualified by the owner (DBO) and database (master) names.

**! These sp_ objects must be created under the ownership of DBO in order to have global scope. Objects created under other ownerships in the master database don't have global scope, even if they begin with sp_.**

Under SQL Server 2000 and SQL 7, system stored procedures are technically defined by setting a bit in the status integer column of the sysobjects table in the master database. If we look at the description of SYSOBJECTS table in SQL Server Books Online, we will notice a column called status that is described as Reserved. For internal use only. Microsoft uses this and several other similar columns, such as a bit map, to turn control the functionality of system stored procedures. When we say bit map, we mean that the column will be in sums of powers of 2.

For example, when a procedure is created with QUOTED_IDENTIFIER turned on, the status column will have the integer value of $2^{30}$ (or 1073741824). Other powers of 2 included in the column have different functionality. Microsoft has reserved a special status column setting for system stored procedures.

A system stored procedure will have the integer value of $-2^{31}$ (that is -2147483648) added in the status column. In terms of bit notation, we would refer to this as 0x80000000. Thus, if a stored procedure had a status column value of -1073741824, Microsoft would interpret this as $2^{30}$ (QUOTED_IDENTIFIER on) plus $-2^{31}$ (a system stored procedure).

Another way of looking at the effects of setting a status bit is to look at the object properties. If the system status bit is set, the object will have the property of isMSShipped.

In SQL 2000 Service Pack 2, there are over 900 procedures with this special status bit set. One such procedure is an undocumented procedure called sp_MS_marksystemobject. If we delve into the details of this procedure, we will see that its status column in sysobjects has the value 0xC0000000. This marks it as a system stored procedure with QUOTED_IDENTIFIER on.

To see which stored procedures have the status bit set, execute the following code:

```
SELECT status, objectproperty(id,'IsMSShipped'), name
FROM master.dbo.sysobjects
WHERE status & 0x80000000 = 0x80000000
ORDER BY name
GO
```

*Change the = sign in the above code to <> to see which ones don't have the system stored procedure bit set.*

However, Microsoft usually doesn't use sp_MS_marksystemobject for setting the status bit. When Microsoft creates a system stored procedure, an undocumented trace flag 1717 is turned on by using the sp_MS_upd_sysobj_category procedure. We can see examples of this in the INSTALL directory of any Microsoft SQL 2000 installation.

For example, look at the UPGRADE1.SQL file. In the proc sp_MS_upd_sysobj_category, we can see a warning from Microsoft; it is embedded in a comment. We have quoted it below, word-for-word:

```
NOTE: THE IMPLEMENTATION (i.e. using trace bit 1717) IS *VERY* LIKELY
TO CHANGE, SO DONT EVEN *THINK* ABOUT USING THIS TRACE BIT DIRECTLY!!!
```

Later on in this chapter, we'll talk about using the undocumented features of SQL Server. However, this is a good warning to remember when using any undocumented SQL Server functionality.

## *Effect of the 0x80000000 Status Bit*

As mention in the last section, system stored procedures in the master database beginning with sp_ can be called from any local database, and they will execute in the context of the local database. Furthermore, while we are in the context of a local database, if we precede the system stored procedure name with any other database name and owner name, they will execute in the scope of that other database.

Now, here's a tricky part. If the status column bit 0x80000000 is set, as discussed above, either by running the sp_MS_marksystemobject on the procedure after we create it or by setting the 1717 trace flag with the sp_MS_upd_sysobj_category procedure before creation, the system stored procedure will act differently from other stored procedures in master, even if the other stored procedures begin with sp_.

The best way to explain this is to create two different stored procedures with identical names, one in master and one in a local database such as pubs. We'll name the two procedures sp_test. In the master version of sp_test, we will execute the command PRINT 'master', while in the local (pubs) version of sp_test, we will execute the command PRINT 'pubs'.

Here are the two versions:

```
USE master
GO
CREATE PROCEDURE sp_test AS PRINT 'master'
GO
```

```
USE pubs
GO
CREATE PROCEDURE sp_test AS PRINT 'pubs'
GO
```

We'll create the master version without setting the 0x80000000 STATUS column bit. Now execute the procedure in the local pubs database, in Query Analyzer. The statement for this is EXEC sp_test. We'll see that the output is pubs. Then, execute the sp_test script from any other database, for instance Northwind; it will return master.

Now, drop both versions of the stored procedure. We will create them again; however, this time before creating the master database version, execute the following script:

```
USE master
GO
EXEC sp_configure 'allow updates',1
GO
Reconfigure with override
GO
EXEC sp_MS_upd_sysobj_category 1
GO
```

Setting the server configuration to `allow updates` on is included for completeness, in case you need to manage any system table values or expose some specialized functionality. `Reconfigure with override` makes the `allow updates` setting to take immediate effect. The parameter 1 for `sp_MS_upd_sysobj_category` turns on the trace flag 1717.

Don't let us mislead you into thinking that we manage system table functionality often; we do it extremely rarely. Generally, Microsoft does a good job of taking care of these objects. However, one case does come to mind where we have managed system table functionality. With integrated security, we can go into User Manager and disable a user, thereby giving us the option to re-enable that user later on. No such option exists for the SQL Server standard logins.

However, we've written our own procedure that renames the existing logins, for example we will rename `JohnSmith` to `JohnSmith-Disabled`. It also goes and gives `JohnSmith-Disabled` an unusable 128-character password. If we've allowed John Smith to own any tables, views, procedures, or, worse still, user-defined data types, we don't have to worry about rebuilding those objects. Later, if John Smith's login needs to reactivated, we simply run the same system stored procedure to change `JohnSmith-Disabled` back to `JohnSmith` and give him a reasonable password. To do this we had to modify the `sysxlogins` system table in the `master` database. That's where `allow updates` comes into play.

Next, create the `master` version of `sp_test` and then execute the following script:

```
EXEC sp_MS_upd_sysobj_category 2
GO
Exec sp_configure 'allow updates',0
GO
Reconfigure with override
GO
```

This time, the parameter 2 for `sp_MS_upd_sysobj_category` turns off the trace flag 1717. Similarly, we turn off the setting for `allow updates`. Then create the `pubs` database version, without any changes. Now, no matter which database context we execute the procedure in (even if it's `pubs`) the version of the stored procedure from the `master` database will always be used over any other version in the local database. Even if we explicitly run the script `EXEC pubs.dbo.sp_test`, it will still return `master` as the result.

The significance of this difference in functionality between a procedure beginning with `sp_` and the `status` bit set and one beginning with `sp_` and the `status` bit not set is very important.

For example, we could write a local version of a procedure called `sp_password`, having the same input parameters as that of the system stored procedure; in our localized version, we can include some code that will cache the new password and login to a known place for later curious eyes. This will be a security hole, but by setting the `status` bit for a `master` database system stored procedure, we can completely eliminate the possibility of anyone else making a different version of the stored procedure, in another database.

> **By setting the 0x80000000 status bit, we can always make
> our system stored procedures execute the master database
> version thereby forestalling a very serious security hole.**

## Making System Stored Procedures with the 0x80000000 Bit

Microsoft 'strongly recommends' that we don't make any stored procedures beginning
with sp_. For all we know, in future, Microsoft may do away with the automatic global
scope of sp_. Instead, they may throw in a status bit that, when set, gives a procedure
global scope. Truly speaking, the global scope of sp_ is really an undocumented
functionality. Use it at your own risk.

This said, most of the DBAs who make their own stored procedures in master end up
naming them with the prefix sp_. However, they don't make them as true system
stored procedures, since they may not know the 0x80000000 status column bit
phenomena, which we just discussed.

To make your own system stored procedures, simply wrap your procedure script (or
scripts) in the scripts that we discussed in the previous section, begin the procedure
name with the three characters sp_, and you will have created your own system stored
procedure.

It is advisable to create our own system stored procedures, as in certain situations they
can be quite helpful. Nevertheless, how do we ensure that we will not overwrite (or be
overwritten) by a later Microsoft system stored procedure? One way of ensuring this is
by beginning our system stored procedures with the four characters sp__ (note that it's
a double underscore).

In doing this, we get three advantages:

❑   We can guarantee that our procedures will always have a different name
    from that used by Microsoft.

❑   We can make a localized version of a Microsoft system stored procedure
    that has different or additional functionality. For example, if we want to
    customize the results of sp_helptext, we can write a procedure called
    sp__helptext, which can do the job for us (note that the latter name has
    two). This new system stored procedure can also have input parameters.

❑   Finally, when we look at the list of stored procedures in the Query
    Analyzer's or SQL Enterprise Manager's Object Browser list, these
    procedures are at the top of the list.

**!** **We strongly advise you to only create system stored procedures only on servers where you have authoritative control over what goes into the master database – servers that you directly manage.**

We would like to give you many of the system stored procedures that we use; however they don't belong to us. They belong to the companies that we work for and not Apress. Therefore, we can only tell you about the features of our system stored procedures but they are quite easy to develop.

One such stored procedures is called `sp__database$create`. As mentioned before, our system stored procedures start with the double-underscore `sp__`. Non-system stored procedures don't have this prefix, they generally have `object$method`. `sp__database$create` allows us to create databases the same way, every time. It is parameterized and designed to do the common things that we need to do for every database that we create.

The default parameters demand that we make certain extended properties for a default table in our database. These extended properties define who created the database and what it was created for. It automatically creates the underlying file structure for the three database-related files and their associated filegroups. It does this by querying the registry for specific data values, which we code into it. These values will vary from server to server depending on the makeup of the disk structure of the server. If these values aren't there, then it looks for Microsoft's default locations.

If the server's disk is compressed, then it makes sure that the folders where we create our database files are uncompressed. Our system tables go in the first or PRIMARY filegroup, transaction logs on the second, and all other tables on the third, by making the third the default filegroup right when the database is created. It creates each file in each file group with the desired file size and growth rates.

We don't like to use the default commands in the CREATE DATABASE command, since, by default, it changes the database owner from our integrated login to the sa login for standardizing database ownership issues. Also, our custom-made procedure has parameters that help us to make the backup model simple, bulk-logged, or full (the default). By default, it simulates all this and produces the scripts for accomplishing this. Only when we set another parameter flag does it actually perform the database creation and subsequently runs `sp_helpdb` to provide us with information regarding our new database. Remember, Microsoft provides us with the basic system stored procedures and system commands, such as CREATE DATABASE, to handle the required functionality, not the nice-to-have functionality.

**!** **Professionals *always* thoroughly document the stored procedures that they write because they write so many that they will forget what they did earlier if they don't document well. Make sure that your system stored procedures are properly documented.**

Some of us will argue that we shouldn't design such things into servers. Their argument is, what happens when you, who have read this book and really sharpened your skills, move on to a better position and the company has a less ambitious DBA, who may get bewildered by the work you have done?

Our argument is that, firstly, your company should recognize your skills and make your job enjoyable enough (often translated as more pay and perks) to keep you from moving on to greener pastures. Besides, if you are as good as you think you are, you are adequately documenting everything that you are doing, aren't you? Our stored procedures, user-defined functions, and the triggers that we write have tons of documentation built into them, both in the form of a header description, as well as throughout the code.

Our header description includes:

❏   The purpose for the procedure

❏   A description of its normal usage

❏   A description of every parameter and their default, normal, and acceptable values

❏   A description of the expected output and the error code output

❏   A change log to tell who made modifications to the procedure and what the modifications were

❏   It also includes a note about any unsupported functionality that we might use in the procedure, such as Microsoft's system extended stored procedures that manage the registry

The cost of this documentation in terms of process cache memory space is negligible compared to the benefit of having it there for later review and analysis.

**!** **Remember that, we should *never* create a stored procedure in the master database for a product that we are going to ship. Chances are that it might be overwritten by someone else; besides, most DBAs consider it extremely bad and unprofessional for a vendor to sell them an application that puts any objects in the master database.**

## An Important Feature of System Stored Procedures

Microsoft exposes the functionality of some undocumented functions by limiting their usage to objects where the 0x80000000 bit is set in the sysobjects.status column.

We discovered this feature by accident. We were attempting to record the history of our domain; we wanted to extract the domain SID for a user and store it into a SQL database. Naturally, one of the first places we looked into was the stored procedure sp_grantlogin. This system stored procedure adds a reference for a domain user into the SQL sysxlogins table.

`sp_grantlogin` uses an undocumented stored procedure called `sp_MSaddlogin_implicit_ntlogin`. This procedure uses an undocumented function called `get_sid` to return the SID from either the domain or the computer. We started playing around with `get_sid`. No matter how often we ran the query, in exactly the same way that `sp_grantlogin` used `get_sid`, instead of getting a VARBINARY SID to stick in our database it kept on returning NULL.

We ran our standard query to find out where `get_sid` was used:

```
SELECT DISTINCT object_name(id) FROM SYSCOMMENTS
WHERE text LIKE '%get_sid%'
ORDER BY 1
```

Feel free to use this query over and over in your investigations of stored procedures. Just substitute `get_sid` with the phrase that you are look for.

When we executed this query, ten system stored procedures, including some very well known ones, such as `sp_changedbowner`, popped into the list. Then we generated the scripts for each of these procedures. All ten used `get_sid` exactly the way we were doing in our testing.

Now, we knew that the only thing these ten documented and undocumented system stored procedures had in common was that they had the 0x80000000 status bit set in their `status` columns. So, we created a very simple stored procedure that used `get_sid`, when we fed it the input parameters of a domain and user account name. Wrapped around this stored procedure, we ran the `sp_MS_upd_sysobj_category` toggle on/off script (we had discussed it earlier in the section on *The Effect of the 0x80000000 Status Bit*). All of a sudden, the `get_sid` function worked, as expected. The 0x80000000 status bit was a hidden switch, which allowed the GET_SID function to work.

If you are planning to use the `get_sid` function or other 0x80000000 functions, you might ask the question – "Can I use them in stored procedures in other databases, besides `master`?" The answer is – yes. Just wrap the stored procedures, which they contain, in the `sp_MS_upd_sysobj_category` toggle script before you create them.

**❗ Note that, when you upgrade your servers to a later version of SQL Server, to certify their continued functionality you will have to perform regression testing on your stored procedures.**

By the way, here's our procedure for `sp__getsid`:

```
CREATE PROCEDURE sp__getsid (@loginame sysname)
-- Note: This procedure uses UNDOCUMENTED
-- functionality compatible with SQL 2000 SP2
AS
DECLARE @newsid VARBINARY(85)
SELECT @newsid = get_sid('\U'+@loginame, NULL)     -- NT user
```

```
IF @newsid IS NULL  -- the loginame is not a user
SELECT @newsid = get_sid('\G'+@loginame, NULL)   -- NT group

IF @newsid IS NOT NULL
BEGIN
  SELECT @newsid
  RETURN 0
END
ELSE   -- the login is not a user or group
BEGIN
  SELECT 'No SID was available for '+ @loginame
  RETURN 1
END
```

# Other Features of SP_: Global Tables and Views

In the section on *System Stored Procedures*, we had mentioned that certain types of objects, beginning with sp_ in the master database, could be accessed from any other database, as if they were in that other database. This doesn't apply only to stored procedures and extended stored procedures; it also applies to tables and views created in the master database with the sp_ prefix. If you've been working in SQL Server for any length of time, initially it may seems strange to create a table or view beginning with sp_. Some purists will cry heresy; however, we saw it as a solution to many issues. It shouldn't be discounted.

For example, let's assume we have a database, called Geodemog, common to all our servers, storing common data for many of our applications. This database holds country, state, mailing code, area code, and enterprise-wide people lookup tables. We replicate it around our enterprise from a single master point. We could create views to it in our databases; instead, we will create the views in master, such as sp_vw_People that in turn points to the Geodemog.dbo.People table.

Now, when we reference sp_vw_People from a stored procedure in the telephone billing application in our enterprise, we gain a level of indirection. This indirection is quite helpful, as it gives us the flexibility to change underlying objects without having to recompile our code.

In future, if we want to store this data in a different database or even in a different medium, such as Active Directory for our enterprise-wide people lookup tables, we can easily make the change. All we need to do is to simply go into the master databases in our enterprise and quickly recode sp_vw_People view to point to the new database or data source. We don't have to reach out and change all those stored procedures spread across our enterprise; with this simple technique, we can save enormous amounts of time.

Unlike stored procedures, the 0x80000000 status bit setting doesn't apply for sp_ tables and views. If we create a table or view in a local database with the same name as the one in the master database, then the one in the local database will be referenced first.

# Common Documented System Stored Procedures

As we mentioned in the beginning of this chapter, we are going to give you our list of top 25 documented system stored procedures. Note that, there are some pairs in our list, as we consider them indispensable in the day-to-day job of a DBA.

As mentioned earlier, we will not repeat the information given in SQL Server Books Online. Rather, drawing upon our experience, we are going to highlight these procedures and make you aware of the values and problems that SQL Server Books Online doesn't mention or hides in the small print. At the same time, we always encourage you to refer to SQL Server Books Online for examples and detailed information about their input parameters and so on:

| Stored Procedure | Description |
| --- | --- |
| sp_who2 | It is an indispensable proc and inevitably the first one that we run in a production environment, when troubles occur. Pay attention to the BlkBy or Blocked By column of its output. This column tells us who is blocking whom. When a user complains about a process not running, run sp_who2 quickly to look for blocking. Follow it up with DBCC INPUTBUFFER (spid) to gain information about the guilty BlkBy spid. |
| sp_lock | It is another invaluable system stored procedure from our troubleshooting kit. It is used to cross reference blocking problems found in sp_who2. |
| sp_password | This procedure adds or changes a password for a SQL Server login. Note that the first parameter can be NULL for sas. Thus, to quickly set a password run:<br><br>sp_password NULL, newpassword, loginname |
| sp_configure | When run without any parameters it's a great way of gauging the setup of a SQL server. It's necessary for a DBA to know the general settings of every parameter; don't forget to set the show advanced options to 1. |
| sp_dboption | It is the database equivalent of sp_configure. It's suggested that you get to know the meaning of each option. |

*Table continued on following page*

| Stored Procedure | Description |
|---|---|
| sp_changedbowner | Inevitably, we will have databases created by users (including ourselves) with integrated security. We need to make sure that these databases are changed to an owner who will not be later disabled; we recommend either the sa account or the server system account. This system stored procedure accomplishes this. |
| sp_attach_db<br>sp_detach_db | These two procedures are very handy for taking a database out of the system catalog, without deleting its files. We can then copy the files to another location or server; reattach the original and the copy. We can even use a new name for either. Note that, while running sp_attached_db if the file names and paths haven't changed from when we detached our database, we only need to attached the primary file. It will look in the sysfiles table and find out where to attach the other files from. However, if we move any file from its original location, we will have to explicitly list the new location. |
| sp_change_users_login | When we do copy database files (don't forget the transaction log) over to another server and reattach it, any standard login SIDs will be out of sync between the database sysusers table and the server sysxlogins table; use this procedure to resynchronize them. |
| sp_rename | This made it into our top 25 not because we like it, but because we wanted you to understand the dangers involved in using this on stored procedures. When we rename a stored procedure, the original definition of the stored procedure with the original name is still stored in the syscomments table. For example, if we rename a proc called Database$SaveAll to Database$SaveAll_Old, then make a new system stored procedure call Database$SaveAll and finally script out Database$SaveAll_Old in Query Analyzer; the script will generate a warning message. |
| sp_spaceused | It's very handy to calculate the space used by the whole database or a single table. For a single table, it can also give us the row count and the relative amounts of space used by both data and indexes. |

| Stored Procedure | Description |
|---|---|
| sp_procoption | This procedure has one use – to make startup procedures in the master database. Startup procedures can be extremely powerful (and dangerous); make sure they are well tested and don't have any output results or input parameters.<br>If you do get in trouble, for example, if the SQL Server doesn't start or hangs when a startup procedure runs; rather than starting the SQL Server as a service, run the SQLSERVR.EXE executable from a command prompt with the 4022 trace flag.<br>The command is:<br><br>**SQLSERVR.EXE /T4022**<br><br>Then go in and rebuild the procedure, without making it a startup procedure. |
| sp_help | This procedure reports information about a database object. |
| sp_helptext | Use this to script out the text of stored procedure to the Query Analyzer's result pane; then, we can copy it to a new pane for analysis, with those nice colors on. |
| sp_helpdb | Use it without a parameter to list all databases, and with a parameter to find file information for a particular database. |
| sp_helpserver | It lists all the servers that your server has a relationship with, and mentions what the relationship is all about; it is very handy in a multi-server environment. |
| xp_msver | This extended stored procedure returns build and environment information about the SQL Server; don't be afraid to store the contents in a temporary table for later use. See the sp_addqueued_artinfo stored procedure for an example of how to do this (just run:<br><br>EXEC sp_helptext sp_addqueued_artinfo<br><br>in a Query Analyzer window). |
| sp_grantlogin<br><br>sp_addlogin | These two procedures add integrated and standard logins to a server, respectively. sp_grantlogin supports groups as well as users. Microsoft treats integrated and standard logins quite differently, even to the point of having two different procedures for their implementation. |

*Table continued on following page*

| Stored Procedure | Description |
| --- | --- |
| sp_grantdbaccess<br>sp_adduser | These procedures add integrated and standard logins, as database users, respectively. Again, sp_grantdbaccess works with groups as well as users. |
| sp_addrole<br>sp_addrolemember | There are huge advantages to creating your permission structure around roles instead of users in a database. The first procedure creates the role, while the second sets up the relationship between that role and either a user or another role; that's right, a role can be contained in another role. |
| sp_xml_preparedocument<br>sp_xml_removedocument | XML in SQL 2000 is still in its infancy; then why have we listed these procedures here? There's an important reason, as mentioned in SQL Server Books Online, behind it.<br>A parsed document is stored in the internal cache of SQL Server 2000. The MSXML parser uses one-eighth of the total memory available for SQL Server. To avoid running out of memory, run sp_xml_removedocument to free up the memory. |
| sp_cycle_errorlog | We can use this procedure to keep our SQL error logs in order, without having to restart our SQL Server. We will be looking at an example later on. |
| xp_sendmail | SQL Server uses this stored procedure to send a message and a query result set attachment to the specified recipients. It is capable of mailing us with various notifications and exception conditions. |
| xp_cmdshell | This stored procedure has its set of proponents and opponents. Some will say that we should never have it on a production server; however, in our opinion, we should lock it down tightly but have it available. We've had instances where NetBIOS was dead on our production server, and the only way into the server was through SQL port 1433 using TCP/IP sockets. In such a situation, having this procedure at our command was invaluable for system diagnosing.<br>Removing this stored procedure will break some features, such as replication. In short, never let anyone but a sa to run this procedure. |

| Stored Procedure | Description |
| --- | --- |
| xp_logininfo | This stored procedure is not used frequently but it can be invaluable in hunting down permission-related problems. |
| sp_executesql | We can use this procedure to execute dynamic SQL. This procedure is preferable to using an EXECUTE statement for two reasons:<br>1. It allows for parameter substitution, and<br>2. There is a good chance that for repeated usages, as in a loop, the execution plan will get cached and reused; something that is guaranteed not to happen with the EXECUTE statement. |

# Other Important System Stored Procedures

In its *System Stored Procedure* section, SQL Server Books Online lists 17 categories of system stored procedures. For brevity's sake, we won't cover them in detail; feel free to refer to SQL Server Books Online.

Here are some quick pointers to guide you:

❑ If you are a DBA, then you should have some knowledge about each of the procedures mentioned in the *System Stored Procedure* section of SQL Server Books Online. Take a few minutes every day to read one or two articles from this section.

❑ You should know that SQL Server 2000 is capable of linking to other servers. The *Distributed Queries Procedures* will get you there.

❑ You can *and* should script out replication when you move your server into production. This is well documented in SQL Server Books Online.

❑ Make sure you are familiar with the *Log Shipping Procedures*. In log shipping, transaction logs from one database on a server are applied to the same database on a second server. The second database is considered to be **in standby**. This state is read-only with only restoration of logs allowed. Log shipping is only available in the Enterprise version of SQL Server. If you have the Standard version and think you might want to do log shipping, get hold of the SQL Server Resource kit. It has a **log shipping lite** solution. If you do have the Enterprise edition, use the Database Maintenance Plan to start testing and then move to scripting out your log shipping solutions using these stored procedures. If you log ship to tape, you'll have to use the stored procedures only.

❑ Only members of the sysadmin role can execute any of the procedures in the *OLE Automation Extended Stored Procedures* section. This is for good reason, as they are quite powerful. Essentially any DLL registered on the server is available to these stored procedures, with all its methods and functionality. The next version of SQL Server (known before its release as Yukon) fixes this, as well, by creating security environment levels to give more granular control to such functionality.

❑ Your developers should be intimately familiar with the *Catalog Stored Procedures*. They should be able to use them for interfacing their applications with SQL security.

❑ Although sp_validatelogins in the *Security Procedures* section didn't make it to our top 25 list, you should become familiar with its usage for cleaning up orphaned NT user logins.

❑ We will be discussing about the XP_TRACE logins later in the section on *Tracing Object Creation and Deletion*. Make sure you are familiar with it.

❑ SP_Start_Job and SP_Stop_Job in the *SQL Agent Procedures* can be very helpful. Anything we can do in the Jobs GUI can be done with the procedures from this section.

# Mining System Stored Procedures

One of the neat things about system stored procedures is that we can easily examine them to learn 'how Microsoft does it'. Often, we have ended up digging through system stored procedures for an insight into how Microsoft writes their T-SQL code. At times, we have come across code nuggets that can be quite handy; we can easily add to them our repertoire. It's always a profitable idea to learn the techniques employed by Microsoft for carrying out complex jobs.

While mining Microsoft techniques in their system stored procedures, you need to keep one thing in mind – generally, system stored procedures are not designed for high frequency, high concurrency applications. However, note that this doesn't mean that adding a login as a user ID in a database or creating a distribution database for replication are high frequency tasks. While the T-SQL code nuggets are certainly good for examples of how to code T-SQL, it may not be the most efficient at minimizing resource conflicts.

There are over 900 stored procedures and more than 170 extended stored procedures in an out-of-the-box SQL Server 2000's master database. Don't stop there; be sure to look in the msdb database and, after installing replication, the distribution database. There are more than 350 system-supplied stored procedures in these two databases.

It's also worth having a look at the SQL scripts Microsoft uses to set up SQL server (these are available in the `Install` folder of your SQL Server installation). These scripts are particularly good for mining when you need to set up your own database installations. Further, they are valuable to look at when you are trying to understand what Microsoft is doing with a particular extended stored procedure. Quite often, they will have hints about what the extended stored procedure is used for.

# Undocumented Functionality

Now that we have examined the important documented system stored procedures, let's move on to discuss about the undocumented functionalities provided in SQL Server. Before we begin our discussion, here's a word of caution – while working with undocumented functionality, apart from indicating that we are using undocumented functionality we should always ensure that our code is well documented.

We've heard some people saying that if you are going to use undocumented functionality, when a documented SQL-DMO function is available by writing an extended stored procedure, you should write the extended stored procedure. This is usually not true in our camp; others will differ. When you do version regression testing, you are still going to have to test your extended stored procedure just as much as you have to test your usage of undocumented functionality. It is a whole lot easier to test the SQL function than to pull through the C++ code. As often as not, both will work, but which would you prefer to debug?

In all likelihood, in the next version of SQL Server stored procedures and assemblies exposing the C# and VB.NET coding environments will be available. In such a situation, when given the choice between undocumented functionality in SQL and rolling your own in a VB.NET assembly our resolve will weaken. However, as of now, we aren't there yet.

Documentation of any undocumented functionality used in our code is critical. We will always include the word UNDOCUMENTED in a comments section at the top of our stored procedure that use undocumented functionality. This enables us to easily execute a simple search through the `text` column of the `syscomments` table for each database for this word. This will give us a list of all the places that need to undergo regression testing before moving a new stored procedure or patch into production.

We should not shy away from using undocumented functionality in our production and development environment, where we manage the system. As an example, we had described the `sp__database$create` procedure earlier (refer to the section on *Making System Stored Procedures with the 0x80000000 Bit*).

Such usage is responsible and desirable. DBAs shouldn't have much problems in using undocumented functionality in their homemade system stored procedures and on their company's proprietary utility database. However, outside this scope they should be reluctant to use undocumented functionalities. They should be used only if there is no other way of performing the task, and this will happen very rarely.

# Finding Undocumented Extended Stored Procedure Functionality

As we mentioned before, we can mine system stored procedures to see 'how Microsoft does it'. Generating their code through SQL Query Analyzer can easily accomplish this. However, extended stored procedures behave in a different matter. About the only thing that we can see in SQL Query Analyzer is the DLL on which the extended stored procedure relies. So how can we figure out what a procedure does?

We begin by selecting the extended stored procedure we are interested in then we run the following query in the `master` database:

```
SELECT DISTINCT object_name(id) FROM syscomments
WHERE text LIKE '%extended stored procedure name%'
```

As we mentioned earlier, `syscomments` table is where the code definitions of stored procedures, views, functions, table functions, check constraints, computed columns in tables, and defaults live. Here, we are looking for procedures using the particular extended stored procedure we are attempting to mine. Quite often, we will strike out in querying the `master` database. This is because the functionality of that extended stored procedure may not be used in the `master` database.

Remember that only the `master` database can have extended stored procedures. Other databases will make use of these procedures. Particularly, if the extended procedure begins with `sp_`, run the above query in both `msdb` database and the `distribution` database (we have looked at it the section on *Mining System Stored Procedures*). More often than not, we'll discover that many of the extended stored procedures exist for replication, and are called by a stored procedure in the `distribution` database.

# Windows-Registry Related Stored Procedures

Microsoft routinely reads the registry with probably the most 'well-known' undocumented system stored procedures. They all begin with the characters XP_Reg. Here, we'll examine each of them in detail. By default, these procedures are only available to system administrators; we encourage you to keep it that way.

## The Windows Registry

Before we start our discussion, let's have a brief look at the registry. The registry is a hierarchical database of relatively unchanging information that controls almost all aspect of our machine's operation and user's environment. It is unforgiving if you mess it up, so use extreme caution while making any changes to it. If you've never explored the registry before, it can be fascinating to see how things are put together.

For beginners, we recommend using the REGEDT32.EXE program. In this program, you can set an option for making the registry read-only – from the Options menu, choose Read Only Mode. We can also use this program for changing the security settings on a registry key or when we want to connect to the registry of a remote machine. REGEDIT.EXE is another program that we can use to edit the registry, its search capabilities are much more robust than REGEDT32.EXE. In Windows XP, these two programs have been merged together into a single application, callable with either name.

The registry is composed of hives, keys, sub-keys, values, and data. In the following figure, we can see the HKEY_LOCAL_MACHINE hive, the SOFTWARE key, the _Test sub-key in the left pane:

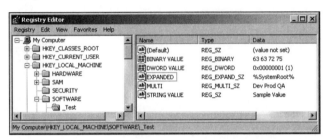

In the right pane, we can see the values and their corresponding data settings. Values will generally be one of several different types. The most common are String Value (REG_SZ) and DWORD Value (REG_DWORD). String values are just that, while the latter are 4-byte integers.

> **!** **Editing the registry can be dangerous even if you think you know what you are doing. You should not use any of these registry procedures until you have thoroughly tested them on a development machine.**

In the course of our discussions, we will be working with a key called Software\_Test in the HKEY_LOCAL_MACHINE hive. If you start the registry editor with the command REGEDT32.EXE, you will be able to make the various keys shown in the previous screenshot.

## XP_RegRead

The most commonly used registry-related system stored procedure is XP_RegRead. It has two functions:

- ❑ The first is to determine if a registry key exists or doesn't exist
- ❑ The second is to read data for a specific value

> **!** **When you are doubtful about the existence of a key, you should always test its existence before attempting to read data from it.**

To determine if a key exists, use the following code:

```
CREATE TABLE #keyexist (keyexist INT)
DECLARE @regkey NVARCHAR(1000), @hive NVARCHAR(1000),@keyexist INT
SELECT @hive = 'HKEY_LOCAL_MACHINE'
SELECT @regkey = N'SOFTWARE\_Test'
INSERT INTO #keyexist
EXECUTE master.dbo.xp_regread 'HKEY_LOCAL_MACHINE', @regkey
SELECT @keyexist = keyexist FROM #keyexist
IF @keyexist = 1
... -- continue with your code once you determine the key exists
```

If the key exists, the XP_RegRead returns an integer value of 1, else it returns 0.

To read a registry DWORD, STRING, or BINARY value using XP_RegRead, use the following code:

```
DECLARE @data SQL_VARIANT, @regvalue NVARCHAR(1000), @rc INT
DECLARE @regkey NVARCHAR(1000), @hive NVARCHAR(1000)
SELECT @hive = N'HKEY_LOCAL_MACHINE'
SELECT @regkey = N'SOFTWARE\_Test'
SELECT @regvalue = N'String Value'

EXECUTE @rc = master.dbo.xp_regread @hive, @regkey, @regvalue,
        @data OUTPUT, N'no_output'
SELECT @rc,@data
```

MULTI-STRING values store multiple 0 to n strings. Each stored string is known as an item.

To read a MULTI-STRING value using XP_RegRead, we use the following code:

```
DECLARE @regvalue NVARCHAR(1000), @rc INT
DECLARE @regkey NVARCHAR(1000), @hive NVARCHAR(1000)
CREATE TABLE #regmultistring
  (Item NVARCHAR(1000),
   Value NVARCHAR(1000)
   )

SELECT @hive = N'HKEY_LOCAL_MACHINE'
SELECT @regkey = N'SOFTWARE\_Test'
SELECT @regvalue = N'Multi'

EXECUTE @rc = master.dbo.xp_regread @hive, @regkey, @regvalue
SELECT Item,Value FROM #regmultistring
DROP TABLE #regmultistring
```

This returns a record set of the MULTI-STRING values; here, we have called it Multi.

**Usage Notes**

While using this code snippet, please keep the following things in mind:

❏ Acceptable values for the @hive parameter for all XP_Reg procedures are:

- HKEY_LOCAL_MACHINE

- HKEY_CURRENT_USER

- HKEY_USERS

- HKEY_CLASSES_ROOT

❏ The XP_RegRead stored procedure will not read a registry value of type REG_EXPAND_SZ (expanded string). An expanded string has an embedded environment variable; an attempt to read such a value will return NULL.

❏ If you have REG_EXPANDED_SZ or REG_BINARY in the key, it may throw an extra column or two when attempting to populate a temporary table by reading from a REG_MULTI_SZ value. This can be found out only by testing.

❏ Sometimes when you read a REG_MULTI_SZ value, it may return an extra column. You need to pad your temporary table with this column; its data should be NULL. Only testing can reveal this.

❏ As a rule of thumb, when you use an NVARCHAR data type in XP_Reg procedures, it will be NVARCHAR(1000). This is what Microsoft does in their usage of XP_RegRead.

# XP_RegWrite

The system stored procedure XP_RegWrite writes to the registry. There are quite a few examples in both the master and msdb databases that make use of this procedure. The trick in using this procedure lies in knowing the type of value that will be written:

| Key type | Data type |
|----------|-----------|
| REG_SZ | NVARCHAR |
| REG_DWORD | INT |
| REG_BINARY | VARBINARY |

Here are some examples of each. It shows us how to make a key with only a default, blank value:

```
DECLARE @retcode INT
EXECUTE @retcode = master.dbo.xp_regwrite N'HKEY_LOCAL_MACHINE',
    N'SOFTWARE\_Test',
    N'', -- the default, non-named value
    N'REG_SZ',           -- the value type
    N''                  -- this is the blank data
SELECT @retcode
```

For adding or changing a `REG_DWORD` value:

```
DECLARE @intDWORD INT, @retcode INT
SELECT @intDWORD = 0
EXECUTE @retcode = master.dbo.xp_regwrite N'HKEY_LOCAL_MACHINE',
                   N'SOFTWARE\_Test', N'DWORD VALUE', N'REG_DWORD',
                   @intDWORD
SELECT @retcode
```

For adding or changing a `REG_SZ` value:

```
DECLARE @value_string NVARCHAR(1000),@retcode INT
SELECT @value_string = 'Sample Value'
EXECUTE @retcode = master.dbo.xp_regwrite N'HKEY_LOCAL_MACHINE',
                   N'SOFTWARE\_Test', N'STRING VALUE', N'REG_SZ',
                   @value_string
SELECT @retcode
```

Adding or changing a `REG_BINARY` value:

```
DECLARE @value_binary VARBINARY(1048),@retcode INT
SELECT @value_binary = 0x63657273
EXECUTE @retcode = master.dbo.xp_regwrite
  'HKEY_LOCAL_MACHINE',
  N'SOFTWARE\_Test',
  N'BINARY VALUE',
  'REG_BINARY',
  @value_binary
SELECT @retcode
```

**Usage Notes**

Keep the following things in mind while running these scripts:

❑ The acceptable hive definitions are the same as those for `XP_RegRead`.

❑ If the key and/or value are not present, they will be created. If the value exists, it will be changed to the new value and type (if different).

# XP_RegEnumKeys

`XP_RegEnumKeys` is commonly used to seed nested cursors while mapping the keys or sub-keys. We will not use `XP_RegEnumKeys` for checking the existence of a key, as `XP_RegRead` works much better here:

```
DECLARE @regkey NVARCHAR(1000), @retcode INT
CREATE TABLE #keylist (key_name NVARCHAR(1000))
SET @regkey = 'SOFTWARE'
INSERT INTO #keylist
EXECUTE @retcode = master.dbo.xp_regenumkeys
'HKEY_LOCAL_MACHINE', @regkey
SELECT @retcode
SELECT key_name FROM #keylist
DROP TABLE #keylist
```

## XP_RegEnumValues

XP_RegEnumValues will usually return a two-column result set for REG_SZ, REG_MULTI_SZ, and REG_DWORD value types. It may return ragged column result sets if we have REG_EXPAND_SZ or REG_BINARY types in the registry. Extensive testing is needed for getting around this potential error.

Here's an example that uses our Software\_Test key (refer to the earlier screenshot):

```
CREATE TABLE #values
   (value NVARCHAR(1000) NULL,
    data NVARCHAR(1000) NULL
    )

EXECUTE xp_regenumvalues N'HKEY_LOCAL_MACHINE', N'SOFTWARE\_Test'
SELECT value,data FROM #values
DROP TABLE #values
```

For this example, you may get a ragged column. This will be characterized by a column number mismatch error. If you do, delete the REG_EXPAND_SZ and the REG_BINARY values during your testing. Obviously, in a production situation, this would be a concern:

**Usage Notes**

Here's the usage note:

❑ Similar to XP_RegRead for REG_MULTI_SZ, the presence of REG_BINARY or REG_EXPAND_SZ value types can cause errors, causing the output of XP_RegEnumValues to have ragged columns. The extra columns would show up as extra value columns. As a result, testing the code is necessary.

## XP_RegDeleteKey

Before explaining this procedure, it is worth repeating here to be extremely careful when making changes to the registry.

**!** **Rollback isn't available when you are executing these procedures. This is a particularly dangerous procedure, as it can to wipe out your entire registry in very short time.**

Except for some parts of the HKEY_LOCAL_MACHINE\System key, backups aren't easily available.

In this example, we will first check for the existence of the key and then try to delete it:

```
CREATE TABLE #keyexist (keyexist INT)
DECLARE @regkey NVARCHAR(1000), @keyexist INT, @retcode INT

-- regdelete returns 'Access Denied' message if key does not exist;
-- check before delete
SELECT @regkey = N'SOFTWARE\_Test'
INSERT INTO #keyexist EXECUTE master.dbo.xp_regread
                                'HKEY_LOCAL_MACHINE', @regkey

SELECT @keyexist = keyexist FROM #keyexist
IF @keyexist = 1
BEGIN
   EXECUTE @retcode = master.dbo.xp_regdeletekey 'HKEY_LOCAL_MACHINE',
                  @regkey
   IF @@error <> 0 OR @retcode <> 0
   BEGIN
      SET @retcode = 1
      GOTO FAILURE
   END
END
FAILURE:
DROP TABLE #keyexist
```

If you try to delete a non existent key, you will get the error message:

```
Msg 22001, Level 1, State 22001
RegDeleteKey() returned error 2, 'The system cannot find the file
specified.'
```

## XP_RegDeleteValue

This stored procedure is used to delete a single value:

```
DECLARE @retcode INT
EXECUTE @retcode = master.dbo.xp_RegDeleteValue N'HKEY_LOCAL_MACHINE',
                  N'SOFTWARE\_Test', N'Multi'
SELECT @retcode
```

**Usage notes**

While using this procedure, keep the following point in mind:

❑    Whether you actually delete a value or not, the return code from the
     procedure will be zero if the three parameters of hive, key, and value are
     included with the correct data types

## XP_RegAddMultiString

This and XP_RegRemoveMultiString are the least understood of the registry extended
stored procedures. Multi-string values, REG_MULTI_SZ, are essentially lists of strings in the
registry. Each separate string in a multi-string value is called an item. Implicit to a multi-
string value is an item count. The first item will be item 1, the next item 2, and so on. As
the name implies, these procedures add and remove items from a multi-string value list.

What you are going to see here is new ground. None of Microsoft's system stored procedures has ever used it. Frankly speaking, we are unsure why Microsoft added it into their code; nevertheless, we've found uses for it in our production scripts.

Here's the only correct example of this procedure that we've ever seen:

```
DECLARE @data_item_multi NVARCHAR(1000),@retcode INT
DECLARE @value_multi NVARCHAR(1000)
SELECT @data_item_multi = N'ItemX', @value_multi = N'MULTI'
EXECUTE @retcode = master.dbo.xp_regaddmultistring
                N'HKEY_LOCAL_MACHINE', N'SOFTWARE\_Test',
                @value_multi, @data_item_multi
SELECT @retcode
```

### Usage notes

These are the usage notes for this stored procedure:

❑ When you run XP_RegAddMultiString, you are adding a new item to a registry array value of type REG_MULTI_SZ.

❑ If the registry value doesn't exist previously, it will be created with item value of 1.

❑ Subsequent additions to an existing value will increase the item count by 1.

❑ If you add the same data item again to the same value, it will show up as a second item with the same data. This is particularly important to note when discussing XP_RegRemoveMultiString.

## XP_RegRemoveMultiString

Like XP_RegAddMultiString, this is the first time you will be seeing an accurate working demo of XP_RegRemoveMultiString in publication, either print or electronic. The syntax is similar to XP_RegAddMultiString:

```
DECLARE @data_item_multi NVARCHAR(1000),@retcode INT
DECLARE @value_multi NVARCHAR(1000)
SELECT @data_item_multi = N'ItemX', @value_multi = N'MULTI'
EXECUTE @retcode = master.dbo.xp_regremovemultistring
                N'HKEY_LOCAL_MACHINE',N'SOFTWARE\_Test',
                @value_multi, @data_item_multi
SELECT @retcode
```

### Usage notes

Let's look at the usage notes for this stored procedure:

❑ If no data string matches the string specified in the @data_time_multi variable, nothing will be deleted and the return code will be zero.

- ❑ If there is one or more data items equivalent to the data item specified, all such data items will be deleted, not just the first one.

- ❑ When all data items are deleted from a value, the value will not be deleted itself. In order to delete the value, you should use XP_RegDeleteValue.

## XP_Instance_Reg Extended Stored Procedures

As you probably know by now, SQL Server 2000 can have multiple instances. This is a change from SQL 7 and earlier versions, which only allowed one instance. In the registry, the default instance of SQL Server is always found under the key:

```
HKEY_LOCAL_MACHINE\ Software\Microsoft\MSSQLServer.
```

In Windows 2000, the named, non-default instances are found under the key:

```
HKEY_LOCAL_MACHINE\Software\Microsoft\Microsoft SQL Server\instance
```

where instance is the name of the instance provided at installation time.

In order to handle multiple instances, Microsoft put together the set of XP_Instance_Reg stored procedures. They have a one-to-one correlation with the XP_Reg stored procedures that we have just discussed. What happens is that you always specify the second key parameter as if you were specifying the key parameter for the default instance. However, if you are in a named instance the stored procedure senses this and redirects you from the \Microsoft\MSSQLServer key to the \Microsoft\Microsoft SQL Server\instance key. You don't have to specify the instance name. You can see that XP_Instance_Reg is used frequently in the msdb database when actions are being taken with the SQL Server Agent.

When the key specified is outside the scope of \Microsoft\MSSQLServer key, the XP_Instance_Reg stored procedures act exactly like their XP_Reg stored procedure equivalents. Interestingly, there is a set of keys in

```
HKEY_LOCAL_MACHINE\System\CurrentControlSet\Services
```

for both the SQL Server service and the SQL Agent service.

The XP_Instance_Reg procedures will not automatically detect the correct service keys for these keys. A good example of how Microsoft resolves these service names can be found in the msdb procedure sp_get_sqlagent_properties. Here, to build the SQL Agent service key name, the function SERVERPROPERTY('INSTANCENAME') is used.

# *The File System*

A number of undocumented extended stored procedures exist for working through the file system. We will discuss some of them, as they can be quite helpful for getting things in and out of the file system and also, for checking the existence of files, folders, and drives.

Like the registry procedures, it's advisable to make sure that these procedures are only available to system administrators. If you have to open them up to an application for users write wrapper procedures, which can control the input parameters.

## XP_AvailableMedia

XP_AvailableMedia returns a result set listing the available drives on the host server for SQL Server. It has a single optional input parameter, TINYINT, that can be interpreted as a bitmap variable for the drive type.

The result set has four values – name, low free, high free, and media type. The combination of the low free and high free columns describes a 64-bit number representing the free space on the disk. If the low free is greater than zero, then it represents that number of bytes. If it is less than zero, then it represents $2^{32}$ plus the low free value bytes. This result is then added to $2^{32}$ times the high free value to get the total number of bytes on the disk. To make the number more meaningful, in the following example, we have divided the result by 1MB to get the number of megabytes.

The media type appears to be some sort of a TINYINT bitmap. The XP_AvailableMedia can take a single parameter of type TINYINT. The valid values for it are:

| Value | Description |
|-------|-------------|
| 1     | Both floppy drive and fixed disks are shown in the output |
| 2     | Only fixed disks are shown in the output |
| 8     | Only CDROM drives are shown in the output |
| 255   | This shows all media types in the output |

Here is a good example, which shows the output of the procedure. This example will also calculate the available free space for the media:

```
SET NOCOUNT ON
CREATE TABLE #availablemedia
   (name CHAR(3),
    [low free] INT,
    [high free] INT,
    [media type] TINYINT
   )
```

```
DECLARE @mediabitmap TINYINT
SELECT @mediabitmap = 255
INSERT #availablemedia
EXECUTE xp_availablemedia @mediabitmap

SELECT name, [low free], [high free],
  (CAST((CASE when [low free] >= 0 THEN [high free]
  ELSE [high free] + 1 END) AS FLOAT) * 4294967296.0 +
  CAST([low free] AS float))/1048576.0 AS 'Available MBytes',
CASE WHEN [Media Type] = 2 THEN 'Fixed Disk'
WHEN [Media Type] = 8 THEN 'CDROM'
WHEN [Media Type] = 1 THEN 'Floppy'
ELSE 'Unknown Media Type' END AS 'Media Type'
FROM #availablemedia
DROP TABLE #availablemedia
```

## XP_SubDirs

XP_SubDirs returns a single column result set called subdirectory. The values are the immediate subdirectories of the single input parameter, which is the parent directory of the subdirectories.

Here's an example:

```
DECLARE @parentdir NVARCHAR(4000)
SELECT @parentdir = N'c:\temp'
EXEC xp_subdirs @parentdir
```

## XP_DirTree

XP_DirTree returns a two-column result set. The first column is called subdirectory and is of type NVARCHAR. The second column is called depth and is of type INT. The procedure has a required input parameter of type NVARCHAR representing the parent directory and an optional input parameter of type INT representing the depth to return. If the second parameter is specified, then only subdirectories with a depth equal to or less than the specified depth will be returned in the result set. If the second parameter is omitted then all subdirectories of any depth are returned in the result set.

Here is an example that returns the immediate subdirectories of the C:\temp folder:

```
CREATE TABLE #dirtree
  (subdirectory NVARCHAR(1000),
   depth INT
  )
INSERT #dirtree
EXECUTE xp_dirtree N'c:\temp',1
SELECT subdirectory, depth FROM #dirtree
DROP TABLE #dirtree
```

## XP_FixedDrives

XP_FixedDrives is quite similar to XP_AvailableMedia, except that it will list only fixed disks and its precision on available free space is only an integer number of megabytes. It returns a two-column result set. The first column is called drive and is of CHAR(1) data type. The second column is called MBFree and is of type INT. It has no input parameters.

Let's look at an example:

```
CREATE TABLE #fixeddrives
    (drive CHAR(1),
     MBFree INT
     )
INSERT #fixeddrives
EXECUTE xp_fixeddrives
SELECT drive, MBFree FROM #fixeddrives
DROP TABLE #fixeddrives
```

## XP_FileExists

XP_FilesExists is a flexible stored procedure. It is always called with a first parameter containing the path and file name. If the path is omitted from the first parameter and only a file name is given, it will default to the system root folder.

It can be called with a second optional OUTPUT parameter. In this case, it will be a Boolean flag specifying whether the file exists or not. If the second optional OUTPUT parameter is omitted, the procedure returns a single record of three columns. The three columns are File Exists, File is a Directory, and Parent Directory Exists. Each column is a Boolean flag.

Here are two examples, the first with the optional OUTPUT parameter:

```
DECLARE @fileexists INT
EXECUTE xp_fileexist 'c:\windows\explorer.exe', @fileexists OUTPUT
SELECT @fileexists
```

This second example doesn't use the optional OUTPUT parameter; use it to test the existence of a folder:

```
CREATE TABLE #fileexist
    (FileExists BIT,
     FileIsDirectory BIT,
     ParentDirectoryExists BIT
     )
INSERT #fileexist
EXECUTE xp_fileexist 'c:\windows'
SELECT * FROM #fileexist
DROP TABLE #fileexist
```

# XP_ReadErrorLog

After reading its name, you might think that XP_ReadErrorLog is designed for just reading the SQL Server's error log. This is only partly true; this undocumented stored procedure has the capability to return any text readable file in its entirety. It can return specific rows from the text file that match one of two string search parameters. It is a very flexible and useful stored procedure.

Generally and by default, only system administrators should be allowed to access this procedure. In some instance, you may want to write a wrapper procedure around this that would tightly control the filenames it can read. Since it runs in the SQL Server memory space, it has permissions to read any file that the SQL Server service system account has access to.

The syntax of this procedure is:

```
xp_readerrorlog
{@errorLogNumber{,@filename{,@searchstring1{,@searchstring2}}}
}
```

The procedure takes four input parameters. They are:

❑ @errorlognumber TINYINT
It is optional and accepts numbers between 1 and 99. If omitted, all other parameters should also be omitted, and it will return the current SQL Server error log. If it is added and no other parameters are used, it should be between 1 and 6 and will return the corresponding ERRORLOG.n from the SQL Server's log folder. If the second @filename parameter is specified, it should have a value between 1 and 99.

❑ @filename
This is parameter optional and is of type VARCHAR(255). It consists of the fully qualified name of the file that is to be read. You can pass it a non-text file, but the results may be somewhat bizarre and unpredictable.

❑ @searchstring1
It is an optional parameter of type VARCHAR(255). If this and @searchstring2 are omitted (or NULL), then every line from the file will be returned in the result set. If the value of this parameter is an empty string (' '), then it will return all non-blank lines that have a space in them. If it is a string of characters, then it will return all lines that have that string of characters in them. For example, a value of 'the' would be analogous to using the T-SQL comparison function of LIKE '%the%'.

❑ @searchstring2
This parameter is also optional, and is of type VARCHAR(255). It acts like @searchstring1. If @searchstring1 and @searchstring2, are both specified, then the result set is a Boolean AND of their string matches.

The result produced by this procedure is quite interesting. It consists of two columns – a `Line` column of data type `VARCHAR(256)` and a `RowContinuation` column of type `BIT`. Normally the `RowContinuation` bit is 0. If the row from the file is more than 256 characters, it will wrap to the next row and subsequent rows and the `RowContinuation` bit will flip to 1. You can think of it this way: when the `RowContinuation` bit is equal to 1, the row appends to the end of the previous row in a continuous chain until you get to a row with a `RowContinuation` bit of 0.

Here are three examples that make use of this stored procedure:

Example 1 returns the current error log:

```
DECLARE @retcode INT
EXECUTE @retcode = xp_readerrorlog
```

Example 2 returns the error log file `ErrorLog.5` from the log folder

```
DECLARE @retcode INT
EXECUTE @retcode = xp_readerrorlog 5
```

Example 3 will read the file named `hosts` from the `C:\Temp` folder and returns only rows having a space and the character string `the` in them:

```
DECLARE @errorlognumber TINYINT, @retcode INT
DECLARE @filename VARCHAR(255)
DECLARE @searchstring1 VARCHAR(255)
DECLARE @searchstring2 VARCHAR(255)
CREATE TABLE #filerows
   (ident INT IDENTITY,
    line VARCHAR(256),
    continuationRow INT
   )

SELECT @errorlognumber = 1
SELECT @filename = 'C:\Temp\hosts'
SELECT @searchstring1 = ''  -- returns non-blank lines with a space
SELECT @searchstring2= 'the'

-- searches for the three characters 'the' in a line
INSERT #filerows (line, continuationRow)
EXECUTE @retcode = xp_readerrorlog @errorlognumber, @filename,
                  @searchstring1, @searchstring2

SELECT line, continuationRow FROM #filerows
   ORDER BY ident
DROP TABLE #filerows
```

# Performing Complex Tasks with System Stored Procedures

In our list of top 25 documented system procedures, we had mentioned about `sp_cycle_error_log`. Now we will see an example that makes use of this stored procedure.

In our office, we use a process that every night cycles our SQL Server Error log and makes an ISO labeled file with the day's error log. We have a SQL Agent job that runs this stored procedure at 23:59 every night. Making it a startup procedure, by using the `sp_procoption` system stored procedure, ensures that an error log after a reboot is added to the error log copy. It uses both documented and undocumented (`sp_instance_regread`) system stored procedures. We've given the production quality script below:

```
SET QUOTED_IDENTIFIER ON
GO
SET ANSI_NULLS ON
GO

CREATE PROCEDURE sp__errorlog$archivelog
-- ----------------------------------------
-- sp__errorlog$archivelog
-- ----------------------------------------
-- WARNING: This procedure uses UNDOCUMENTED functionality compatible
-- with SQL Server 2000 GA, Service Pack 1, and Service Pack 2.
-- ----------------------------------------
-- Description:
-- Create an ISO log from the "errorlog.1" file each time errorlog is
-- cycled or server restarts. An ISO log is a 'date-named' file named
-- like: errorlog.yyyymmdd

-- This proc is run at each sql server startup (which creates a new
-- errorlog.1 file).

-- It is also run by a SqlAgent task that runs at midnight, and right
-- before it calls this proc, it issues "dbcc errorlog" to cause a new
-- "errorlog.1" to be built.

-- If this proc is run accidently before a new "errorlog.1" is
-- created, it will just append the current errorlog.1 to the ISO
-- log file again. No harm is done as it's just duplicate data.

--    Run this job from SQL Agent at 23:59 every night.

-- Implementation
-- IMPORTANT:  Each time you re-create this procedure, it needs to be
-- made a startup procedure. Run the command:
-- exec sp_procoption N'sp__errorlog$archivelog', N'startup', N'true'
-- ----------------------------------------
```

In the documentation for the procedure, we can see the capitalized word UNDOCUMENTED. This is a key word for searching SYSCOMMENTS table later, during version and stored procedure upgrades for regression testing.

```
AS
DECLARE @PathNoExt NVARCHAR(1000), -- path to error log from the
                                    --registry
@PathISO VARCHAR(255),      --the ISO format log, errorlog.YYYYMMDD
@DosCmd VARCHAR(255),       --Dos command to append errorlog.1 to make
                            --date-name errorlog
@RC INT                     --The return code
--  ----------------------------------------
-- Only cycle the errorlog between 23:59 and 24:00, otherwise just
-- append current errorlog.1 to an existing file
--  ----------------------------------------

WAITFOR DELAY '000:00:02'   -- wait for two seconds to ensure we are
                            -- well into the 23:59 minute.

IF GETDATE() BETWEEN DATEADD(N,-1, DATEADD(D,1,CONVERT(DATETIME,
   CONVERT(VARCHAR(20),GETDATE(),101)))) AND
   DATEADD(D,1,CONVERT(DATETIME,CONVERT(VARCHAR(20),GETDATE(),101)))
BEGIN
   EXEC @RC = master.dbo.sp_cycle_errorlog

   IF @RC <> 0
   BEGIN
     RAISERROR 50000 'Errorlog did not cycle'
     RETURN -1
   END
END
```

Next, we test to see if the time is between 23:59 and 24:00. If so, we will cycle the error log. The other time the procedure runs is on SQL Server startup and you can already assume that the error log has been cycled.

```
--  ----------------------------------------
-- Get the Path to the Sql ErrorLog from the registry
--  ----------------------------------------
Exec @Rc = master.dbo.xp_instance_regread N'HKEY_LOCAL_MACHINE',
          N'Software\Microsoft\MSSQLServer\ MSSQLServer\Parameters',
          N'SQLArg1', @PathNoExt OUTPUT, N'no_output'

IF (@PathNoExt is null) or @RC <> 0
BEGIN
   RAISERROR 50000 'sp_errorlog$archiveLog cannot obtain Sql ErrorLog
     Path'
   RETURN -2
END
```

Then, we get the path to the error log from the registry and generate the path string to our ISO `ErrorLog.YYYYMMDD` file:

```
-- ------------------------------------------
-- Create Output FileName based on date (ISO name)
-- ------------------------------------------
-- Trim off the first two characters and append a backslash and the --
- file name
SELECT @PathISO = SUBSTRING(@PathNoExt,3,998)+ N'\errorlog.' +
    CONVERT(CHAR(8), GETDATE(), 112)
SELECT @PathNoExt = SUBSTRING(@PathNoExt,3,998) + N'\errorlog.1'

-- ------------------------------------------
-- Build commands to append new errorlog.1 to the Date-Name (ISO)
-- file. @DosCmd will look like:
-- TYPE "C:\MSSQL\LOG\errorlog.1" >>"C:\MSSQL\LOG\errorlog.20010605"
-- The >> will create the output file if it does not exist. if it
-- exists it will append it to the output file
-- Use double-quotes around file names in case they have embedded
-- spaces.
-- ------------------------------------------
SELECT @DosCmd = 'TYPE "' + @PathNoExt + '" >>"' + @PathISO + '"'

-- ------------------------------------------
-- Run TYPE command to append new errorlog.1 to the Date-Name (ISO)
-- file.
-- ------------------------------------------
EXEC('xp_cmdshell ''' + @DosCmd + ''',no_output')
GO

-- Make the procedure a startup procedure
EXEC sp_procoption N'sp__errorlog$archivelog', N'startup', N'true'
GO
```

Finally, we append the contents of the new `ErrorLog.1` file to the `ErrorLog.YYYYMMDD` file, creating the `ErrorLog.YYYYMMDD` if it is not already created.

**!** **Don't forget to wrap this procedure in the `sp_MS_upd_sysobj_category` procedure to toggle on and off the `0x80000000` status bit.**

# Tracing Object Creation and Deletion

The vast majority of functionality improved from SQL Server 7.0 to SQL Server 2000. However, the system stored procedures supporting the scripting of tracing lost some important functionality. In SQL Server 7, we could grant execute rights to users on the trace procedures and they could run SQL Profiler. This was particularly useful in allowing developers to run Profiler on a development server. In SQL Server 2000, when Profiler is started the first command issued after the login is:

```
SELECT is_srvrolemember('sysadmin')
```

Therefore, unless we give our developers sa rights on the development server, they will not be able to run SQL Server 2000 Profiler. This is one of the few disappointments that we've encountered in SQL Server 2000.

In addition, the SQL Server 2000 SP_TRACE extended stored procedures are limited in functionality, as compared to the SQL Server 7.0 XP_TRACE procedures. In SQL Server 7.0, it was possible to send a procedure-generated trace to a SQL Server table. In SQL Server 2000, we can only send a procedure-generated trace to a flat file. While SQL Server 2000 does expose a system function to read the flat file back into a table, we lose the real time value of the trace. All that said, we've coded a small application that uses system stored procedures to write object creation and deletion events to a flat file. Every hour, a SQL Agent job then wakes up to consume the flat file into a object history table. Changes of interest are then mailed out to us.

In the code bundle (you can download it http://www.wrox.com) you will find a script for writing the trace to a file named as Object\Objects_Created_ YYYYMMDD_HHMMSS in the SQL Server error log folder. Before the new trace file is created, any current file is consumed and loaded into a table called object_hist. For our purposes, we placed the table in the master database, but you could easily redirect it to the database of your choice. You will also find scripts to create two tables and a notification procedure.

# SQL Mail

Most DBAs have a love-hate relationship with SQL Mail. We often rely upon it for reporting of our server's vital status. At the same time, this very tool has the capability of bringing down our server.

SQL Mail, which is really the procedure XP_SendMail, runs in memory with the SQL Server service, like all other extended stored procedures. This means that if something goes wrong with SQL Mail, its Outlook client, or the Exchange Server that they both depend upon, the server could be in big trouble. Quite often, the problem lies not in SQL Server but with the Exchange Server.

Before we go any further, let's clarify that we've never discovered any good reason for opening up SQL Mail to consume incoming mail from outside the server. Ideally, the data flow should be one-way – from the SQL Server to us. We've heard of (but never met) people who use the SQL Mail system to send messaging to their server, in other words, a kind of quasi-MSMQ. However, if you are going to do this, you might as well implement MSMQ for all the trouble it is worth.

In this section, we will concentrate only on outgoing SQL Mail from the SQL Server.

## *Best Practice Tips for SQL Mail*

Let's now look at the best practices to be followed while setting up the Outlook client:

❑ Make the service account with the same name, as that of the server – when you get mail, you'll know whom it is from. Also, while you are at it make the password for the service account really difficult.

❑ Whatever you do, don't auto-archive the Outlook client; we've had to completely rebuild profiles where the auto-archive had kicked in and messed things up.

❑ Don't have the Outlook client save sent items. Exchange administrators are notorious for setting mailbox size limits and you don't want to push these limits.

❑ Have the Outlook client only send out plain text messages unless you have an overriding reason to do otherwise.

❑ Have your Exchange administrators do two things:

• Add your login to the administrators of the service account mailbox

• Automatically delete items from the Sent Items folder; even if you don't save sent items, some sent mail items will still be placed in the Sent Items folder

❑ After you set up the profile, close Outlook. Then go in and copy the existing profile. Give the new copy the same name as the service account and the SQL server instance. Then delete the original profile with its cumbersome name. Use this new profile when setting up SQL Mail. We'll talk more about this later.

In our discussion regarding SQL Mail, we will look at:

❑ XP_SendMail recursion

❑ Ensuring that our XP_SendMail calls don't fail

❑ Replacing XP_SendMail with Gert Drapers' XP_SMTP_SendMail procedure

## *XP_SendMail Recursion*

Here, the word 'recursion' means that when we use XP_SendMail to send out mail by running a query, we will have the procedure first call XP_SendMail by setting an @sendmail flag on. The @query parameter of the XP_Sendmail command is the procedure itself; however, with the @sendmail flag off.

The nice thing about this is that for quick testing, we can run the procedure with the @sendmail flag off to just run the query. It is a nice set of packaging. This is the way we do it:

```
CREATE PROCEDURE ourjob$notification
  (@sendmail TINYINT = 0,
   @recipients VARCHAR(255) = NULL
  )

AS

-- check to see if we need to keep on going
IF NOT EXISTS (query to count rows to send off and determine if
  notification is needed)
RETURN 0

DECLARE @query VARCHAR(8000)
IF @sendmail = 1 -- we're going to send mail
BEGIN
    -- check to make sure a good recipient was sent in
    IF @recipients IS NULL
    ...Handle the error and RETURN -1

    -- recursively call itself with a @sendmail flag of 0 to go to the
    -- query portion of the procedure
    SELECT @query = EXEC ourjob$notification, 0, NULL
    Specify the subject and any other message you want to add;
    Specify whether the query will be attached or included

    -- Call the XP_SENDMAIL proc
    EXEC master.dbo.xp_sendmail @recipients, @subject = @subject,
      @message = @message, @query = @query, @attachment = 'true',
      @width = 2000, @no_output = 'true'

-- make sure that the width is sufficient and @no_output is true
END
ELSE -- @sendmail = 0;
BEGIN
    Here you put the query logic to return a single record set
END
GO
```

Here, we'll let you fill in your query. Another good trick is to get into variables the maximum lengths, such as @maxlenColName, of your VARCHAR columns in your result sets. Then run an sp_executesql proc to have the final results sent in formatted fashion and run a Left function across the column, Left(column,@maxlen).

By putting the query through sp_executesql, the final output of your attachment will be formatted with the contents of @maxlenColName, instead of the full listed length of the VARCHAR column. This makes for a much prettier attachment.

## XP_SendMail Bullet-proofing

What is the number one reason for Send Mail failures? It happens when the SQL Server is up and running a MAPI connection to an Exchange Server. Then, unbeknown to the SQL Server, the Exchange Server goes away for whatever reason. A piece of mail is sent with the XP_SendMail procedure; so far, it's not a problem. However, when the second piece of mail is sent to the nonexistent Exchange Server, most probably we will have a full scale MAPI failure, which can often only be cleared by a restart of the SQL Server.

The key word in the previous paragraph is "unbeknown". If we could examine the availability of the Exchange server before firing the XP_SendMail procedure, it would remove the uncertainty. With the undocumented xp_test_mapi_profile system stored procedure, we can precisely do this. Microsoft uses this procedure to test Send Mail in the SQL Enterprise Manager GUI.

This xp_test_mapi_profile system stored procedure takes a single input parameter, sysname of type NVARCHAR(128), which is the profile name of the Outlook client for the SQL Server service account. By default, this profile name is somewhat cumbersome. However, if you had followed our last best practice tip, your profile's name is the same name as the server. So, just run the following script snippet prior to running xp_sendmail:

```
DECLARE @rc int, @profilename sysname
SET @profilename = @@servername

-- If you profile name isn't your server name, you need to adjust
EXEC @rc = master.dbo.xp_test_mapi_profile @profilename
IF @rc = 0
   Run XP_SENDMAIL
ELSE -- you have an error condition with your MAPI Server
   Try running a Net Send to one of your DBA's with XP_CMDSHELL
```

## Breaking the Exchange Umbilical Cord – XP_SMTP_SendMail

All DBAs owe an eternal debt of gratitude to Gert Drapers. While Gert didn't write this under the auspices of Microsoft as an officially supported procedure, we think that it has the equivalence of functionality that you would find in the SQL Server resource kit. In fact, we are told that many SQL Servers inside Microsoft already use this stored procedure.

You can find XP_SMTP_SendMail for free download at http://sqldev.net/xp/xpsmtp.htm. Follow the instructions provided on this site for downloading and installing it.

To implement it on our servers, we first turn on the SMTP service for our SQL Server and then add the 127.0.0.1 IP address in the allowed relay addresses. It should be the only address. Then we went into the HOSTS file (it's located in the \System32\Drivers\Etc directory) and added a line for a host called STARHOST with the 127.0.0.1 address.

In XP_SMTP_SendMail procedure, STARHOST is the default relay agent. This means that the procedure will look for an SMTP server to relay the mail through. With the 127.0.0.1 address, it will always find itself. Even if it doesn't have network access, the mail will queue up as a .EML file.

Although it doesn't have all the functionality of XP_SendMail, XP_SMTP_SendMail is quite promising. Most noticeably, at the time of this writing, query functionality had not been made available within the product.

However, we've written a wrapper procedure around the XP_SMTP_SendMail. The wrapper has all the same input parameters, as the existing SQL 2000 XP_SendMail. In order to run a query, it writes a query script file out to C:\Temp with a DATETIME name. Then it uses ISQL to run the script back against itself and places the .OUT file with the same DATETIME name back in C:\Temp. As long as everything else works, the two files are later cleaned up. If something doesn't work, the files will remain undeleted for later analysis.

On some servers, particularly those outside the firewall and in contact with a MAPI server, we have ended up renaming the existing XP_SendMail and instead called our wrapper stored procedure as XP_SendMail. Next, we turn off SQL Agent Mail and add failure mail steps to all our jobs and success mail steps if we want to be notified of the successful completion of a job. We also write alert jobs that correspond to each of the alerts that we want to get mail about.

Below is our wrapper script for XP_SMTP_SENDMAIL:

```
CREATE PROCEDURE xp_sendmail
  (@recipients VARCHAR(8000) = NULL,
  @message VARCHAR(8000) = NULL,
  @query VARCHAR(8000) = NULL,
  @attachments VARCHAR(8000) = NULL,
  @copy_recipients VARCHAR(8000) = NULL,
  @blind_copy_recipients VARCHAR(8000) = NULL,
  @subject VARCHAR(8000) = NULL,
  @type VARCHAR(255) = NULL,
  @attach_results VARCHAR(5) = 'FALSE',
  @no_output VARCHAR (5) = 'FALSE',
  @no_header VARCHAR(5) = 'FALSE',
  @width INT = 80,
  @separator CHAR(1) = ' ',
  @echo_error VARCHAR(5) = 'FALSE',
  @set_user VARCHAR(255) = NULL,
  @dbuse SYSNAME = 'MASTER'
  )

/*
Purpose: Replaces xp_sendmail with a same name wrapper around
xp_smtp_sendmail procedure; use when Exchange is not availble.
```

```
Version: 1.0
Author: C.Hawkins*/

AS
SET NOCOUNT ON
```

These are the declarations for out script:

```
DECLARE @cmd VARCHAR(4000),
  @PRIORITY NVARCHAR(10),
  @SERVER NVARCHAR(4000),
  @RC INT,
  @messagefile VARCHAR(8000),
  @outfile VARCHAR(255),
  @infile VARCHAR(255),
  @marker VARCHAR(255)
```

We have to make sure that we have to have a recipient for the mail:

```
IF @recipients IS NULL
BEGIN
  RAISERROR('No Recipient was given.',16,-1)
  RETURN -1
END

-- Check to see if there is a query to run
IF @query IS NOT NULL
BEGIN -- @query IS NOT NULL
  -- set up an ISQL outfile; form of outfile is
  -- ISQLYYYYMMDDHHMISSMMM.OUT
  SELECT @marker = 'c:\temp\ISQL'+REPLACE(convert(varchar(32),
    GETDATE(),102),'.','') +
    REPLACE(CONVERT(VARCHAR(32),GETDATE(),114),':','')
  SELECT @infile = @marker + '.sql'
  SELECT @outfile = @marker + '.out'

  -- write the query out to the infile because it makes it easier to
  -- deal with single quotes
  SELECT @cmd = 'echo '+@query+ ' >'+@infile
  EXEC @RC = master.dbo.xp_cmdshell @cmd,no_output

  IF @RC <> 0
  BEGIN
    RAISERROR('Error writing @infile for xp_sendmail',16,-1)
    RETURN -2
  END  -- @query IS NOT NULL
```

Then we may need to specify the ISQL path; here, we hardcode it for simplicity and then execute the command line:

```
-- build the ISQL command line
SELECT @cmd = '"C:\Program Files\Microsoft SQL Server\80\Tools\Binn\
              isql.exe" -E -n -b -d '+@dbuse+' -t 600 -h'+
              CASE WHEN @no_header = 'TRUE' THEN '-1' ELSE ' 0' END
              + ' -w'+CONVERT(VARCHAR(10),@width)+ CASE WHEN
              LTRIM(@separator) <> '' THEN ' -s '+@separator ELSE
              '' END + CASE WHEN @echo_error = 'TRUE' THEN ' -e'
              ELSE '' END + ' -i '+ @infile+ ' -o '+@outfile

-- Execute the ISQL command line
EXEC @RC = master.dbo.xp_cmdshell @cmd,no_output
IF @RC <> 0
BEGIN
  RAISERROR('Error running ISQL for @query',16,-1)
  RETURN -3
END
```

If attach_results is false, the output file will be the message file:

```
IF @attach_results = 'FALSE'
BEGIN
  SELECT @messagefile = @outfile
  IF @attachments IS NULL
  BEGIN
    SELECT @attachments = ''
  END
END
-- The output file will be one of the attachments
ELSE
BEGIN
  SELECT @messagefile = ''
  IF @attachments IS NULL
  BEGIN
    SELECT @attachments = @outfile
  END
  ELSE
  BEGIN
    SELECT @attachments = @attachments + ';' + @outfile
  END
END
END
```

Then, we ensure that we have got the other necessary details right:

```
IF @message IS NULL SELECT @message = ''
IF @query IS NULL SELECT @query = ''
IF @attachments IS NULL SELECT @attachments = ''
IF @copy_recipients IS NULL SELECT @copy_recipients = ''
IF @blind_copy_recipients IS NULL SELECT @blind_copy_recipients = ''
IF @subject IS NULL SELECT @subject = ''
```

Finally, we send the mail:

```
EXEC @rc = master.dbo.xp_smtp_sendmail
@FROM = @@servername,
@TO = @recipients,
@CC = @copy_recipients,
@BCC = @blind_copy_recipients,
@priority = NORMAL,
@subject = @subject,
@message = @message,
@messagefile = @messagefile,
@type = 'text/plain',
@attachments = @attachments

IF @RC <> 0
BEGIN
  RAISERROR('Error sending mail for xp_smtp_sendmail',16,-1)
  RETURN -4
END

-- temporary: set @marker to NULL to save the files; comment out in
-- production.
-- select @marker = NULL

-- clean up the temp files from @query
IF @marker IS NOT NULL
BEGIN
  SELECT @cmd = 'del '+@marker+'.* /Q'
  EXEC master.dbo.xp_cmdshell @cmd,no_output
END
GO
```

# Summary

In this chapter, we have discussed SQL Server's system stored procedures. We've avoided repeating much of the details given in SQL Server Books Online; it does an excellent job of outlining the routine use of the system stored procedures and should always be your first reference. However, Microsoft's system stored procedures give only the required functionality to manage SQL Server and not the desirable nice-to-have functionality.

In the course of our discussions, we have covered some of the most popular system stored procedures and their uses. We looked at some of the undocumented system stored procedures and their benefits. Then, we went on to discuss extended stored procedures. The examples that we discussed should spur you to develop and DOCUMENT your own system stored procedures.

SQL Server 2000

Stored Procedures

Handbook

6

# 6

# User Defined Functions

User defined functions, known more commonly as **UDF**s, are routines called from T-SQL code to return either a single value or a rowset. Although they are, perhaps, the least used of specialized stored procedures, they are powerful tools in a database developer's armory. They provide the developer with the ability to create their own customized functions, which can then be re-used in other parts of their T-SQL code.

UDFs have some features that are common to stored procedures, but there are a number of restrictions as well. In this chapter, we will begin by looking at what a UDF actually is, and then move onto look at:

- ❏ The different types of UDFs
- ❏ Building and calling functions that return different types of data
- ❏ Using schema binding with UDFs
- ❏ How UDFs differ from stored procedures

# UDFs

UDFs are subroutines developed by us (the users), to implement some common functionality. If there is a set of code that is common to two or more stored procedures, or if there is a business function, calculation, or data retrieval which will be used as either part of a JOIN or a filter or even as a value in a column when returning a rowset, then we can use a UDF to implement it.

For example, we can use a UDF to return a set of orders placed by a client. This UDF can form part of a JOIN condition. The data thus generated, could then be used for producing an invoice, or a delivery note, or outstanding delivery note, and so on; with just one routine we can easily cater to all these scenarios.

> **Note that, UDFs cannot modify data; they are simply there to return information.**

The earlier versions of SQL Server didn't have the concept of a UDF. Any functionality that was common and called from different stored procedures had to be implemented itself as a stored procedure. This approach wasn't always ideal; the value returned from such a stored procedure had to be placed into a variable and then the variable used in the T-SQL statement. Also, it was not possible to return a tabular set of data that could form part of a subset of data. With a UDF we can do all these, as well as other tasks, such as formatting the text of a column within a SELECT clause.

Some people argue that the UDFs of SQL Server 2000 are more powerful than in the other databases, as they can return a special set of data type, which looks just like a table of data within our database. In the *Table Data Type* section of this chapter we will discuss this data type in more detail.

# *In-Built Functions*

SQL Server comes with many in-built functions, ranging from ones that provide us with system information to those performing some sort of complex calculation or variable manipulation. Some of the commonly used functions are:

- ❏ GETDATE()
  This function returns the current system date and time

- ❏ AVG()
  This is used to return an average value of a set of grouped rows

- ❏ COUNT()
  This function returns the number of rows that meet our join and filtering criteria

- ❏ ISNULL()
  This is used to test whether a column contains a null value or not

Unlike SQL Server's system stored procedures, we cannot inspect the T-SQL statements making up these in-built functions. However, we can easily find out the existing functions by using Query Analyzer; here, they are also grouped into relevant sections. This can be seen in the following screenshot:

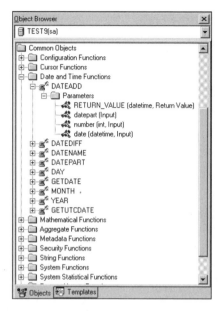

Here, we can see the **Object Browser** of Query Analyzer. It not only lists the functions but also tells us what parameters need to be passed in and the function's return type. It saves us from having to refer to SQL Server Books Online for this information, thereby speeding up our development time.

# Creating a UDF

Creating a UDF is similar to creating a stored procedure. To being with, we use the CREATE FUNCTION statement, followed by the name of the function we are creating. This is followed with any incoming parameters, although there are no output parameter definitions, as you would find with stored procedures. Any output data is placed in a RETURNS statement that follows the input parameter definition. The remainder of building a function then follows a similar manner to that of building a stored procedure.

It is important to know that functions can be defined in two different ways, and before we can create a UDF we need to know about these two types. Now, let's discuss them.

## *Types of Functions*

No matter how the information is returned, functions fall into two categories – deterministic and non-deterministic. It is important to know what type of function you are creating, as this affects the design of the function, such as the code that can be placed into the function. Based on the T-SQL placed within the function SQL Server decides if the function is deterministic or not.

## Deterministic Functions

Deterministic functions will always return the same information each time they are called, providing that the parameters passed remain the same. The *Factorial* stored procedure of Chapter 1 is one such example. Another example would be a function that returns the area of a circle when we pass in the radius.

The requirements for a function to be deterministic are:

❑ The function must be schema bound (even if it doesn't access any schema objects).

❑ All functions (in-built or user-defined) called by it must also be deterministic.

❑ No external objects can be used. In other words, the function can only reference objects having local scope.

❑ They cannot call any extended stored procedures.

## Non-Deterministic Functions

Non-deterministic functions can return different results each time they are called with a specific set of input values. For example, a function retrieving the price of a share on the stock market or the balance of a customer's bank account would be non-deterministic. Keep in mind that between calls a non-deterministic function may not return the same information.

We can tell if a function is deterministic or not by checking the value of its OBJECTPROPERTY through a SELECT statement. This property is defined and set by the SQL Server.

We can check the determinism of the function by executing the following code (execute it on the Northwind database):

```
SELECT OBJECTPROPERTY(OBJECT_ID('dbo.fn_EmpName'),'IsDeterministic')
```

A return value of 0, false, indicates the function is non-deterministic, while 1, true, indicates that it is deterministic.

# *Computed Columns*

Deterministic functions are important when creating an index on a view or computed column.

> **If an index on a view or computed column refers to a user defined function, then that function must be deterministic.**

**182**

When you create an index on a computed column, the index must calculate the values for the computed column to enable it to build the keys for the index. The index will then only work while any data modification on the column follows exactly the same algorithm; in other words, the function used to calculate the value needs to be deterministic. An error will be raised if you try to modify key values that use a algorithm different from that used when the index was originally created. If you do want to alter the computation, for example if you have a column that computes a tax amount, and the tax rate alters, then you need to drop the index and recreate it.

## Example of Creating a UDF

Now, let's create a simple UDF. It will format an employee's name from the Employee table of Northwind database and return the employee's title, initial of first name, and last name. This is a deterministic function:

```
CREATE FUNCTION fn_EmpName (@EmpID INT)
RETURNS VARCHAR(50)
AS
BEGIN
  DECLARE @NewName VARCHAR(50)
  SELECT @NewName = RTRIM(TitleOfCourtesy) + ' ' + LEFT(FirstName,1) +
    '. ' + RTRIM(LastName)
  FROM dbo.Employees
  WHERE EmployeeID = @EmpID
  RETURN @NewName
END
```

Creating functions requires some amount of planning, as UDFs have some limitations, as compared to stored procedures. We will be discussing these limitations in the next section.

For now, we will attempt to convert a non-deterministic function into a deterministic one.

## Converting a Non-Deterministic Function to Deterministic

This process is somewhat tricky, as we are trying to include a non-deterministic function within our UDF, which is not allowed.

> **Any system function, used within a UDF must be deterministic. If you create a UDF which is non-deterministic, it can be used within another UDF.**

The follow example demonstrates how to get around such a problem.

The non-deterministic function, in our example, adds the number of business days, which we pass as a parameter, to the current date and return the new date. Note that our business day won't include weekends. The value returned by our UDF is a DATETIME data type and will be the new date. Our function makes use of the GETDATE() function, which is non-deterministic:

```
CREATE FUNCTION fn_AddWorkDays (@NoDays INT)
RETURNS DATETIME
AS
BEGIN

  DECLARE @Today DATETIME
  SET @Today = GETDATE()

  -- This should not happen but just in case the function is
  --called on a weekend
  IF DATEPART(dw,@Today) IN (1,7)
  RETURN NULL

  --Main Part of the function
  WHILE @NoDays > 0
  BEGIN
    IF DATEPART(dw,@Today) = 6
    SET @Today = DATEADD(day,3,@Today)
    ELSE
    SET @Today = DATEADD(day,1,@Today)

    SET @NoDays = @NoDays - 1
  END
  RETURN @Today
END
```

When we execute this code in Query Analyzer we will receive the following error:

```
Server: Msg 443, Level 16, State 1, Procedure fn_AddWorkDays, Line 7
Invalid use of 'getdate' within a function.
```

This error occurs because of the GETDATE() function, which is non-deterministic, and as we mentioned earlier we cannot have non-deterministic functions inside of a UDF.

Now, to get around this problem we need to modify the function, so that it contains only deterministic function calls. This means we cannot use the GETDATE() function; instead, we will have to start with our own date. In other words, we will have to pass it in as a parameter.

Now, take a look at the modified function:

```
CREATE FUNCTION fn_AddWorkDays (@NoDays INT, @InDate DATETIME)
RETURNS DATETIME
AS
BEGIN
  IF DATEPART(dw,@InDate) IN (1,7)
  RETURN NULL
  DECLARE @Today DATETIME
  SET @Today = @InDate
  . . .
```

Here, the caller is required to provide the current date. This might be something that you would want to put in the function's documentation, so that any future amendments don't try to put GETDATE() in. Of course, this implies that the function's caller passes in the necessary date.

Although we may view this as a deterministic function, SQL Server sees this as non-deterministic. The reason is that DATEPART() is non-deterministic, even although it will always return the same value for the same input parameters. DATEADD() is also seen by SQL Server as being non-deterministic. However, using these wouldn't stop your UDFs from being deterministic.

As with stored procedures, the BEGIN and END statements surround multi-statement lines of code, and you code functions as you would code any other stored procedure, with one or two exceptions.

Errors cannot be raised using the RAISERROR statement and functions must have an explicit RETURN statement, compared to stored procedures which can have an explicit or implicit RETURN.

In our above example, we return a NULL value if the date is invalid. You have to be aware of this if you are coding functions, as returning a bad value can cause problems. For example, in our above example if we didn't return a NULL value and we happened to pass an invalid date, then it might be difficult to interpret the output of this function. If the return value was used in a WHERE clause, then you could even find erroneous data being processed.

Keep your function as short and succinct as possible, as the function could be called against every row of returned data in a rowset; for example, if the function is formatting text, such as concatenating the initial of an employee's first name and last name into a single column. If the function is deterministic and the value returned is constant, then it would be better to call the function and place the value in to a local variable, rather than calling the function many times. This is quite a performance gain, especially when working with a large number of rows.

Now let's look at calling a UDF.

# Scalar Valued Functions

A scalar valued function simply returns a single value, such as the result of a mathematical calculation or of formatting some text. Many of SQL Server's in-built functions are based on this, such as returning a date through GETDATE() or returning a string with the trailing blanks removed with the RTRIM() function.

*Scalar functions cannot return any of the following data types – cursor, rowversion, timestamp, table, text, ntext, or image. Any other data type is valid.*

Scalar functions can form the value for a column within a rowset, return a value that is used as part of a WHERE statement, or simply return a value that is placed in a local variable. Basically, they can be used anywhere a scalar expression can be used.

Note that any T-SQL errors within a function will stop the trigger as well as cancel the invoking statement. For example, if we get a NULL value in an unexpected place and a T-SQL error is thrown, then the function will stop, as will the calling T-SQL, and therefore, our whole stored procedure that invoked the UDF will stop executing.

Calling a UDF is relatively straightforward, when working with scalar values. We just have to provide the name of the function's owner, the function name, and the parameter values (if any) that are to be passed in.

In our previous example (where we added business days), if we wanted to return the value as a column in a result set then we would call the function as:

```
SELECT dbo.fn_AddWorkDays(2,'3 March 1998')
```

If it were a filter, such as looking for all orders that are two days out, then we could code the T-SQL as:

```
SELECT OrderId, CustomerId, RequiredDate
FROM dbo.Orders
WHERE RequiredDate > dbo.fn_AddWorkDays(2,'3 March 1998')
```

Or would we? The value returned from this function will always be the same, so, in this instance, it would be better to call the function prior to the SELECT statement, place the value in to a local variable and then use the local variable as the filter. However, in cases where the parameter being passed to the function is going to have a varying value, such as a different value for each row in the rowset, we can't use this approach.

An example of this would be when we are working with different employee names. Another example would be using different dates and amounts for calculating interest. To clarify this further, let's look at a concrete example:

**186**

If we wanted to get a list of orders from the Northwind database that shipped more than 10 working days after the order was placed, then the way we can code this is the following:

```
SELECT OrderId, CustomerId, OrderDate, ShippedDate
FROM dbo.Orders
WHERE ShippedDate > dbo.fn_AddWorkDays(10,OrderDate)
```

Of course, there will be performance degradation with this query, as every row from the Orders table will be passed into the function. One way to improve this would be to add a second condition to the filter for removing rows that would not fit in the returned rowset. In this case, we can add the following conditions to the WHERE statement of the SELECT statement defined above:

```
AND ShippedDate IS NOT NULL
AND ShippedDate > DATEADD(dd,10,OrderDate)
```

Here, SQL Server will have to take the function into its query plan, although it will be working with a small number of rows, and since we are not completing any further table access within the function itself, the function should not cause any undue overhead. The optimizer will, itself, figure out the best plan to use.

As far as possible, always try to reduce the number of rows by adding in subsequent filter conditions. If we alter the function to include a SELECT statement where we look up the order again and return the OrderDate within the function, it will be slower. Therefore, wherever possible pass in the value from the column, rather than making the function do the work:

```
CREATE FUNCTION fn_OrderShipDays (@NoDays INT, @OrderId INT)
RETURNS DATETIME
AS
BEGIN
   DECLARE @Today DATETIME

   SELECT @Today = OrderDate
   FROM dbo.Orders
   WHERE OrderId = @OrderId

   WHILE @NoDays > 0
   ... -the remaining part is same as in the fn_AddWorkDays example
```

Scalar functions can be used just as we would use a column value or a local variable within SQL Server, and the same constraints exist for UDFs as for columns and variables. These constraints are:

❑　If we are using a function as a value in a RETURN statement in a stored procedure, then the function must return an integer number

❑ When using a function in a PRINT statement the return type must be a string or such that they can be CAST to a character value

❑ If used as part of an assignment operator on either side of the = sign then the data type should match that on the other side of the equals sign, or be of a data type that can be automatically converted

Scalar functions can also be used in CASE statements, flow control statements, default definitions, and constraints. For a constraint we can access the data in the row in the parameters; with a default definition this is not possible.

Scalar functions are pretty straightforward, but what about if we wanted the function to return a row, or a set of rows of data? This is where the TABLE data type comes in handy.

# TABLE Data Type

The TABLE data type is a specialized data type that has some similarities to a table within a database. It's more like a temporary table than a permanent table, as it is created on the fly and has a limited life span.

Two types of UDF definitions exist – single statement table function and multi-statement table function. As the name suggests, a single statement table function doesn't have a function body and the whole SELECT statement returning the data table is placed within the RETURN statement.

The second type is more like other UDFs, where we wish to complete processing before actually returning the data. This data type is not unique to functions and can be found in stored procedures or inline (as a part of) T-SQL (statements). By defining the TABLE data type as a local variable we can populate it from within any T-SQL statement, just as we would do to any other table.

The TABLE data type provides a rowset of data, as you might find from a temporary table, or even from a view. When used within a function it can provide a predefined subset of data for a query.

**! Temporary tables, such as those defined within stored procedures or ad-hoc T-SQL, cannot be defined within UDFs.**

## Single Statement Table Function

To demonstrate the TABLE data type in action, let's create a function returning a set of unshipped orders from the Northwind database. The function receives a customer ID and returns one row per order date, required date, and shipping company.

*When coding a function such as this, it is advisable to check the T-SQL first, including checking the execution plan, before placing it into a function.*

```
CREATE FUNCTION fn_CustUnShippedOrders (@CustId NCHAR(5))
RETURNS TABLE
AS
RETURN
    (SELECT o.OrderDate, o.RequiredDate, s.CompanyName AS 'Shipper',
        ROUND(SUM((UnitPrice * Quantity) - Discount),2) AS 'Order Value'
    FROM dbo.Orders o
    JOIN dbo.[Order Details] d ON o.OrderId = d.OrderId
    JOIN dbo.Shippers s ON o.ShipVia = s.ShipperId
    WHERE o.ShippedDate IS NULL AND o.CustomerId = @CustId
    GROUP BY customerid, o.OrderDate,
                o.RequiredDate, s.CompanyName)
```

We can execute the above statements as if we were returning data from a view, or a table.

This following statement should return two rows:

```
SELECT OrderDate, RequiredDate, Shipper, [Order Value]
FROM fn_CustUnShippedOrders('ERNSH')
```

The output is:

```
OrderDate                RequiredDate             Shipper
                                                  Order Value
------------------------------------------------------------- -------
1998-04-08 00:00:00.000  1998-05-06 00:00:00.000  Federal Shipping
                                                  4903.3999999999996
1998-05-05 00:00:00.000  1998-06-02 00:00:00.000  United Package
                                                  5218.0
```

Please note that we have formatted this output to fit it onto our page.

The above function is written in such a way that it assumes the input value is always known and is passed in through the parameter. Suppose we wanted to cater for a specific customer or a list of all customers who have unshipped orders; in other words, what if we didn't know the customer ID (that is, the customer ID is NULL)?

The following example demonstrates this situation. First, we need to modify the function so that it can work with either a valid or a NULL customer ID. Also, in the previous example we did not list the CustomerId column, as it wasn't needed. If we call the function with NULL then we need to know what customer each row relates to, so here we have added an extra column to the TABLE data type being returned:

```
CREATE FUNCTION fn_CustUnShippedOrders (@CustId NCHAR(5))
RETURNS TABLE
AS
RETURN
  (SELECT o.CustomerId, o.OrderDate, o.RequiredDate,
     s.CompanyName AS 'Shipper',
     ROUND(SUM((UnitPrice * Quantity) - Discount),2) AS 'Order Value'
   FROM dbo.Orders o
   JOIN dbo.[Order Details] d ON o.OrderId = d.OrderId
   JOIN dbo.Shippers s ON o.ShipVia = s.ShipperId
   WHERE o.ShippedDate IS NULL
   AND (@CustId IS NULL OR o.CustomerId = @CustId)
   GROUP BY o.CustomerId, o.OrderDate, o.RequiredDate, s.CompanyName)
```

*Note tha, the execution plan for this function will differ depending on whether a customer ID is entered or not.*

# Multi-Statement Table Functions

In the above example, we simply received a parameter and then returned a table of information within the RETURN statement, but things change when more processing is involved. If we have to perform more processing, within the function, prior to returning the table data, then the function is known as a **multi-statement table function**.

Multi-statement table functions are quite similar to stored procedures, in that you can process any information and use any functions within the T-SQL statements. The difference between a single statement function and multi-statement function is that we have to define a table variable, as part of the RETURNS statement, and then place data into that table, which is then returned.

**!Remember that within a function we cannot define temporary tables other than the table variable itself.**

# Table Variables

It is possible to create a table within a function, work with it as if it were a temporary table, and then pass the rowset out of the function from the defined table variable. We come across this in a multi-statement table function rather than a single-statement table function.

The syntax for a multi-statement table function is:

```
CREATE FUNCTION name (@parametername datatype[(datalength)][,…])
RETURNS @tablename TABLE (column datatype[(datalength)][, …])
AS
BEGIN
...
-- There must be some sort of population of @tablename in here
RETURN
END
```

We would define the table in the RETURNS statement itself, as you can see in our altered procedure shown below. This method is quite a bit slower, when compared to our last example. This comes from building the table and then having to insert data, instead of the server creating the table on the fly.

**!Unless it's necessary to have a multi-statement table function avoid using them; whenever possible, aim for a single statement function.**

Now, let's look at the implementation of the fn_CustUnShippedOrders function by using multi-statement tables:

```
CREATE FUNCTION fn_CustUnShippedOrders (@CustId NCHAR(5))
RETURNS @UnShipped TABLE (CustomerId NCHAR(5),
                          OrderDate DATETIME NULL,
                          RequiredDate DATETIME NULL,
                          Shipper NVARCHAR(40),
                          [Order Value] MONEY
                          )
AS
BEGIN
   INSERT INTO @UnShipped
   SELECT o.CustomerId, o.OrderDate, o.RequiredDate,
    s.CompanyName AS 'Shipper',
    ROUND(SUM((UnitPrice * Quantity) - Discount),2) AS 'Order Value'
   FROM dbo.Orders o
     JOIN dbo.[Order Details] d ON o.OrderId = d.OrderId
     JOIN dbo.Shippers s ON o.ShipVia = s.ShipperId
   WHERE o.ShippedDate IS NULL
     AND (@CustId IS NULL OR o.CustomerId = @CustId)
   GROUP BY customerid,o.OrderDate, o.RequiredDate, s.CompanyName
   RETURN
END
```

This function inserts the data into the table variable, as we would with any temporary table. However, the link between this table variable and its return to the calling T-SQL is through the RETURNS statement of the CREATE FUNCTION statement.

An example of using the above function for joining data from the multi-statement table UDF is given below. We perform a JOIN operation on the CustomerId column from both the function's table variable and the Customer table to give the relevant result:

```
SELECT c.CompanyName, f.OrderDate, f.RequiredDate,
       f.Shipper, f.[Order Value]
FROM dbo.Customers c
JOIN fn_CustUnShippedOrders(NULL) f ON f.CustomerId = c.CustomerId
```

Multi-statement table functions can help stored procedures to remove the need for creating a temporary table within the calling procedure. Consider the above example; if this processing was being done in several stored procedures by using a temporary table, it would be better to create a single function and place all the code within this, to reduce the amount of duplicate code. It would also give us one central code repository for carrying out any changes.

As we can see from the table definition, there are many similarities to building any other table, such as allowing NULL values. It is also possible to place keys and CHECK and DEFAULT value constraints on columns, but it is not possible to place a foreign key reference to this table from any other table.

**!** **Just like any other local variable, the table is scoped to the function in which it is defined. Indexes cannot be added at a later stage, once the function has returned the data.**

# In-built Functions with Table Data Type

As we mentioned earlier, there are in-built functions that return a scalar value, but there are also in-built functions that return a TABLE data type. It is easy to distinguish them, as they all have the prefix fn_. These functions are:

- ❏ fn_helpcollations
  This lists all collations supported by SQL Server

- ❏ fn_listextendedproperty
  If you use extended properties in your database, then you can use this function to return this information in a table

- ❏ fn_servershareddrives
  This function lists the names of shared drive on the clustered server

- ❏ fn_trace_geteventinfo
  When using tracing, this function will return information about the events

- ❏ fn_trace_getfilterinfo
  When using tracing, this function will return information about the filters in place

- ❏ fn_trace_getinfo
  If you are using tracing, this function will return information about it, such as the options, file name of the trace, current trace status and so on

- ❏ fn_trace_gettable
  This function returns trace information in a table format

- ❏ fn_virtualfilestats
  This provides Input/Output statistics for database and transaction log files

- ❏ fn_virtualservernodes
  This lists all the nodes on which the virtual server can run

Working with functions such as these is a bit different to scalar system functions. It is necessary to prefix the function name with a double colon mark : :. For example, here's how we can use the fn_helpcollations function:

```
SELECT *
FROM ::fn_helpcollations()
```

This statement will return a list of all the collations that are available in SQL Server, along with a description of each collation. It might have been more useful if the function could either take a NULL parameter to list all the functions, or a collation identifier so that you could list either a specific collation or even a subset of collations based on the input. This is where not being able to work with the source has a downfall, and we have to write our own function for doing this. However, you could write your own wrapper around this function to complete the filtering of the collations.

# Schema Binding

There is an option available with UDFs, which is similar to that for views, for binding the columns used in any SELECT statement creating a TABLE data type to the underlying table. Schema binding will stop a table, a referenced column within a function, or a view from being dropped or altered from the underlying table and therefore keep our existing functions working.

Note that generally any good DBA will check existing dependencies by running sp_depends before dropping a column. However, by making our function schema-bound we can add in a layer of extra safety.

> *The system function sp_depends lists all dependencies for a given object. It allows you to find out what things might break if you alter an object.*

To make a function schema-bound we need to use the WITH SCHEMABINDING statement after the RETURNS statement. Apart from this, we have to meet a few other requirements:

❑ All objects must be from the same database

❑ All objects must be referenced by two part names (<ownerName>.<objectName>)

❑ User must have REFERENCE permissions to the tables, views, and user-defined functions used in code

❑ We cannot use the SELECT * syntax for returning values, even in an EXISTS expression

❑ All objects employed are schema-bound

If we look at our `fn_CustUnShippedOrders` function again, we can make this schema-bound by simply adding the `WITH SCHEMABINDING` statement, as we have already fulfilled all the other criteria:

```
ALTER FUNCTION fn_CustUnShippedOrders (@CustId NCHAR(5))
RETURNS @UnShipped TABLE (CustomerId NCHAR(5),
                          OrderDate DATETIME NULL,
                          RequiredDate DATETIME NULL,
                          Shipper NVARCHAR(40),
                          [Order Value] MONEY
                         )
WITH SCHEMABINDING
AS
... -- rest of the code is similar to the previous listing
```

Another important point concerning schema-bound functions is that the function itself would have to be deterministic to be able to apply schema binding.

> *Remember from earlier in the chapter that for a function to be deterministic, it must be schema-bound; however, a schema-bound function need not be deterministic.*

# Stored Procedures versus UDFs

System and user stored procedures are managed by SQL Server in a similar fashion. They can be accessed in the same way through the system tables, such as `sysobjects` and `syscomments`. UDFs are stored in the system tables; in-built system functions are not. As a result, the code for system functions is not contained in any system table; therefore, we cannot access them, unlike system stored procedures where we can learn much from the way Microsoft has implemented them.

UDFs represent new functionality, so you may find that some of your stored procedures can be altered to functions, which will make them more accessible to your T-SQL code. Converting our system stored procedures to functions, in the right cases, will make them friendlier and easier to use, and will also reduce the lines of code in the T-SQL statements. It may also make our T-SQL less complex, as we won't be returning our data to a temporary local variable and then operating upon it.

Also, having the ability to return a table directly into another set of T-SQL is a great advantage, as it reduces the lines of code and awkward processing otherwise required to get a set of data returned from a called stored procedure to be included with the calling procedure.

Stored procedures can create temporary tables but this is not possible from within the body of a function. Also functions cannot perform any data modification operations on the permanent tables. This is not the aim of functions; data modification should remain in stored procedures.

As with stored procedures, if we placed UDFs into the SQL Server master database and prefix their name with sp_, then these functions will be available to all other databases within the installation. If you do write a function that you wish to be system-wide then stick to SQL Server's naming conventions of using all lower case, prefixed with fn_, and owned by the system_function_schema and not dbo.

To create functions owned by system_function_schema you must run the following command from the master database first, and then build your function in the master database:

```
EXEC sp_configure 'allow updates', 1
```

# Summary

In this chapter, we have examined the different types of UDFs and looked at creating reliable functions. We examined both deterministic and non-deterministic functions and discussed the requirements for a function to be deterministic.

We then looked at calling UDFs and scalar valued functions. Our discussions also included the Table data type and the advantages and pitfalls in using it. We also looked at the SQL Server's in-built functions that return Table data types.

We then discussed schema bindings and finally went on to examine the similarities between stored procedures and UDFs. UDFs share a number of similarities with stored procedures, but as we saw there are a number of restrictions too. None is more restrictive than the inability to modify data in existing tables; however, data modification isn't what a UDF is about. UDFs are there to provide us with a value or a set of data based on a set of criteria.

# SQL Server 2000

## Stored Procedures

## Handbook

**7**

# 7

# Triggers

As we approach the conclusion of this book, we come to an important topic in the specialized stored procedure arena – triggers. Triggers are best used for enforcing business rules as well as performing validation or data modifications, when other methods are not sufficient.

We will see that triggers are mainly used in two areas:

❑    Creating audit records and reflecting changes to crucial business tables

❑    Validating of changes against a set of business rules coded in T-SQL

In this chapter, we will cover:

❑    What a trigger is and why it exists

❑    Performance considerations

❑    How to create a trigger and its different types

❑    Transactions and rollbacks within triggers

❑    Recursive triggers

❑    Good and bad programming practices

# What is a Trigger?

A trigger is a specialized stored procedure which fires automatically when an alteration occurs to an underlying table due to an action like deleting, inserting, or updating of a row, or a batch of rows, within the single table that the stored procedure is linked with, or potentially multiple tables if the trigger is linked to a view. To clarify the statement of 'batch of rows' – if we have an UPDATE statement that modifies several rows, for example, then the trigger will not fire for each row updated, but only once when the batch completes. If we needed to fire the trigger for each row being updated, then we would need to construct some sort of loop processing within our T-SQL to do this.

Triggers can be assigned to tables or views. However, although there are two types of triggers, INSTEAD OF and AFTER, as we will see later in the *Types of Triggers* section, only one type of trigger can be assigned to views. Briefly, an INSTEAD OF trigger is the one that is usually associated with a view, and runs on an UPDATE action placed on that view. An AFTER trigger fires after a modification action has occurred.

It is possible to have more than one trigger firing for the same action, if they are AFTER triggers. So it is quite possible and perfectly valid for two or more separate triggers to fire on the same table modification action. This will allow separate processing to take place, rather than having different underlying functionalities in the same procedure. It is also possible to define the order in which triggers will fire. Both these areas are covered in detail, in the *Types of Triggers* section.

From a performance viewpoint, the fewer the triggers, the better, as we will invoke less processes. Therefore, do not think that having one trigger per action to make things modular will not incur performance degradation. A trigger's main overhead is referencing either two specialist tables that exist in triggers – deleted and inserted or other tables for business rules. Modularizing triggers to make the whole process easier to understand will incur multiple references to these tables, and hence a greater overhead.

> *It is not possible to create a trigger to fire when a data modification occurs in two or more tables. A trigger can be associated only with a single table.*

Care has to be taken in areas such as **DTS** or **BCP**, when loading data into tables, as we may wish to switch off the firing of the triggers. DTS (Data Transformation Services) is a tool within SQL Server to allow bulk loading of data, data manipulation, and many other useful processes surrounding data. BCP is the predecessor of DTS, and is a simple prompt-based utility for bulk loading from a source to SQL Server. Dropping the trigger from the database, or using the DISABLE TRIGGER option of the ALTER TABLE statement, may be needed in such cases. We can then complete the bulk loading and reapply the trigger. If the trigger remains in place, and we bulk load a number of rows, then a trigger could be fired once for each row being placed into SQL Server, and hence it should remain only if we need this. For example, loading 100,000 rows will slow down a normally fast process. If a trigger exists as part of auditing, then we may remove it.

*Disabling the trigger is the preferred option; otherwise, we will need to
recreate the trigger once it has been dropped.*

**!** **Care must be taken to ensure that we perform the** DROP **or** DISABLE **only
when there are no other tasks being performed at that time. If we drop the
trigger when a valid task is running, then we may corrupt the data, especially
if the trigger is performing a business function. Triggers should be dropped
only when they will not be invoked.**

One way to ensure this is to change the database Access property through the Restrict
Access clause, to a Single User in the Properties page of the desired database, in the
Enterprise Manager.

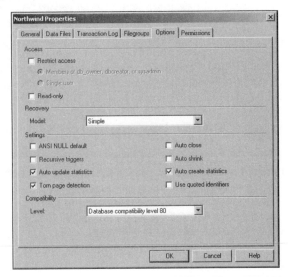

Later, in the *Replication* section, we will also look at triggers in places where
replication of a database is involved.

*Triggers are not designed for returning any information. No parameters
can be passed to them, and returning a rowset of information will cause
logistical problems in the invoking procedure. If you are concerned that a
rowset may be returned, then use the SET NOCOUNT statement at the start
of the trigger to ensure that no rows are returned.*

# Why use Triggers?

Using triggers can greatly improve data integrity. When an action is performed on data, it is possible to check if the manipulation of the data concurs with the underlying business rules, and thus avoid erroneous entries in a table.

For example:

❏ We might want to ship a free item to a client with the order, if it totals more than $1000. A trigger will be built to check the order total upon completion of the order, to see if an extra order line needs to be inserted.

❏ In a banking scenario, when a request is made to withdraw cash from a cash point, the stored procedure will create a record on the client's statement table for the withdrawal, and the trigger will automatically reduce the balance as required. The trigger may also be the point at which a check is made on the client's balance to verify that there is enough balance to allow the withdrawal. By having a trigger on the statement table, we are secure in the knowledge that any statement entry made, whether withdrawal or deposit, will be validated and processed in one central place.

Note that we discuss only data integrity here, and not referential integrity.

We may also wish to replicate changes in one database into another; a trigger on the table that is being updated will be ideal to place the changes from the 'live' database to the 'audit' database. We use this scenario to create an audit on specific tables, but the audit is kept in a separate database. When we discuss building triggers, in the *Creating and Using a Trigger* section, we will see this scenario in action. This is different from replication, which we will discuss later in the *Replication* section.

Another use of trigger can be to carry out an action when a specific criterion has been met. One example of this is a case where an e-mail requesting more items to be delivered is sent, or an order for processing could be placed, when stock levels reach a preset level. However, if we insert data into another table from within a trigger, we have to be careful that the table we insert into doesn't have a trigger that will cause this first trigger to fire. It is possible to code triggers that result in an endless loop, as we can define a trigger on TableA, which inserts into TableB, and a trigger for TableB, which updates TableA. This scenario will ultimately end in an error being generated by SQL Server. The following diagram will demonstrate this:

**Figure 1**

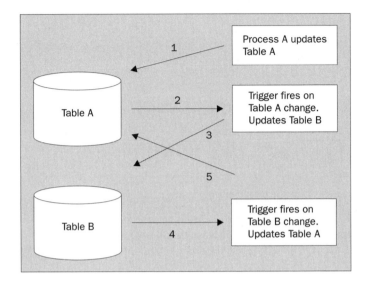

1. A stored procedure, A, updates TableA.

2. This fires a trigger from TableA.

3. The defined trigger on TableA updates TableB.

4. TableB has a trigger which fires.

5. This trigger from TableB updates TableA.

# Performance

Remember that for every trigger, since we execute more code than for a simple insertion, keep trigger code minimal. Triggers are also 'hidden' from a developer, as it is not immediately visible that a table has a trigger on it, unless the developer knows the system, or there is good documentation around. They may create a new process that refreshes the data every night and may not immediately realize this slows down the process.

For example, if we have a number of records to load from a data repository, a stored procedure or DTS process loads the data into the main table that has an audit trigger on it. This trigger modifies the audit table with the notified changes. The overall process will slow from a straightforward load due to the trigger, the extra insertion, and any other work SQL Server has to index on the audit table. We may try removing the trigger itself and then updating the audit table as a separate batch process later in the overall cycle, if possible.

**Figure 2**

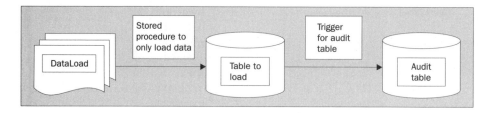

## Deferred Updates and Direct Updates

While modifying rows in a table, SQL Server can employ any of the two different methods – **direct update** or **deferred update**.

As the name suggests, a direct update will modify the table directly with the data that is already there. Once this is done, the transaction log is then created. Every modification to a row in the modified table will then create a record of the row in the transaction log, and the altered column values of the underlying table will simply have their information overwritten in the transaction log.

In a deferred update, the row to be modified is placed into the transaction log as a delete, and then an insertion with the modifications is placed in the transaction log. The row is then deleted from the table, and then reinserted into the table with the new information, with the last two actions taking the information from the log. This is obviously slower than the first method as we have to re-read the data from the transaction log, as well as removing and inserting whole rows of data.

As soon as we place a trigger on a table, we force SQL Server to use the deferred update method of table modification. Therefore, although we may find that the code within the trigger itself is very quick, we will degrade performance of the data modification by placing the trigger.

# Creating and using a trigger

A trigger is created by a CREATE statement. The syntax follows:

```
CREATE TRIGGER name ON table
[WITH ENCRYPTION]
[FOR/AFTER/INSTEAD OF]
[INSERT, UPDATE, DELETE]
[NOT FOR REPLICATION]
AS
BEGIN
...
END
```

We will look at the two options for the type of trigger, AFTER and INSTEAD OF, in the *Types of Triggers* section. When naming a trigger, it is best to follow the naming standard of prefixing the name with tr_, followed by actions the trigger is for, like ins for insert, upd for update, del for delete, and lastly, the name of the table that the trigger is attached to. If we create more than one trigger for a table, for the same set of actions, which is possible with AFTER triggers, then we will suffix each trigger with other information to identify each one. If we had a trigger on the orders table, which will fire on an INSERT only, then it will be called tr_i_orders or tr_iorders. Many people prefer the first method, as it makes the associated trigger action clearer.

As a trigger fires on an action (unlike procedures, which are invoked), it is obvious that it is not possible to pass in any parameters. All of the information for a trigger has to come from table information. If we need to pass in some sort of parameter information, then prior to executing the triggering action, we need to create a temporary table that can then be referenced by the trigger.

There are two occasions when a trigger will not fire on a modification action:

❏ Triggers fire on logged actions, such as an INSERT, when the action is placed in the transaction log. TRUNCATE TABLE statements are non-logged actions, which is one reason for TRUNCATE TABLE being faster than a DELETE with no WHERE statement, as a TRUNCATE TABLE will not fire any underlying triggers.

❏ The second occasion is when we use WRITETEXT to write information to a TEXT data type column. This is also a non-logged action, and therefore cannot fire a trigger.

Code within triggers needs to be short. Any trigger that fires on a table modification will reside in the same transaction as the modification action that fired it. Therefore, the longer a trigger takes to run, the longer the lock on any rows or tables is held.

It is possible to reference any tables within the database in which the trigger resides, tables outside the containing database, or any temporary table created in the calling batch. Remember that every such action will degrade performance, and hence it is crucial to create optimal T-SQL code.

We will look at replication and triggers, but it will be useful to make the point about using the NOT FOR REPLICATION option in the trigger. If we code our trigger with this option, we are indicating that if the database is replicated, this trigger will not fire when the update coming into the table is from a replication action.

**! When we set up replication within SQL Server, we can automatically transfer triggers from the publisher to the subscriber database. If the publisher is marked NOT FOR REPLICATION, and placed in the subscriber. If the trigger does not have this option, then the triggers will also be replicated without the option, which may not be what we want.**

Although not a mandatory option, it is best to keep this in mind in case our company decides to replicate a production database to another location.

*We can encrypt a trigger for security, as with stored procedures, hence the* WITH ENCRYPTION *option in the syntax.*

# The Conceptual Tables within Triggers

When a trigger fires, there are two conceptual tables available for use to check data changes. For example, let's say we are updating a row in TableA in some database. SQL Server knows we have an update trigger on this table, so it takes an image of the row before the modification takes place, then allows the modification to occur, and finally takes an image of the row. This pre-modification image is placed into a table called deleted, as we delete the values in the old row. The post-modification row is placed into a table called inserted. Remember that these tables only exist within a trigger. A deletion will have a row in the deleted table and an insertion will have a row in the inserted table, per row modified.

We can demonstrate this in the following trigger:

```
CREATE TRIGGER tr_upd_OrdersCount
ON orders
AFTER UPDATE
AS
BEGIN
  DECLARE @Rc VARCHAR(20)

  SELECT @Rc = CAST(COUNT(*) as VARCHAR(10)) FROM deleted
  SET @Rc = 'Rows Updated ' + @Rc
  RAISERROR(@Rc,1,1)
END
```

If we update the data with the following, we will see that Rows Updated as well as the COUNT for the UPDATE command comes to 5.

```
UPDATE orders
SET RequiredDate = RequiredDate
WHERE CustomerId = 'VINET'
```

The output of the UPDATE is:

Msg 50000, Level 1, State 50000
Rows Updated 5

(5 row(s) affected)

When working with multiple modifications, it is necessary to have a method to match the rows in the deleted table with the rows in the inserted table. Normal practice will be to use the primary key, providing that this gives unique rows, without which we may need to alter our underlying table.

These conceptual tables are held in memory, and hence are fast. If a trigger fires after a large number of row modifications, it is not possible to index these tables to speed up the trigger.

## Triggers Fired on an Update

When a trigger fires on an UPDATE or INSERT action, it is possible to find out if a specific column value has been modified. If the IF UPDATE clause is used, SQL Server will compare the values in that column from the deleted table with those in the inserted table, to determine if a modification has taken place. If every column in the IF statement has been updated or inserted, then this will return a TRUE value, and the trigger will then drop in the relevant code block for the decision. This is faster than multiple IF...ELSE IF..., where we will need one IF per column. Computed and TEXT data type columns cannot be placed in the UPDATE test.

There is another similar function called COLUMNS_UPDATED that returns a **bitmask** of the column number of every column that has also been modified. A bitmask is simple binary positioning for the columns in a table.

We can see the bitmask value against each column in the table:

| Column in table | Bitmask value |
|---|---|
| First | 1 |
| Second | 2 |
| Third | 4 |
| Fourth | 8 |
| Fifth | 16 |
| Sixth | 32 |
| Seventh | 64 |
| Eighth | 128 |

If we want to check if the second, fifth, and seventh columns have been updated, then add 2, 16, and 64 (result is 82), and the SQL statement will be IF COLUMNS_UPDATED(82). It will not matter if the other columns have also been updated, as this statement will only consider the three columns mentioned.

As we can see, we have mentioned the first eight columns only. What if we want to check if the ninth column has been updated? The value will not be 256 because we are going from one byte to two bytes, and COLUMNS_UPDATED() works on the bit settings of one byte only. Well, we can still do this, but we have to SUBSTRING that second byte from COLUMNS_UPDATED(), and then use the POWER function.

Code to test columns 4, 7, 10, and 12 is as follows:

```
IF  SUBSTRING(COLUMNS_UPDATED(),1,1) = POWER(2,4-1) + POWER(2,7-1)
AND SUBSTRING(COLUMNS_UPDATED(),2,1) = POWER(2,10-8-1) + POWER(2,12-8-1)
```

This can be clarified as $2^{4-1} + 2^{7-1}$ (as we want to test column 4, and $2^0$ is 1). In the second test, it is $2^{10-8-1} + 2^{12-8-1}$ (as the first eight were covered in the first SUBSTRING).

If a column is inserted in the middle of an existing table, then our bitmask tests will no longer be valid. The same reason for not coding SELECT * applies here – our related processes will no longer work. if the column order changes.

# Types of Trigger

There are three main types of triggers that fire on INSERT, DELETE, or UPDATE actions. Like stored procedures, these can also be encrypted for extra security, and more on this will be covered in the next chapter.

## FOR

This is the most basic trigger found in virtually all corporations where versions of SQL Server prior to SQL Server 2000 exist. This syntax has been replaced with the AFTER trigger action.

## AFTER

This is the default definition while creating a trigger. AFTER triggers will fire after checking the concerned constraint once the deleted and inserted tables have been created, after the data has been modified, but before it has been committed to the database. Whether the underlying data modification is surrounded by a BEGIN TRANSACTION or not, it is not until completion of this trigger that the transaction takes effect.

*If we have NTEXT, TEXT, or IMAGE data types within our triggered table, then we will not be able to reference those columns from the inserted and deleted tables. If we need to reference these data types, then it is necessary to use INSTEAD OF triggers.*

To demonstrate the AFTER trigger, we will place records into an audit table, which will be populated from triggers on the orders table. Note that northwind is used as the default database in all the code snippets in this chapter. The description of the table is:

```
CREATE TABLE Orders_Audit (
   OrderID INT ,
   CustomerID NCHAR (5)  NULL ,
   EmployeeID INT NULL ,
   OrderDate DATETIME NULL ,
   RequiredDate DATETIME NULL ,
   ShippedDate DATETIME NULL ,
   ShipVia INT NULL ,
   Freight MONEY NULL ,
   ShipName NVARCHAR (40)  NULL ,
   ShipAddress NVARCHAR (60)  NULL ,
   ShipCity NVARCHAR (15)  NULL ,
   ShipRegion NVARCHAR (15)  NULL ,
   ShipPostalCode NVARCHAR (10)  NULL ,
   ShipCountry NVARCHAR (15) NULL ,
   DateAdded DATETIME NOT NULL DEFAULT GETDATE()
)
```

The new column that was absent in the orders table is a simple DATETIME stamp of when the record was inserted. While creating audit records, it maybe necessary to record under which login the modification was made, depending on how our users connect to the database. We can record which connection made the modification by using SELECT USER. There are ways of getting the UID into a trigger table, like having a user column on the underlying table that is populated using a parameter passed to the calling stored procedure.

The following T-SQL code will create a record of how the modified orders rows looked before any update or deletion took place (only the shipping or required dates are altered):

```
CREATE TRIGGER tr_iud_Orders
ON Orders
AFTER INSERT,UPDATE,DELETE
AS
BEGIN
-- If either of these two dates altered, then create the audit record
-- If either are not altered, then no audit record
IF UPDATE(ShippedDate) OR UPDATE(RequiredDate) THEN
INSERT INTO Orders_Audit (OrderID ,CustomerID ,EmployeeID ,OrderDate ,
  RequiredDate ,ShippedDate  ,ShipVia ,Freight ,ShipName ,ShipAddress ,
  ShipCity ,ShipRegion ,ShipPostalCode ,ShipCountry )

SELECT OrderID , CustomerID , EmployeeID , OrderDate , RequiredDate ,
     ShippedDate , ShipVia , Freight , ShipName , ShipAddress ,
     ShipCity , ShipRegion , ShipPostalCode , ShipCountry
  FROM deleted
END
```

This is a case where we might wish to have more than a trigger for each action, depending on how we want to use the table; but if there will be a high volume of inserts, compared to updates and deletes, we will slow down our insertion as we will work with the deleted table that will have no rows. The trigger simply places a row in the audit table; therefore, we might not have an INSERT action fire the trigger.

We can make a trigger as complex as we wish for our auditing. If we want to audit INSERT records, then we can modify this trigger so that if @@ROWCOUNT in the deleted table was 0, we can make the trigger insert rows into the audit table from the inserted table. The dark side is that the first modification to the row will generate a duplicate row of the same data. Therefore, if we want to modify every row in the audit table there is no straightforward solution, but we can have an indicator on the audit table to show whether the row is an insertion, modification, or deletion, and ignore any insertion records for the unique key if there are any subsequent rows for the key.

Here, we have a table showing how the audit table and the underlying table will look, for each action:

|  | Orders | Orders_Audit |
| --- | --- | --- |
| INSERT | New row | No row |
| UPDATE | Updated Row | Previous rows values |
| DELETE | No row | Previous rows values |

**!** **AFTER triggers will only fire if all constraints placed on the associated table are valid. When building a trigger it is crucial that the code does not violate any constraint validation placed on a column if it completes any data modification. Otherwise, this will result in an error.**

## Ordering Trigger Actions

We can have more than one trigger for each action, to make modularisation of functionality and maintenance of our code easier. For example, having a trigger specifically for auditing records, such as creating an image of the record in an audit table, and another to perform any business logic validation is better than having a single trigger to do both.

It is also possible to define when the AFTER trigger should fire. If we have a trigger defined to fire first and wish for a different one instead, we will have to remove the existing first trigger before adding a new one. It is not possible to simply replace the name of the trigger.

Taking the audit and business rules validation scenario one step further, we could create an audit table with the same rules as the main table, and add a column for DATETIME of the row generated, and then another column for an audit message. If we have the audit record insertion as the first trigger, we can add in any business failure message into this record when the second business rules validation trigger fires. However, we can also have the audit trigger fire last so that all eventual modifications to the data are picked up. In addition, if any other triggers cause a rollback, then no audit record will be created, which might be the scenario we wish to have. It all depends to how we want to create audit records, and the better practice will be to have rollbacks in triggers to fire sooner rather than later.

Another scenario could be when a price rise is placed on inventory. A stored procedure can run, which will update the tax value on each stock item. The first trigger can be an audit trail, the second trigger can check if the new cost of the item is above a certain level and apply a new level of discount or shipping charge, and a third can modify a table holding statistics on stock, value, taxation levels, and so on.

We can call `sp_settriggerorder` system stored procedure to set the order of triggers:

```
sp_settriggerorder @triggername, @order, @stmttype
```

**!** **If there are three or more AFTER triggers, those not named as first or last will fire in any order.**

# INSTEAD OF

Until SQL Server 2000, it was not possible to have a trigger on a view. Prior to SQL Server 2000, a view was simply to provide a specialized view on a set of data. However, it is now possible to modify the underlying data displayed in a view. Modifying data through a view doesn't need a trigger necessarily, but it's use gives control over the modifications. By defining an INSTEAD OF trigger, we can prevent any modifications through a direct T-SQL statement on a view, and control those modifications through the trigger.

> *INSTEAD OF triggers differ from AFTER triggers as they run before any constraint checking. Therefore, these can supplement any constraint checking, if required.*

Unlike AFTER triggers, we can only define one INSTEAD OF trigger per table or view. If we want to follow the scenarios defined earlier in this section, with multiple triggers, then we can get the trigger to either have all the code in one place, or call other stored procedures if necessary. This also means that we cannot set a trigger default order for INSTEAD OF triggers, as there is only one.

Although INSTEAD OF triggers fire before constraint checks, we should not replace constraints with triggers. More on this will be discussed in the *Triggers Versus Constraints* section.

If we have cascading actions defined when a foreign key is placed on the underlying tables, then we cannot have a corresponding INSTEAD OF trigger defined. Therefore, if we have cascading DELETEs, we cannot have an INSTEAD OF DELETE trigger.

# Cascading

It is possible for one trigger to alter data in another table and the trigger on that table to fire. This is known as **cascading triggers**. Cascading triggers do not exist on INSTEAD OF triggers, but only on AFTER triggers. Cascading triggers execute in the sequence:

❑   If there are any cascading actions selected when creating a foreign key on the table with the trigger, then these will fire first

❑   Then, the trigger associated with the modified table will fire

❑   Each table modified in order will then fire any trigger associated with it

Cascading triggers have obvious performance hits on our application. We can use cascading triggers only if a trigger is performing either some audit action or an update, such as summing a set of orders for a product into a sales audit table. If the potential cascading triggers perform only validation, then cascading should not be allowed.

To allow nested triggers, we need to configure the database. This can be done in T-SQL as:

```
sp_configure "nested triggers",1
```

# No Rows Updated

A trigger will fire on the triggering action even if no rows have been affected. Take a look at the following update trigger. This will fire on an UPDATE action on the orders table.

```
CREATE TRIGGER tr_upd_OrdersNoRows
ON Orders
AFTER UPDATE
AS
BEGIN

  RAISERROR('Update occurred',1,1)

END
```

**210**

If no rows in the `orders` table are actually updated, the `RAISERROR` statement will run.

```
UPDATE Orders
SET RequiredDate = Null
WHERE CustomerId = 'NOROW'
```

Once the above code is executed, we will see the following output. It looks as if a row has been updated but the `(0 row(s) affected)` line says that there have been none.

Msg 50000, Level 1, State 50000
Update occurred

(0 row(s) affected)

The correct method of writing a trigger is to use `@@ROWCOUNT` to check how many rows were affected. We can do this as the first statement in the trigger, or by checking the `deleted` and `inserted` tables.

> **If we want to check the triggered table, then we must put `@@ROWCOUNT` first in the trigger.**

Let's rewrite the above trigger accordingly to fire the trigger if no update occurs:

```
ALTER TRIGGER tr_upd_OrdersNoRows
ON Orders
AFTER UPDATE
AS
BEGIN
   IF @@ROWCOUNT = 0
      RETURN

   RAISERROR('Update occurred',1,1)

END
```

# Transactions and Triggers

It is possible to work with transactions within a trigger issuing `COMMIT TRANSACTION` or `ROLLBACK TRANSACTION` statements. This may seem similar to having these statements within a T-SQL transaction, but it is not so with `ROLLBACK`.

Within a T-SQL batch, a `ROLLBACK` will undo any changes made from the start of the transaction, and processing will continue with the next statement after the `ROLLBACK` within the batch, or the next batch.

If we issue a ROLLBACK within a trigger, the changes are undone for the transaction including changes made in the trigger and the stored procedure at the BEGIN TRAN statement, but the batch will terminate and processing will move on to the next batch irrespective of any statements. The reason behind this can be seen in this section of dummy code:

```
BEGIN TRANSACTION
UPDATE TableA
SET Column4 = Value1
WHERE column1 = Value2

INSERT INTO TableA (Column1,Column2,Column3,Column4)
  VALUES (1,2,3,4)

COMMIT TRANSACTION

SELECT Column4 FROM TableA
```

If we have a trigger on TableA and a problem arises within this batch, SQL Server will not assume that we have an UPDATE trigger, INSERT trigger, or both. The trigger with the ROLLBACK statement may be any of the ones set up for TableA, or on any combination of table updates. Therefore, the trigger itself may have been fired for the UPDATE or the INSERT. If a ROLLBACK is issued from the trigger, then SQL Server will not know whether it is allowed to run the INSERT or any further statements, so it takes the safe route and will not run the SELECT statement either (in the example).

# Trigger versus Constraints

When it comes to enforcing integrity, we have to get the right tool for the right job. Later in the *Good Practices* section, we will look at good and bad practices for triggers and talk about the right tools there. One of the issues is enforcing the different levels of integrity, one of which is domain integrity, enforced through CHECK constraints.

Enforcing domain integrity through CHECK constraints is not always possible. Foreign key constraints may also provide insufficient processing complexity and this is where a trigger fits in.

We will use a trigger instead of a CHECK constraint when the validation required is not against another column within the table or a value. So if we had an order total which checks that the total matched the order plus tax and shipping, which cannot be done as part of a CHECK constraint. Instead, we will have a trigger that fires when the order table is updated or inserted, and validates those specific columns. Validating against a column in another table could be done in a case where clients are given credit rating. When an order is being placed, a join to the credit rating table from the client table is placed and a check is made that the client has enough credit to place the order. We will compare the value in the client table's credit outstanding column with the level in the credit rating table, to ensure that it falls within acceptable bounds.

Finally, when working with a CHECK constraint, if an error occurs, we have no control over the message; this depends on the SQL Server. If we wished to have a custom error message, we will have to implement this through a trigger, but if it is possible to stick with the generic message, then do so.

# Triggers versus Stored Procedure

We may ask why not use a stored procedure instead of a trigger? Well, there may be times when it is the more appropriate choice, as the stored procedure code will work with sets of data at a time, while the trigger will work with rows of data at a time. Therefore, any validation or extra processing when a record is modified can be performed in the trigger, rather than altering the stored procedure to use a cursor, or completing a pass-through of the records at least twice – once for validation and then for an update. It may be possible to have some of the validation in the JOIN and WHERE statements, but this may not cover every scenario.

In addition, we can get the exact columns that have been modified with a trigger and see the value before or after any column, which can aid in the validation. The main difference between triggers and stored procedures is that stored procedures are controlled and invoked by the user, whereas triggers are controlled totally by the actions performed on the underlying table, and we have no control over their firing except dropping them.

Finally, by using a trigger rather than placing the validation within a stored procedure, we can have the validation or any further script actions in a central place. Therefore, as the database owner, when an ad-hoc query is being executed, or a number of different stored procedures modify the same underlying table, we can be assured that the business validation is being performed.

This is an uncommon, but useful scenario for more complex stored procedures, where we attempt to debug the activities of the stored procedure in the temporary table. If the stored procedure is updating a table at several points within a procedure, we might be able to see which section of the stored procedure has the problem, and the time when the problem occurred, by having an audit trigger.

# Replication

Although we are not here to teach replication, it is necessary to know a bit about replication, if our database contains triggers. We will cover the more salient points when looking at replication with user-defined triggers.

Three possible types of replication are possible:

❑ **Transactional** – We have one `master` database, the `publisher`, where all changes are made and are passed to the `subscribers`, which are any other databases set up to receive any replicated information.

❑ **Merge** – We still have a `publisher` database that sends out changes, but the `subscribers` can also send out changes.

❑ **Snapshot** – The `publisher` database is copied as a whole to all `subscriber` sites.

With snapshot replication, triggers are not a problem as the whole database is replicated as a snapshot at a particular time, however we have to design carefully with the other two.

With transactional replication, we will be aware of what data is being replicated and how. Triggers on the `subscribers` do not need to contain any business validation necessarily, but contain updates to tables that are not replicated, such as tables in a different database.

Finally, with merge replication, we will have triggers on both tables with business rules and cascading actions. When data published on one system propagates through to the replicated systems, any trigger in place has to cater to data coming either from its own system, or from replicated data. Merge replication use triggers created by the Snapshot Agent to place any changes in the replicated tables into the system replication defined tables.

When replication is created for a table that is defined as **immediate** or **queued update subscriber**, then the replication sets up a default trigger that will fire first. Therefore, any change completed on that table will be replicated before any other trigger, when replication is allows `subscriber` databases to modify data to be passed back to the `publisher` database.

> *Immediate or queued update subscriber is an update mode for* `subscriber` *databases to replicate any changes to the* `publisher`*.*

One other point to note is that the **nested trigger** option must be enabled while using immediate or queued update subscriber replication. This is the default setting, but if we have disabled this option as some sort of safety check in our system, we will have to enable it again.

**!** **If we already have a trigger defined as the first trigger, we must remove this before making the table an immediate or queued update subscriber, otherwise an error will occur. We cannot make any other trigger a first trigger, once this replication is set up.**

While replicating, any trigger that has been defined as WITH ENCRYPTION will never be published. We either have to remove the encryption, which is probably not the best action, or manually place the trigger on each subscriber with the encryption included.

If we have user-defined triggers on the subscriber database, they have to be replicated to ensure that they are really needed there. We may find that moving the logic to the stored procedures defined for the replication itself makes the code more efficient, but will have to be controlled in a very tight source code fashion if we ever have to recreate the database with replication, for example when moving from a test setup to the live setup. Preferably, this option of moving code should only be considered if we find the replication slow, and there are lags in the updates.

# Recursion

As with stored procedures, we can set up recursive triggers. Although rare, there can be scenarios when this can be acceptable. We saw a direct recursion with the Factorial stored procedure in Chapter 1, it is possible to have recursion on triggers as well.

There are two types of trigger recursion:

❑ **direct** – A trigger updates the same table that the trigger has been fired on and therefore fires itself again.

❑ **indirect** – A trigger is fired on one table, which updates a different table with a trigger on it, which then updates the original table again.

To clarify the indirect trigger, one example would be when a new order comes in, and a trigger fires which updates the stock levels. This fires a trigger on the Stock table to reduce the stock level. If the stock falls below a certain level, then this might update the order table with an indicator that we are out of stock. This will re-fire the trigger on the order table. In this scenario, we have to be careful not to end up in an endless loop, and fire the update on the Stock table only if there is a stock movement. The second time the order trigger is fired this will not be the case, and therefore we will test this, and just let the trigger recursion stop.

To enable direct recursion to take place, then we need to set the RECURSIVE_TRIGGERS SQL option to ON.

```
ALTER DATABASE Northwind
SET RECURSIVE_TRIGGERS ON
```

*As soon as we place a trigger on a database, whenever another trigger is added, there is always the danger that recursion could exist. Keep this in mind, it is better to have RECURSIVE_TRIGGERS set to OFF, and ensure that we do not code a 'cover all' and bolt down what the trigger is actually there for, while building it.*

If we have a trigger that updates the same table that caused its firing, then the same trigger will fire again if RECURSIVE_TRIGGERS was ON. If we do have this option on, and we are updating the same table, perhaps with summary info, then we have to consider the fact that recursion will occur and code defensively for it, otherwise we may get into an infinite loop.

# Good Practice

The most important point is to keep the trigger as short as possible to execute quickly, just like stored procedures. The longer a trigger takes to fire, the longer the locks will be held on the underlying tables. To this end, we could place cursors within a trigger, but good practice dictates that we don't. Cursors are not the fastest of objects within a database, and we should try and revisit the problem with a different solution, if we feel the need for cursors. One way around the problem may be to run two, or perhaps, three updates, or even use a temporary table instead.

Use triggers to enforce business rules, or to complete actions that have either a positive effect on the organization, or if an action will stop problems with the system. An example of this is creation of a trigger that will e-mail a client when an order is about to be shipped, giving details of the order, and so on.

> Use an @@ROWCOUNT, where required, to check the number of rows that have been affected.

If we have a trigger on a table, watch out if our code invoking the trigger uses the @@IDENTITY value. If we have a stored procedure that inserts an order and returns @@IDENTITY to give the order number created, and we have an audit trigger that inserts into the audit table, which also has an IDENTITY column, the @@IDENTITY value returned by the stored procedure will be that from the audit table and not the orders table. To get around this, we will perhaps have to use a MAX() function to find the last order ID.

# Bad Practice

Firstly, don't substitute a constraint with a trigger, as we covered much of this in the *Triggers Versus Constraints* section. Within a database solution, there are different levels of integrity, and at each level, there is an appropriate method of enforcing that integrity.

❏ **Entity Integrity** – No row has a NULL in the primary key, all tables have primary keys, and no two rows have the same primary key value. The solution to enforcing this is to build a primary key as a UNIQUE constraint, and no column that forms the primary key allows NULLs.

❑ **Domain Integrity** – When all values in a specific column are valid, whether this is a range of values or specific values, the solution is to place a constraint on a specific column, known as a CHECK constraint

❑ **Referential Integrity** – Where all foreign keys are valid, the solution is to place foreign key constraints on the relevant tables.

These solutions for each integrity type will cover most scenarios. We will consider using a trigger only when they are not sufficient. It is unusual, if not rare, to run into a different database solution, and find that triggers have replaced these natural methods of enforcing integrity. Although overheads of using triggers are low normally, we create a performance overhead if we use a trigger when one of these options would have been sufficient. Therefore, any code violating these recommendations should be removed and replaced.

There are other problems with a ROLLBACK in a trigger too if we use cursors and nested transactions; we looked at some of the problems in Chapter 3.

There are no restrictions on the T-SQL code placed within a trigger. Therefore, it is possible to place a SELECT statement within code to return a rowset, which is an unusual action, since we should return data within a stored procedure when we need to.

# Summary

Triggers are excellent tools for a developer to have when building a database solution. Care has to be taken that the right trigger and the right code is placed within a trigger though. But the skill lies in knowing when to have cascading triggers, whether to work with transactions within a trigger, what to do when replication is involved, and what isolation levels to have.

Once a database solution is in place with working triggers, any alteration to that database environment, such as replication, will require a great deal of thought and planning. Testing should be intensive with an emphasis placed on areas such as performance. We may need to alter what happens within triggers, and maybe even split an AFTER trigger on one table action into two, with only one working on the replication.

# SQL Server 2000

## Stored Procedures

### Handbook

**8**

# 8

# Security

By now you will have realized that using stored procedures is the best way for making data available from an SQL database. In the earlier chapters, we have seen that there are several reasons for preferring this approach. One such major reason is security. In this chapter will examine this aspect of SQL Server stored procedures.

We will first analyze security threats and the core security requirement of SQL Server – allowing data access only to explicitly authorized users. Then, we will look at the proper implementation of stored procedures for adequately countering these threats. Finally, we will examine some general methods for securing our SQL Server implementation; we will be giving special emphasis on SQL Server stored procedures and the system stored procedures that Microsoft ships with SQL Server.

## Increased Need for Security

Whenever we deal with a threat, we not only analyze the degree of the vulnerability, but also the gain-to-loss ratio that a hacker has for taking advantage of that vulnerability. If the gains are high and the losses are perceived to be low, the hacker is more likely to hack the system. Note that, the gains can be subjective or abstract. Until a few years ago, the vast majority of SQL Server applications were client-server applications, which were totally contained within the firewall of an organization. In such a scenario, the potential hacker was an employee of the company itself. The gains in successfully hacking the application and not getting caught were significantly counter-balanced by the perceived loss of losing their job and the fear of being prosecuted.

However, in today's web-enabled world, two significant things have happened:

❑ The quality of the data that we are collecting is getting both more valuable and more liquid (for example, credit card numbers).

❑ Secondly, with the increasing penetration of the Internet, the potential hacker is sitting miles away and has no direct relationship with the organization. You can't fire them, since they usually aren't an employee or contractor. Getting their name, address, and phone number to turn them over to a law enforcement authority is much more difficult.

As a result, the gains for the hackers have gone up considerably while the perceived losses have gone down dramatically. In such a scenario, hacking is bound to be more attractive to a crooked conscience.

# SQL Server Vulnerabilities

To minimize the risk of hacking, it is essential for a DBA to minimize (if not completely eliminate) the vulnerabilities of SQL Server. In this section, we will be looking at three different vulnerabilities and how stored procedures can be used to minimize them. We will look at:

❑ Misconfiguration of SQL Servers, particularly regarding permissions on objects

❑ SQL injection attacks

❑ SQL buffer overflows

## *Misconfiguration of SQL Servers*

This can be broken down into two categories – problems arising due to a weak setup and problems related to permissions paths.

### SQL Server Setup

By far, the most damage that can ever be done to your IT enterprise is by a rogue DBA, so judge wisely!

> **Security Tip #1: This is the first step in SQL Server security. You have to trust your DBA. If you can't, find another DBA. There is no alternative.**

Even though we have said that there is no alternative, in reality, you could implement C2 security tracing. However note that the overhead is extraordinarily high in terms of resource (CPU, disk, memory, and so on) usage. Additionally, it is quite hard to configure a system where the trace occurs without the DBA having access to it.

> *For more details on setting up a C2-level auditing you can refer to SQL Server Books Online.*

Apart from a rogue DBA, the first real threat of unauthorized data access happens when the SQL Server security infrastructure is not properly configured. By this, we mean that a DBA doesn't know what they are doing and inadvertently end up leaving a hole in their server configuration. Closely related to this is the improper assignment of permissions in an application, such that a user has more permissions than they should be allowed to have.

The security settings of an out-of-the-box SQL Server 2000 installation are certainly better than those in SQL Server 7.0. However, still, a lot is left to be desired. In the summer of 2002, Microsoft finally woke up to SQL Server's security concerns. With virtually no exceptions, development at Microsoft came to a screeching halt for two months, as code and processes were reviewed line by line. The head engineer of Microsoft's SQL storage engine team, Peter Spiro, stated that 50 man-years of his programming staff were dedicated to security at this time. The results of these efforts can be seen in the SQL Server 2000 Service Pack 3. With the application of this service pack, SQL Server will become one the most secure database product ever produced by Microsoft. This covers both policy implementation, as well as source code review.

At the same time, we need to configure SQL Server properly. Numerous articles have been written about the setting up SQL Server properly. We will not cover these steps; instead we recommend that you refer to the *Microsoft SQL Server 2000 Security* white paper, it's available at http://msdn.microsoft.com/library/default.asp?url=/library/en-us/dnsql2k/html/sql_security2000.asp

This document will give you the basic steps for securing your SQL Server. This said, we must ensure the following:

1. Do not allow a SQL Server to be exposed directly through port 1433 from the Internet; block port 1433 at the firewall. If you expose port 1433, you will be port-scanned, time and again, for known vulnerabilities. Even if you are up to date in applying the service packs, patches, and hotfixes, there is always the likelihood of a hacker finding some new vulnerability (for example, a buffer overflow).

2. Replace the SQL Server's default listen-on port for TCP/IP sockets (port 1433) with some other port and re direct your clients to this new port. This may help in forestalling an internal attack.

To change the server's settings, perform the following steps. Run the Server Network Utility to connect to the server. Then, highlight the TCP/IP entry and click on the Properties button. Change the port number in the pop-up window and click on OK:

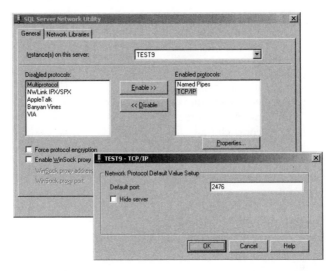

After making the changes to the server, we need to configure the client. This can be done by running the Client Network Utility. In the Alias tab, click the Add button. In the pop-up window, against Server alias enter the name of your server. Then, click on the TCP/IP check box and specifically enter the new port number by unchecking the Dynamically determine port option:

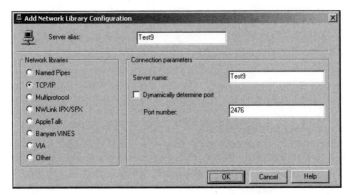

3. Get the service packs, patches, and hoxfixes run through a development server and move into your production environment. This should be one of your highest priorities.

4. If at all possible, use integrated security instead of mixed-mode security for your applications.

5. Make the sa login's (that is, the one with SID of 0x01) password extremely hard and store it away securely. Only use it when it's absolutely necessary. It can have 128 characters in SQL 7.0 and above. Here's an example of one of our sa passwords:

D899î²çûû5Bâ£däöS5¶í9®×zÑZAÀzÂOIËGÔ¼¬ʹÆkNÆÈ¾xôçÃjmÅˆ¦²Ø¬J»J4Uˊ öµAZCDkªA¡ùÎ· ü4Ú6ˊÀ9§ý¼lp§Ú-r8Ô¸OYËi⁄Æ¶ʿR§8qîÏR¥ËÂûÔäÙ5ˊŒ§tWùÈm ßì

A script for making such random passwords is included in our code download; you can get it from http://www.apress.com.

6. If you use applications that require the use of the sa login, audit the use by putting an alert on the successful non-trusted logins (error 18454) with the letters sa. Here's the code snippet which accomplishes this:

```
EXECUTE msdb.dbo.sp_add_alert @name = N'SA non-trusted login',
@message_id = 18454, @severity = 0, @enabled = 1,
@delay_between_responses = 8, @include_event_description_in = 5,
@event_description_keyword = N'''sa''',
@job_name = N'SA login email notify',
@category_name = N'[Uncategorized]'
```

This snippet fires a job which queries SYSPROCESSes for Windows 2000 login ID and application name, logs the usage in a table, and e-mails out the logins made by the sa user. In order for this job to work, you need to be auditing all successful SQL Server logins, but then again, you should be doing that anyway. This job and all the objects necessary for it are included in the code download.

7. We also suggest that all users having access to the sa login use a named pipes connection rather than the usual TCP/IP sockets connection. By making your users use named pipes, you will be able to positively identify their NT account with their connection. There is a small performance trade-off for the connection, but the vast majority of applications and servers will not suffer. In this way, you can also ensure that the operating system approves the security credentials of the users, before they get to SQL Server.

# Permission Paths

Now, let's look at how a person gets access to the database objects, in terms of the following elements – Windows Users and Groups, SQL login IDs, database objects, database users, database roles, object ownership, and object permissions.

### Windows Users and Groups

These are the user accounts and groups that users are assigned to in the operating system. Internally, a binary number, called Security ID or SID, identifies a user or a group. When a user logs into a Windows 2000 computer, they get a security token for their login session. A user in a group will have the SID of that group, on the security token. A user wanting to work with a particular SQL Server presents the token to the SQL Server for access.

The user and group accounts can be either at the domain level or at the local computer level; generally, the user accounts are at the domain level, since a local computer account would provide access only to that single computer. An exception to this is the service accounts for the SQL Server Service and the SQL Agent Service, which may be at the local computer level.

### SQL Login IDs

These logins are present at the SQL Server level, with the data supporting them residing in the sysxlogins table of the master database. They can either be integrated logins with the operating system or standard logins that have no direct relationship with the operating system. If they are integrated, the 28-byte SID in SQL Server is obtained from either the domain or local computer by using the undocumented GET_SID function (we have discussed this function in Chapter 5). This SID directly corresponds to the SID of a particular user or group.

When a user logs into the SQL Server, with an integrated login, they present their token with their SID collection to the SQL Server for comparison with sysxlogins. They can have multiple permission paths since they could be identified with multiple SIDS. A stored procedure, xp_logininfo, shows all the permission paths for an integrated login.

If it is a standard login, the SID in sysxlogins is a self-generated 16-byte binary number. In this case, the password for the login is also stored in an encrypted form, in the password column of the sysxlogins table. Normally, by default the sysxlogins table and its password column for standard logins is only readable to members of the sysadmin role.

**! You should never let normal users access this column, they might download these encrypted passwords and run an offline brute force attack on them by using the undocumented PWDCOMPARE() function.**

When users log in with a standard login, they have to present their password for comparison with the encrypted password stored in sysxlogins. An undocumented function, PWDCOMPARE(), compares the user's password with the encrypted password. The function does this by sending the supplied password through a one-way encrypting function. If the result matches the encrypted password, the function returns a 1, otherwise 0. Normally, the standard password is sent unencrypted to the server, unless the server has a certificate assigned to it in which case the password is automatically encrypted with the public key of the server certificate.

> **Security Tip #2: Get a SSL certificate for your server, so that standard login passwords are encrypted automatically.**

For more details refer to the section on *Installing a SSL Certificate*.

**Database Objects**

Apart from the little bit of configuration data that SQL Server stores in the registry, virtually all data is stored in tables. SQL Server has two types of tables – system tables and user tables. Other objects in the database allow customized viewing (through objects called views), improved sorting (through indexes), customized processing (through stored procedures and functions), limiting table usage (through constraints and defaults), and defining custom data formats (through user-defined data types). Three types of objects are used for customized processing – stored procedures, extended stored procedures, and functions. We'll refer to these collectively as procedures.

The basic record for each object is stored in a system table called `sysobjects`. The definitions for each procedure are stored in one or more records of the `syscomments` system table, in binary format. We'll talk more about the `syscomments` table later on in the section on *Encrypting Stored Procedures*.

> **Security Tip #3: The best practice is to only allow indirect access to table data through stored procedures and, in limited cases, by select rights on views. Doing so increases data control, allows for easier schema modification, and virtually eliminates SQL injection attacks (more on this later).**

**Database User IDs**

Database User IDs are how Windows login SIDs mapped down into the database level. The database user ID can be identified with a SID of a standard login, integrated user, or integrated group. The SID in the `sysusers` table of the database is the same as the SID of the `sysxlogins` table in the `master` database. Usually the names of the login and user ID are the same.

There are two special kinds of user IDs – the database owner or DBO and the guest user ID. The DBO has maximum and irrevocable rights in the database and will always be identified with one of the SIDs in `sysxlogins`. In order for a login to have access to objects in a database, they must be assigned to a user ID in the database. However, there is one exception. If there is a guest user ID in the database, all server logins that do not have an explicit user ID, inherit the permissions assigned to the guest user ID.

> **Security Tip #4: Delete the guest user ID in a database. Always explicitly assign logins to a database if they need to access objects in the database. Note that you cannot delete the guest user ID from the master database.**

**Object Permissions**

There are two types of permissions in a database – statement permissions and object permissions. Statement permissions allow you to do things like creating objects and backup databases. In this chapter, we will focus on object permissions. As the name implies they control permissions to use objects.

> **Security Tip #5: You really need to understand the terminology of action, permission, object, and sysusers record when talking about the application of permissions to objects.**

In T-SQL, a command to setup permissions has the following syntactical structure:

```
Action Permission ON object TO SYSUSER_Rec
```

In the following example, we use the GRANT action to allow the SELECT permission on the sysobjects object to a sysusers record named JERRY:

```
GRANT SELECT ON sysobjects TO JERRY
```

As we mentioned, object permissions include SELECT, UPDATE, INSERT, DELETE, EXECUTE, REFERENCES, and ALL. ALL includes every one of the others. Only the EXECUTE permission applies to stored procedures. If you use ALL for a stored procedure permission statement, it will apply the EXECUTE permission only. EXECUTE and REFERENCES apply to scalar valued functions.

There are three actions for managing permissions – GRANT, DENY, and REVOKE. GRANT allows you to exercise a particular permission on an object, while DENY keeps you from exercising it. REVOKE removes the effects of either a previously defined GRANT or DENY permission setting for an object. If a permission path places both the GRANT and DENY actions on a particular object for a user, the DENY action takes precedence.

Coming back to our above example of Jerry and the sysobjects table, if Jerry is a member of a group called Accounting with an Accounting group login and a corresponding user ID in the database, we can issue the following command:

```
DENY SELECT ON sysobjects TO ACCOUNTING
```

As a result, Jerry will not be allowed to execute SELECT on the sysobjects table because the DENY action override for the Accounting group user ID overrides the earlier GRANT action, which was directly applied to Jerry. In short – any DENY will always override a GRANT.

**226**

The sysuser record can be either a user ID whose SID is mapped to a SQL Server login or a database role.

### Database Roles

The sysusers table in a database stores user IDs and roles. We have already talked about user IDs. Roles differ from user IDs in several ways. Firstly, the UID value for a role record in sysusers is always greater than 16384, while a user ID's UID value is 16383 or less. To see the roles in a database, use this query:

```
SELECT * FROM dbo.sysusers WHERE UID > 16383
```

Alternatively, you execute the system stored procedure sp_helprole:

```
EXEC sp_helprole
```

Roles are also different from user IDs in the sense that roles are essentially containers. There is a system table called sysmembers that maps user IDs and other roles, as members of a role. Members are added to roles by using the sp_addrolemember procedure. Please note that, a role can be nested as a member in another role, but you cannot have circular nesting. If you have nested roles, you need to set up a hierarchical nesting structure, where a node cannot be a parent of any node above or up to itself in the hierarchy.

Microsoft designed security in SQL Server 7.0 and SQL Server 2000 with the idea that permissions would be assigned to roles and not to user IDs. By assigning permissions to a role, we can tremendously increase the flexibility of our database security structure. You can find more on this in the *Putting it all Together* section.

---

**Security Tip #6: Apply permissions to database roles and not to user IDs.**

---

There is a special role called PUBLIC with UID 0. Every user ID in a database is automatically a member of the PUBLIC role, even without being defined in sysmembers. Finally, roles are different from user IDs; the SID column in sysusers for a user ID maps back to a SQL Server login in the sysxlogins table of the master database, the SID column in sysusers for a role is NULL.

> **Security Tip #7: Remove PUBLIC role permissions from all objects in a database. An exception is the master database. Generally, the permission granted to the PUBLIC role in the model database, from which all databases start, are not necessary for an application to run. Rely only on setting permissions explicitly for a role. You will want to try it out in a development environment before implementing it in a production environment, as it may break poorly implemented applications that rely on public permissions instead of explicit role-based permissions.**

For removing all public permissions, we can use the following script:

```
SET NOCOUNT ON
-- We will loop through one record at a time
SET ROWCOUNT 1
DECLARE @i INT, @cmd VARCHAR(1000)
SELECT @i = 1
WHILE @i > 0
BEGIN
   SELECT @cmd = NULL
   -- u.name is the owner of object o.name
   SELECT @cmd = u.name+'.'+o.name
   FROM sysobjects o
   JOIN syspermissions p ON o.id = p.id
   JOIN sysusers u ON o.uid = u.uid
   WHERE p.grantee = 0
-- public grantee UID is 0
   SELECT @i = @@rowcount
   -- the last time through @cmd IS NULL
   IF @cmd IS NOT NULL
   BEGIN
      SELECT 'Revoking PUBLIC perm on '+@cmd
      EXEC ('revoke all on '+@cmd+' to public')
   END
END
```

### Object Ownership

A record in the sysusers table, either a user ID or a role, always owns tables, stored procedures, views, and other objects in the sysobjects table. You can change an object's owner by using the sp_changeobjectowner procedure.

An fully named object consists of four parts:

1. **Object name**
   If there are no objects with the specified name owned by the current user, the DBO owner is assumed. If there are no objects owned by the current user or the DBO with the object name, an invalid object name error is returned. Generally around 97% of databases have all their objects owned by the DBO user ID.

2. **Owner name**

If the owner name is left off, it's assumed to be same as the currently logged in user. This may lend a great deal of convenience, as the owner doesn't have to be explicitly named in an object call, but it is also a security hole.

3. **Database name**

If the database name is left out, the object is assumed to be in the current database.

4. **Server name**

If the server name is left off, the current server is assumed. This would normally be left off, except in cross-server calls.

A fully-qualified name generally has only the first three parts, for example, master.dbo.sysobject. If the database name is left out, the object is assumed to be in the current database.

---

> **Security Tip #8: Create a new role and have all your objects explicitly owned by this role. We commonly create a role called APP in the model database, when we first set up a server, to own all our user objects.**

---

However note that, this is a highly controversial decision. As we said earlier, almost 97% of databases have all their objects owned by the DBO user ID. It is a de facto standard. Using the DBO user ID may make your database susceptible to cross-database hacking, where the databases inadvertently have common owners and the security in the second database isn't tight.

Let's look at an example. First, create a TESTER login (with a blank password), we will use it to run a cross-database view. Before you go any further, make sure that the pubs and Northwind databases are owned by the same login. In our case, it is the sa login with a SID of 0x01.

Look at the sysdatabases table and ensure that the SIDs for the two databases are the same. In the first instance, the DBO will be the owner of both objects. In the second instance, the owner of both objects will be the APP role. First, log in through Query Analyzer, as a user with sysadmin rights for the server. Then run the following script to set up the test environment:

```
EXEC master.DBO.sp_addlogin tester
EXEC pubs.DBO.sp_adduser tester
EXEC northwind.DBO.sp_adduser tester
EXEC sp_defaultdb tester, northwind
EXEC pubs.DBO.sp_addrole app
EXEC northwind.DBO.sp_addrole app
```

```
SELECT * INTO pubs.app.authors
FROM pubs.DBO.authors
USE northwind
GO

CREATE VIEW app.vw_authors AS
SELECT * FROM pubs.app.authors
GO
CREATE VIEW DBO.vw_authors AS
SELECT * FROM pubs.DBO.authors
GO
GRANT SELECT ON app.vw_authors TO tester
GRANT SELECT ON DBO.vw_authors TO tester
```

Next, login through Query Analyzer with the tester login. Remember, that it has a blank password. Now, run the following scripts on the Northwind database:

```
SELECT * FROM DBO.vw_authors
```

You will get the record set of the DBO.authors table in the pubs database. This illustrates the potential cross-database security hole of always using the DBO user ID, as an object owner. Now execute the following query, as tester, in the Northwind database:

```
SELECT * FROM app.vw_authors
```

You will get a SELECT permission denied error on the pubs.app.authors table. By not using the DBO as the object owner, you can forestall a common-owner cross-database hack. The requirements for this hack to occur across the common DBO are:

❑　We need two databases with a common login as owner

❑　In the first database, the login must be a user with very limited permissions

❑　In the second database, the same login must be a user satisfying at least one of these conditions:

• CREATE VIEW statement permission

• CREATE PROCEDURE statement permission

• member of the db_ddladmin fixed database role

• member of the DB_OWNER fixed database role

❑　The login creates a DBO-owned procedure or view in the second database that accesses or changes objects (tables) in the first database that the user shouldn't have access to

Incidentally, in an out-of-the-box installation, the pubs database meets these conditions as the 'second database', such that any login in the server could carry out this hack on a database with the same owner as the pubs database. In a default install, right-click the pubs database in SQL Enterprise Manager and click Properties. Look at the Permissions tab, and you will see that the guest user ID has CREATE VIEW and CREATE PROCEDURE permissions.

> **Security Tip #9: Delete the pubs and Northwind databases from a production server, or, at a minimum, delete the guest user ID from pubs and Northwind databases. For good measure, delete the guest user ID from the msdb database, also.**

**!** **WARNING: Remember, that there may be poorly developed applications that make use of these *guest* security holes. Make sure you test it on a development server prior to doing this on a production instance. Better still, follow *SecurityTtip #8*.**

We have a feeling that Microsoft is really addressing this problem with its system tables, due to poorly implemented applications. After all, even if you make the user objects owned by the APP role in your databases, a hacker can still get a good picture of your schema through this security hole by querying cross-database the system tables. If you run the following query in SQL 2000 having Service Pack 1 or later installed, you will see what we mean:

```
SELECT [DESCRIPTION] FROM
MASTER.DBO.SYSMESSAGES
WHERE ERROR = 15355
```

This query will produce the following output:

```
"'sys' will be a reserved user or role name in next version of SQL
Server."
```

## Putting it all together

Now that you know what a login, user ID, role, object, object ownership, and permissions are, let's look into the correct way for setting up a permission chain for an ideal application. The following diagram shows this:

**Figure 1**

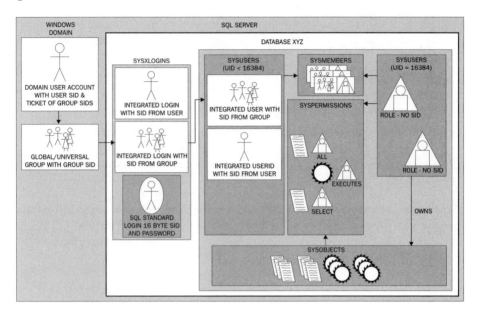

From the diagram, we have the following sequence:

1. Note first that the application uses integrated security.

2. Set up either a domain global group in Windows NT 4.0 domain SAM, or a global or universal group in a Windows 2000 Active Directory. Universal security groups are only available in Active Directory enterprises running in native mode. If you don't know what mode you are in, ask your domain managers.
   We prefer to prefix such groupnames with the letters SQL and then have a meaningful name without any spaces. It lets everyone know exactly what the group is for, and groups all our SQL groups in one area of the (management) GUI.

3. Add the relevant user accounts to the group that you created in step 2.

4. Run SP_GRANTLOGIN to give a SQL Server login to the group you created in step 2. We prefer to script everything out and save them; you never know when they'll come handy for disaster recovery or when you'll have to use them in another server. Plus, they serve as handy documentation. Keep the domain/groupname part for the login name. It keeps all the groups from a domain group together in the GUI.

5. Run SP_ADDUSER to give the login access to the relevant database. We usually strip off the domain names here and make the username just the groupname. Thus, almost all the usernames are SQL plus the "meaningful name without spaces".

6. Add a role to the database using SP_ADDROLE. The role name is the username minus the SQL prefix, that is, just the "meaningful name without spaces".

7. Add a role named APP to the databases if it didn't inherit such a role from your model database.

8. Create all your objects under the ownership of this newly defined role (that is, APP).

9. Grant the minimum permissions necessary for the proper operation of the application to the role created in step 6. To make the application secure, all the data access should be through stored procedures.

10. If, for some reason, you have super users who need to control permission on your APP role objects then give them membership in the APP role. This would be the *ONLY* exception when we would give non-DBO users membership in the APP role.

### Some Notes about this Sequence:

❏ This sequence will give you good indirection between users and roles. To quickly remove a role from an application, just remove the user IDs, representing groups, from the role membership. In this way, the assignments of the permissions to the role remain intact.

❏ When you move a database to another server, either by backing up and restoring or detaching, copying, and reattaching, the permissions will automatically get synchronized if logins are present for the relevant groups. If you install Service Pack 2 (Client Tools module) for SQL 2000, in SQL Enterprise Manager you can readily see orphaned User IDs from databases that don't have a corresponding login with the same SID.

❏ Contrary to Microsoft 'recommended method', we don't make use of local groups on the operating system of the SQL Server to indirect the domain global groups. If we do this, then when we move a database from a development to production instance or vice-versa, SID synchronization is a nightmare. Microsoft made this recommendation because it gives a valid one-to-many relationship solution between the local group and multiple domain global groups. We rarely operate SQL Server in multiple domain environments in NT 4.0.While this was valid in NT 4.0, with the introduction of universal groups in Windows 2000 Active Directory, this is a non-issue.

❏ This sequence applies only to non-system databases (not MASTER, MSDB, or TEMPDB).

# SQL Injection Attacks

SQL injection attack is the single biggest threat faced by SQL-based applications today, especially by those applications which are exposed to the Internet. SQL injection refers to the addition of malicious SQL code to legitimate SQL code, contained within an application. All SQL based DBMSs, and not just Microsoft SQL Server, are potentially susceptible to this attack, as they use SQL. It is a problem with the SQL language.

## The Problem

The attack happens when an application processes user input that forms part of a SQL command. If the application builds executable SQL strings by using unfiltered input, it may be subject to malicious input. A good application builder always operates by the dictum, "never trust user input". By using escape characters, the malicious user can append unintended SQL commands to your intended SQL code.

### Example 1

We'll use the pubs database to demonstrate the problem. Assume that we have an application that takes user input from a textbox called InputBox.Text. Now we need the code for generating the SQL executable code from user input. For this example, it could take one of two forms (the procedure AUTHORLOGIN is a nonexistent fictitious procedure that you could build) The VB code would look something like this:

```
"SELECT au_lname, au_fname FROM authors WHERE au_id = '" & _
InputBox.Text & "'"
```

or

```
"EXEC pubs.dbo.AuthorLogin '" & InputBox.Text & "'"
```

We'll go through the first example in detail; however, the second is an equally valid attack.

Let's set up the scenario. Imagine that you have a web application. The web application or COM+ proxy account under which SQL code is executed has broad rights in the pubs database. In the worst conditions, the proxy account has DBO or even sa rights in the SQL Server. Drill down in the object browser and open the jobs table in the pubs database.

In a default pubs instance, we will see that the table has 14 jobs. To confirm this, run the following SQL query:

```
SELECT * FROM jobs
```

Now, we will simulate a normal user of your web application by executing the following code in the Query Analyzer, on the pubs database:

```
-- Set quoted identifiers OFF so that double-quote work  like in VB or
-- VBScript code
SET QUOTED_IDENTIFIER OFF
DECLARE @InputText VARCHAR(100),
        @command VARCHAR(1000)

-- Imagine that the application is capturing the InputText.Text
-- variable
SELECT @InputText = "527-72-3246"
SELECT @InputText AS 'InputText.Text'

-- Now, imagine that app is VB or VBScript and piecing together a SQL
-- command. The final command is represented by @command
SELECT @command = "select au_fname, au_lname from authors
WHERE au_id = '" + @InputText + "'"

SELECT @command AS 'Executable SQL Command'
-- Imagine that we pass the command to SQL:
EXEC (@command)
```

If this query works, as intended, we will get Morningstar Greene as the output.

Now, we will simulate a malicious user's input into the @InputText variable. In the above example, instead of using 527-72-3246, change the line to:

```
SELECT @InputText = "' ; INSERT INTO jobs (job_desc, min_lvl, max_lvl)
   VALUES ('Important Job',25,100) -- "
```

Notice how we first terminated the current string in our @command statement with ' (the single quotation mark) character. This will close the first statement (in the remainder of @InputText exists) and allows us to start a new statement that we can execute. Our new SQL statement, which is malicious, follows the '. Finally, the -- (double dash) character string tells SQL to ignore the rest of the text, as a comment. In our case it causes the closing ' (single quotation mark) to be ignored, which would otherwise cause the final @command executable to generate a parsing error.

Substitution of the SQL injection code will make our sample code looks like (we'll leave out the previous comments for brevity):

```
SET QUOTED_IDENTIFIER OFF
DECLARE @InputText VARCHAR(100),
        @command VARCHAR(1000)

SELECT @InputText = "' ; INSERT INTO jobs (job_desc, min_lvl, max_lvl)
VALUES ('Important Job',25,100) -- "
SELECT @InputText AS 'InputText.Text'

SELECT @command = "select au_fname, au_lname
FROM authors
WHERE au_id = '" + @InputText + "'"

SELECT @command AS 'Executable SQL Command'
EXEC (@command)
```

After executing this code, right-click and open the jobs table in pubs. The malicious job, which we have added through injection attack, is Important Job.

**Example 2**

Let's look at one more malicious example. Before running this, first make a new table in pubs by running the following command:

```
CREATE TABLE ATEST (testcol INT)
```

Now, change InputText to select a name from sysobjects. The top portion of your code will look like:

```
SET QUOTED_IDENTIFIER OFF
DECLARE  @InputText VARCHAR(100),
         @command VARCHAR(1000)
SELECT @InputText = '' ;
SELECT TOP 1 NAME FROM SYSOBJECTS
WHERE TYPE = 'U' ORDER BY NAME -- "
```

For this example, consider that your web application returns a name. In our case, it is the atest table we just created. The hacker may need to pad the number of columns to produce an improper response, but it is well possible. Once hackers know something about your schema, they are bound to carry out some malicious activity:

```
SET QUOTED_IDENTIFIER OFF
DECLARE  @InputText VARCHAR(100),
         @command VARCHAR(1000)
SELECT @InputText ="';DROP TABLE ATEST -- "
```

In this case it's really nasty – they are dropping a table! Remember that, earlier we had mentioned that usually most of the objects in a database are owned by DBO. If you have your objects owned instead by a non-default role (for example, the APP role ), this injection fails to delete the table, as the object owner was not explicitly called.

What really makes this injection attack possible, though, is not that you relied upon the DBO as the implicit owner, but that the proxy account coming from the web application was all too powerful. Here we made use of DBO privileges. Imagine the consequences of mistakenly granting that proxy account sa privileges. All too often, poor coding techniques on the front end of an application which allow SQL injection are backed up by poor DBO security techniques.

Remember, SQL injection is not a SQL Server problem; it is a vulnerability inherent in front-end applications.

# The Solutions

Now we've seen the problems, let's tackle the solutions.

### Solution 1

For example, let's take VB.NET. In VB.NET, when you build a SQL Statement, instead of building a straight command, use the `Parameters` (syntactically `SqlParameter`) collection to define an `@au_id` parameter.

For a stored procedure running through VB.NET, explicitly define the command string type, as a `CommandType` to `StoredProcedure`. Then, again, use the `Parameters` collection to define the input parameters for the stored procedure.

When you use the `Parameters` collection in VB.NET, as in this case, no matter what malicious input the user provides, it is always treated as a literal string. Also, by using the `Parameters` collection, data type and length checks are more easily enforced.

What happens under the covers, when the `Parameters` collection is used? VB.NET roles together a fully defined `SP_EXECUTESQL` command. Imagine that our `InputText.Text` box was sent to a parameter called `@au_id`, which was `VARCHAR(100)`. This is how our SQL sample code would model the change:

```
SET QUOTED_IDENTIFIER OFF
DECLARE @InputText VARCHAR(100),
        @command VARCHAR(1000)

SELECT @InputText = "527-72-3246"
SELECT @InputText = "' ; INSERT INTO jobs
(job_desc, min_lvl, max_lvl)
VALUES ('Important Job',25,100) -- "

SELECT @InputText AS 'InputText.Text'
EXECUTE sp_executesql N'select au_fname,au_lname
FROM authors WHERE au_id = @au_id', N'@au_id VARCHAR(100)',
   @au_id = @InputText
```

In the above example, we can alternatively comment out the two `@InputText` variable assignments of the good input and the malicious input. No matter which one fires, you will not have a malicious result because in this syntactical structure `InputText.Text` is always treated as a literal.

### Solution 2

Another method of foiling SQL injection attacks is to filter the user input for SQL characters. Use the `REPLACE` function to replace any apostrophe (single quotation mark to SQL) with an additional apostrophe. Within a SQL string, two consecutive single quotation marks are treated as an instance of the apostrophe character within the string, rather than as the unexpected delimiters.

In our Query Analyzer test scenario, notice the line with the REPLACE function that we inserted:

```
SET QUOTED_IDENTIFIER OFF
DECLARE @InputText varchar(100),
        @command varchar(1000)
SELECT @InputText = "' ; INSERT INTO jobs (job_desc, min_lvl, max_lvl)
VALUES ('Important Job',25,100) --"

SELECT @InputText =
REPLACE(@InputText,"'","''")
SELECT @InputText AS 'InputText.Text'
SELECT @command = "select au_fname,au_lname from authors
WHERE au_id = '" + @InputText + "'"
SELECT @command AS 'Executable SQL Command'
EXEC (@command)
```

There are other escape characters that, in addition to the single quotation mark, needs to be routinely replaced in the front-end code. What should bother us now are the pattern matching characters (for example, single quote included for completeness) that would assume importance in a LIKE statement. The REPLACE function converts a character, as shown:

| Character | Replacement Code |
|---|---|
| '  becomes  " | REPLACE ( "'", "''" ) . |
| [ becomes [[ ] | REPLACE ( "[", "[[ ]") |
| %  becomes [%] | REPLACE ( "%", "[%]") |
| _  becomes [_] | REPLACE ( "_", "[_]") |

**A Better Solution**

We've have looked at two choices for avoiding SQL injection attacks. Of the two, using the Parameters collection is preferred. In the REPLACE function instance, a programmer will code a function that passes our notorious InputText.Text input string to be analyzed for all four of the above replacements. VB is notorious for poorly handling string functions in such a situation. As often as not, by the time you are through, you'll have three copies of the string sitting in memory somewhere on your application, one representing the original string, one in the memory space of the function, and one for the final invocation of the SQL code. For a busy web application, this can be burdensome on machine resources.

On the other hand, when your VB programmer uses the Parameters collection, only one instance of the string will reside in the memory space of the application. Additionally, as we pointed out earlier, using the Parameters collection for ad-hoc SQL statements in our call to SQL causes the use of the SP_EXECUTESQL system extended stored procedure. This procedure is designed to cache query plans where possible, giving improved performance.

There are two more best practices for preventing SQL injection attacks. Remember the injection sample that caused the dropping of our ATEST table? This was possible only because the proxy account of the web application, or COM+ middle layer, had permissions that were too broad. This brings up the next best practice:

> **Security Tip #10: Always run SQL code with a least possible privileged account.**

In fact, it is worth repeating here another one of our earlier security tips.

> **Security Tip #3: Allow only indirect access to table data through stored procedures and, in limited cases, select rights on views.**

If the proxy account is capable of only executing stored procedures, all of our previous SQL injection attempts will fail. Generally, a hacker will not have the sophistication to reverse-engineer your application and execute your stored procedures in a way that it harms you. Additionally, following Security Tip #7, whereby you remove default PUBLIC access to the metadata of your database, goes a long way toward thwarting reverse-engineering of your application. This illustrates the real power of using only stored procedures for data access and modification. It very clearly defines what a user can do in your application.

The *Building Secure ASP.NET Applications: Authentication, Authorization, and Secure Communications* white paper issued by Microsoft on front-end application security is a must read for all DBAs and .NET developers. It is available in the online MSDN library http://msdn.microsoft.com/library/default.asp.

# Encrypting Stored Procedures

Even after we've locked down an application, by tightly securing permissions and doing all data access and modifications through stored procedures, it's still advisable to disguise any business rules used in our stored procedures. The best way to do this is by encrypting our stored procedures.

We can encrypt our stored procedures by using the WITH ENCRYPTION clause, immediately before the AS clause of the procedure creation. Doing so will cause the procedure definition to be passed through the CRYPTO API on both read and write.

Why are we dwelling on stored procedure encryption here? It's because we've seen some interesting effort going into encrypted stored procedures. It is important for many DBAs to realize just who can and cannot see this stuff.

## The syscomments Table

While talking about stored procedure encryption, we need to know how Microsoft stores the descriptions for stored procedure objects. While the name of the stored procedure is stored in the SYSOBJECTS table, the actual definition of the stored procedure (as well as all functions, constraints, calculated columns, and views) are stored in the SYSCOMMENTS tables, and cross-referenced by their object ID. Let's take a look at the definition of this table, in SQL Server 2000:

```
CREATE TABLE [dbo].[syscomments]
  (
    [id] [INT] NOT NULL ,
    [number] [SMALLINT] NOT NULL ,
    [colid] [SMALLINT] NOT NULL ,
    [status] [SMALLINT] NOT NULL ,
    [ctext] [VARBINARY] (8000) NOT NULL ,
    [texttype] AS (CONVERT(SMALLINT, (2 + 4 * ([status] & 1)))) ,
    [language] AS (CONVERT(SMALLINT,0)) ,
    [encrypted] AS (CONVERT(BIT,([status] & 1))) ,
    [compressed] AS (CONVERT(BIT,([status] & 2))) ,
    [text] AS (CONVERT(NVARCHAR(4000),
    case IF ([status] & 2 = 2) THEN (uncompress([ctext])) ELSE
    [ctext] END))
  )
ON [PRIMARY]
```

The primary key for this table is the combination of the ID (representing the object ID) and number columns. Essentially, every stored procedure will have at least one record in this table with the number 1. If the stored procedure is longer than either 4000 or 8000 characters, it will have a second record with the number 2, and so on. Note that it could go up to 32,768 records or 250 megabytes. You may not want a stored procedure this large, since your server might have performance issues from the procedure cache being so large, but that's beyond the scope of this discussion.

The key storage area is the 8000 byte VARBINARY CTEXT column. You can see that the human-readable TEXT column is actually a calculated column, based on the CTEXT column. During the CREATE PROCESS function, Microsoft does a quick scan of the data that you want to store in CTEXT. If all the data is in the ASCII 256-character code set, Microsoft will flip the status column $2^1$ bit and stored the data as ASCII. Microsoft calls this as "compressed".

If it has characters outside the 256-character code set, Microsoft will leave the status column $2^1$ bit un-flipped and store the data with a UNICODE 2-byte-per-character representation. This means that when the data is compressed (that is in ASCII), there are up to 8000 characters per record in SYSCOMMENTS. When it is uncompressed (that is in UNICODE), there are only 4000 characters per record.

When Microsoft encrypts the stored procedure, each single character in the definition is represented by one of the 65536 Unicode 2-byte characters; obviously it is uncompressed in the CTEXT column. At the same time, Microsoft flips the encrypted bit in the status column, which is the $2^0$ bit. Although, we haven't been able to completely figure it out, we're convinced that there is an expanding symmetric key that takes an initial seed from a combination of the database name and the object ID and probably some other machine information.

In expanding symmetric key the first Unicode character is encrypted with the seed key. Then the second character's seed key depends upon the seed key and the value of the first character. This an improvement over SQL 7.0, which was easily vulnerable to a brute force attack. However, even in SQL Server 2000, the encryption can be easily broken under certain conditions.

## Breaking Object Encryption in SQL 2000

The condition for breaking the encryption is that you should be able to modify the description for the stored procedure definition. In other words, you have to use the ALTER PROCEDURE statement on the existing stored procedure and replace it with something totally different. However, in doing this, there is a risk that you might end up losing the original definition, thereby messing up the stored procedure and your application.

**! Never try to decrypt a stored procedure on a production implementation. Rather, copy the implementation to a development environment and try there.**

A demo of the process to XOR the encrypted definition with a known definition is readily available after a search on the Internet. The demos that I've seen don't break past the single SYSCOMMENTS record of 4000 characters. However, using the theory behind this demo, we've been able to write a decrypting stored procedure that will decrypt a 40,000-byte (10 SYSCOMMENTS records) stored procedure in about three seconds, on an average server.

As we discussed, when a user could alter an encrypted stored procedure in a database, they can break the encryption rather easily. However, the usage of ALTER PROCEDURE is generally limited to highly trusted users. Nevertheless, it is fairly common for even a limited user to be able to read the SYSOBJECTS and SYSCOMMENTS tables. This gives rise to a question – could a limited user copy the SYSOBJECTS and SYSCOMMENTS records for an encrypted stored procedure to another server, where they have DDL control and crack open your stored procedure encryption in their spare time?

Our testing tells us that this is not going to work. Somehow, the encryption is built into the implementation of the particular database. Obviously, if a limited-rights user can get a backup of the database and restore it to another server, then they could easily reverse your encryption. However, if a limited-rights user can get a copy of your backup tapes or files, you will probably have more serious problems than whether or not she can decrypt your stored procedures.

## A Strategy For Encrypting Your Data

One of the most important data that should generally be stored in an encrypted form is the information pertaining to credit cards. We can think of nothing more damaging or embarrassing for a company than having to go out and explain to its customers that it compromised their credit card information. Now let's look at a strategy for securing vital information, such as credit card information.

We will assume that our regular database is called as SalesOrder, which will hold the encrypted credit card number. Next to it is a very small database, called SalesOrderEncryption.

The SalesOrder and SalesOrderEncryption tables have the same database owner login ID as the master database. Remember, this is a production implementation and there shouldn't be much else on this server, such as the pubs or Northwind database. The SalesOrderEnryption database only has one or more stored procedures; no user tables. These stored procedures use the OLE Automation extended stored procedures to access encryption DLLs on the operating system.

Now, here's the trick. The seed value for the encryption algorithm is encrypted in the stored procedure in SalesOrderEncryption. This seed value is analogous to the PIN for an ATM card – it is not stored anywhere on the server.

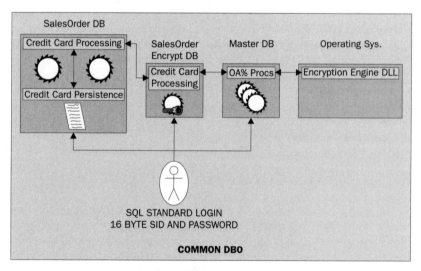

Only users who have a right to access or change the credit card numbers can access the SalesOrderEnryption database and execute the applicable stored procedures. This is very tightly controlled by cross-database EXECUTE permissions. Obviously, you have to trust your DBAs. We suppose you could lock the SalesOrderEncryption database a little more tightly away from your DBAs, but we haven't shown a business need for this. All of this stresses on that fact that your server is properly secured in every respect, especially physical security.

The backup solution, though, is particularly elegant. Since the `SalesOrderEnryption` is so small and unchanging, all we do is backup the database to disk, write the backup to two CDs, give one to the client/owner of the application for safekeeping, and one to a custodian in our company for offsite storage. After deleting this one-time backup, we never backup the `SalesOrder` and `SalesOrderEnryption` database to the same media. Thus, if the media is compromised, it's like your ATM card being stolen. They don't have the PIN, or in our case, the symmetric key encryption seed. In the event of a catastrophic failure of the server, we can rebuild the `SalesOrder` database from backup tapes and the `SalesOrderEnryption` from one of the CD-burned backup copies.

Taking the `SalesOrder` database to a development server is also elegant. We know that development environments are notably less secure than production environments. However, since the production `SalesOrderEnryption` database is not duplicated in the development environment with the same seed value, the production credit card numbers are still secure.

We also recommend that in your environment you also audit all object creation and deletions. Thus, if someone were to try and alter an encryption procedure in the `SalesOrderEncryption` database, this can be recorded and pursued with vengeance.

# SQL Buffer Overflow

Repeatedly, we come across instances where experts will ask us to drop one or the other system stored procedure or system extended stored procedure. This usually happens with an extended stored procedure and is in response to a buffer overflow. A buffer overflow allows a malicious user to execute "code of their choice" on the operating system. This "code of their choice" is usually a privilege elevation, where they give themselves administrator rights on the server.

Generally, the culprit function involved is a non-removable in-built function, such as the `PWDENCRYPT` function or a `DBCC` feature. Rather than trying to remove them, you should apply fixes. Microsoft is extremely quick to fix these types of buffer overflow problems when they appear.

In the *C2 Administrator's and User's Security Guide*, Microsoft does recommend removing stored procedure functionality. It is an excellent document to read. However, remember that when this document was prepared, certain elements of Microsoft functionality were not ready for prime time. Among other things, this includes the Windows 2000 Server operating system.

The *C2 Guide* recommends that two sets of stored procedures be removed. The first set is the Meta Data Services stored procedures found in the `msdb` database. They can be readily identified by the `r_i` prefix. The other set of stored procedures that you might consider removing are the Merge Replication Stored Procedures. These are any stored procedure with `merge` in the name, and the large percentage of the undocumented stored procedures that begin with `SP_MS`. There are ten pages of these stored procedures documented in the *C2 Guide*, so we will not repeat them here.

Remember that you only need to remove these procedures if you need to meet the C2 requirements.

# Installing a SSL Certificate for SQL Server

When SQL Server 2000 first shipped out, it didn't support SSL encryption. We need to have Service Pack 1 installed, to use it. The notes about its use are sparse at best, in SQL Server Books Online. Instead, Microsoft buried this functionality and the SetCert tool necessary for its setup in the SQL Server 2000 Resource Kit.

To set up SSL encryption, you will need to buy the SQL Server 2000 Resource Kit. Alternatively, it is available in a TechNet subscription (which often also has to be bought). Before you get a certificate, you need to know two things:

❑ Every client machine that is going to connect to the server must recognize the certificate authority (CA) that issues the certificate to the server. This is usually a default configuration for such mainline CAs as Verisign or Thawte. If you run your own CA, you will need to make sure that clients recognize it.

❑ The name field on the certificate needs to be the fully qualified DNS name of the SQL Server, for example, server.division.corp.company.com. If you change the server name later on, you'll need to get a new certificate issued.

Installing the certificate and setting up SSL encryption for a SSL server involves two steps:

1. Importing the certificate into the server certificate store

2. Using the SetCert utility to designate the imported certificate for use by SQL Server

## Importing the certificate:

To import the certificate, we need to perform the following steps:

1. Obtain a certificate from a CA. It is usually a single file. Place it in a secure location on the server.

2. Start Microsoft Management Console (MMC) by typing MMC.EXE at the command prompt.

3. Using the Console | Add-Remove Snap-in... choice, add the Certificate snap-in for the Local Computer.

4. Expand the options under Certificate (Local Computer). Right-click on Personal. Click the Import choice.

5. Follow the Import wizard to select the file that we saved in step 1 and import it into the server.

## Using the SetCert utility

To designate the imported certificate for use by SQL Server, follow these steps:

1. Ensure that Service Pack 1 for SQL 2000 is installed

2. Start the SetCert utility from the SQL Server 2000 Resource Kit

3. From the Instance Grid, select the instance of SQL Server you want to modify and click Set

4. From the Select Certificate dialog box, select the certificate you wish to designate for use by the SQL Server instance

5. Click OK and then click Close

This will enable SSL support for your SQL 2000 server.

# Summary

A database administrator should have an excellent knowledge of the permission paths required to attach an end user to the use of an object. Coding stored procedures in an application often takes a little more skill than throwing together a quick SQL statement to fire against a server. Such kind of application development can give rise to vulnerabilities like SQL injection attack. Make sure that your front-end developers are aware of the ins and outs of these attacks. They can be your best friends at securing data.

At the same time, you should always apply security patches expeditiously to your SQL Server environments. Exposure to the web and to e-mail attacks are only going to increase over time. Finally, stored procedure encryption does have both viable uses and weaknesses. If properly implemented, it can be a great help in securing your business rules.

SQL Server
2000

Stored Procedures

Handbook

Appendix A

# Support, Errata, and forums.apress.com

We always value hearing from our readers, and we want to know what you think about this book and series: what you liked, what you didn't like, and what you think we can do better next time. We are committed to supporting you not just while you read the book, but once you start developing applications as well, through our online forums, where you can put your questions to the authors, reviewers, and fellow industry professionals.

## Customer Support

You can send us your comments by e-mailing support@apress.com. Please be sure to mention the book's ISBN and title in your message.

## Errata

We've made every effort to ensure that there are no errors in the text or in the code. However, mistakes can occur. If you find an error in this book, like a spelling mistake or a faulty piece of code, we would be very grateful for feedback. By sending in errata, you may save another reader hours of frustration, and of course, you will be helping us to provide even higher quality information. Go to the book's web page and click the Submit errata link. Please be sure to include your name and email, and the chapter number, page number, and a brief description of the problem, as requested. Queries will be forwarded to the author and editor. You may receive a direct e-mail reply, and/or the erratum will be posted to the web site for all readers to benefit from.

# The Peer-to-Peer Forums at forums.apress.com

For author and peer discussion, join the Apress discussion groups. If you post a query to our forums, you can be confident that many Apress authors, editors, and industry experts are examining it. At **forums.apress.com** you will find a number of different lists that will help you, not only while you read this book, but also as you develop your own applications. To sign up for the Apress forums, go to **forums.apress.com** and select the **New User** link.

# SQL Server 2000

## Stored Procedures

# Handbook

# Index

# Index

## A Guide to the Index

The index is arranged hierarchically, in alphabetical order, with symbols preceding the letter A. Most second-level entries and many third-level entries also occur as first-level entries. This is to ensure that users will find the information they require however they choose to search for it.

## Symbols

**@@ERROR variable**
database logic error handling, 53
examples of using, 54
**@@FETCH_STATUS variable**
accessing cursors from code, 72
**@@NESTLEVEL function**
nested stored procedures, 27, 131
**@@ROWCOUNT variable**
triggers, 211
**@@TRANCOUNT variable**
nesting transactions, 84
**0x80000000 status bit**
creating system stored procedures, 140
care in using, 140
documentation, 141
example, 141
naming guidelines, 140
disabling and re-enabling users, 139
effects of setting, 138
get_sid function, 143
security issues, 139
system stored procedures, 137
toggling on and off, 168
**1433 port**
security problems, 221

## A

**ACID properties, transactions, 82**
atomicity, 82
consistency, 82
durability, 82
isolation, 82

**actions**
triggers and, 203
ordering trigger actions, 208
**administration and stored procedures, 120**
performance tuning, 120
**AFTER trigger, 198, 206**
cascading triggers, 210
compared to INSTEAD OF trigger, 209
complex AFTER trigger, 208
CREATE TRIGGER statement for, 203
description, 206
example of using, 207
ordering trigger actions, 208
replaces FOR trigger, 206
transactions, 207
**ALTER DATABASE command**
CURSOR_DEFAULT setting, 67
scope for cursor, 67
**ALTER PROCEDURE statement**
breaking encrypted stored procedures, 241
modifying stored procedures, 19
**alternate cursor syntax, 70**
variable based cursors, 70
**application logic**
error handling, 52
**atomicity**
ACID properties, 82
**Auto Rollback option**
SQL Server Debugger, 60
**AVG() function, 180**

# B

**batch operations**
Go keyword and, 48
Batch separator option, 49
stored procedures, 78
using cursors for batch operations, 78
**BEGIN DISTRIBUTED TRANSACTION command**
MSDTC, 87
**BEGIN TRANSACTION command**
simple transactions, 82
WITH MARK clause, 83
**BEGIN...END code blocks**
flow control of stored procedures, 21
**blocking**
locks, 94
**buffers**
SQL buffer overflow, 243
**bulk update locks, 95**
**bulk-logged model**
recovery model for database, 81

# C

**C2 security tracing**
auditing DBA, 221
resource costs, 221
**CA (Certificate Authority), 244**
installing SSL certificate, 244
**cached query plans**
performance gain of stored procedures, 11
**cascading triggers**
AFTER trigger, 210
execution sequence, 210
**CASE statements**
decisions, 23
flow control of stored procedures, 23
syntax, 23
**Certificate Authority**
see CA.
**CHECK constraints, 124**
compared to stored procedures, 17, 124
compared to triggers, 127, 212
data validation, 124
domain integrity, 212
**Client Network Utility**
changing client settings, 222
**CLOSE statement**
accessing cursors from code, 73
using as soon as possible, 80
**code, downloading samples, 247**
**COLUMNS_UPDATED test**
firing triggers on INSERT or UPDATE action, 205
POWER() function, 206
SUBSTRING() function, 206
**Command object**

see SqlCommand class.
**command terminator**
Go keyword as, 48
**CommandText property**
SqlCommand class, 117
**commenting stored procedures, 18**
**COMMIT TRANSACTION command**
simple transactions, 82
triggers, 211
**complex AFTER trigger, 208**
**complex result set**
building with RAND() function, 76
formatting result set using cursors, 76
**computed column**
creating index using deterministic function, 183
**conceptual tables**
triggers, 204
**concurrency, 65**
coding for integrity and concurrency, 99
optimistic locking, 101
pessimistic locking, 100
definition, 65
description, 91
guidelines for concurrency, 108
hardware issues, 92
OS (Operating System) issues, 92
SQL Server concurrency controls, 93
**Connection object**
see SqlConnection class.
**Connection property**
SqlCommand class, 117
**consistency**
ACID properties, 82
**constraints**
CHECK constraints, 212
data validation, 124
FOREIGN KEY constraints, 124
**cost**
execution plan, 44
importance of cost analysis, 47
operator cost, 45
query cost, 44
thick arrows as cost measure, 45
example, 46
**COUNT() function, 180**
**CREATE FUNCTION statement**
creating user defined functions, 181
**CREATE PROCEDURE statement**
creating stored procedures, 9
syntax, 9
WITH RECOMPILE clause, 20
**CREATE TRIGGER statement**
creating triggers, 202
AFTER trigger, 203
INSTEAD OF trigger, 203
NOT FOR REPLICATION option, 203
**CRYPTO API**
encrypted stored procedures, 239
**cursor source, 69**

**CURSOR_DEFAULT setting**
ALTER DATABASE command, 67
**cursors, 65**
accessing cursors from code, 70
@@FETCH_STATUS variable, 72
CLOSE statement, 73
DEALLOCATE statement, 73
FETCH statement, 70
OPEN statement, 70
compared to set-based operations, 66
compared to user defined functions, 66
definition, 65
description, 66
guidelines for using, 80
minimizing cursor data set, 80
minimizing use, 108
syntax, 67
alternate cursor syntax, 70
special cursor syntax, 67
temporary tables and, 74, 77, 78, 80
using cursors, 73
batch operations, 78
formatting result set, 73
**customer support, 248**

# D

**data encryption, 242**
strategy for data encryption, 242
stored procedures, 242
**data integrity**
checking data integrity, 15
DBCC statements, 15
recycled procedures, 15
system stored procedures, 15
domain integrity, 14, 212, 217
entity integrity, 14, 216
reasons for using triggers, 200
referential integrity, 15, 217
**data updatability for cursor, 69**
**data validation**
constraints, 124
security for stored procedures, 51
triggers, 126
user interface data validation, 125
using stored procedures, 122
**Database Administrator**
see DBA.
**Database Console Commands statements**
see DBCC statements.
**database locks, 93**
**database logic**
error handling, 52
@@ERROR variable, 53
example, 53
**database objects**
description, 225
permissions issues, 225
syscomments table, 225

sysobjects table, 225
**database owner**
see DBO.
**DATABASEPROPERTYEX() function**
scope for cursor, 68
**DATEADD() function**
non-deterministic functions, 185
**DATEPART() function**
non-deterministic functions, 185
**date-time column**
optimistic locking row based scheme, 102
**DBA**
administration and stored procedures, 120
performance tuning, 120
auditing using C2 security tracing, 221
must be trustworthy, 220
**DBCC statements**
checking data integrity, 15
SQL buffer overflow, 243
**DBO**
objects owned by DBO, 229
compared to alternative, 229
security problems, 229
user ID's, 225
**deadlocks, 95**
**DEALLOCATE statement**
accessing cursors from code, 73
using as soon as possible, 80
**debugging**
dynamic SQL in stored procedures, 50
SQL Server Debugger, 57
debugging stored procedure, 58
**decisions**
CASE statements, 23
flow control of stored procedures, 22
GOTO label, 25
IF...ELSE decision processing, 22
**deferred name resolution**
creating stored procedures, 10
**deferred updates**
compared to direct updates, 202
required for triggers, 202
**deleted table**
conceptual tables for triggers, 204
**DENY action**
object permissions, 226
**deployment and stored procedures, 120**
**deterministic functions, 182**
converting non-deterministic function to
deterministic, 183
creating index on computed column, 183
creating index on view, 183
description, 182
schema binding, 194
user defined functions, 182
**direct recursion triggers, 215**
example, 215
RECURSIVE_TRIGGERS option, 215

**direct updates**
  compared to deferred updates, 202
**direction for cursor, 68**
  FORWARD_ONLY, 68
  SCROLL, 68
**disabling and re-enabling users**
  0x80000000 status bit, 139
**Display Estimated Execution Plan option**
  graphical view of execution plan, 39
**distributed transactions, 87**
  BEGIN DISTRIBUTED TRANSACTION
    command, 87
  MSDTC, 87
  syntax, 87
**domain integrity, 14**
  CHECK constraints, 212
  triggers, 212, 217
**durability**
  ACID properties, 82
**DYNAMIC**
  type of cursor, 68
**dynamic SQL in stored procedures, 50**
  debugging issues, 50
  optimization issues, 50
  security issues, 50

# E

**e-mail support, 248**
**encapsulating logic in stored procedures, 112**
  advantages, 114
  example, 112
**encrypted stored procedures, 239**
  breaking encryption, 241
    ALTER PROCEDURE statement, 241
  CRYPTO API, 239
  storage of stored procedure, 240
  syscomments table, 240
  sysobjects table, 240
  WITH ENCRYPTION clause, 239
**Enterprise Manager**
  system stored procedures, 7
**entity integrity, 14**
  triggers, 216
**errata, feedback on, 248**
**error handling, 52**
  application logic, 52
    example, 52
  database logic, 52
    @@ERROR variable, 53
    example, 53
  RAISERROR statement, 55
    example of using, 56
  return parameters, 56
  returning values from stored procedures, 30
**example databases**
  restoring to default condition, 31
**exclusive locks, 94**

**ExecuteReader method**
  SqlCommand class, 117
**execution plan, 38**
  cost, 44
    importance of cost analysis, 47
    operator cost, 45
    query cost, 44
    thick arrows as cost measure, 45
  performance issues, 39
  stored procedure execution plan, 42
    multiple statement stored procedures, 43
  understanding execution plan, 44
  viewing execution plan, 39
    graphical view of execution plan, 39
    textual view of execution plan, 40
**explicit transactions, 88**
  compared to implicit transactions, 88
**extended stored procedures, 6**
  compared to stored procedures, 136
  sp_ prefix, 136
  system stored procedures, 136
  undocumented features, 152
    file system stored procedures, 161
    finding undocumented functionality, 152
    Windows registry system stored procedures, 152
  xp_ prefix, 136
**extent locks, 93**

# F

**FAST_FORWARD**
  reasons for preferring, 80
  type of cursor, 68
**FETCH statement**
  accessing cursors from code, 70
  FROM clause, 71
  INTO clause, 71, 72
  position options, 71
  syntax, 70
**field formatting**
  formatting result set using cursors, 73
**file system stored procedures, 161**
  XP_AvailableMedia system stored
    procedure, 161
  XP_DirTree system stored procedure, 162
  XP_FileExists system stored procedure, 163
  XP_FixedDrives system stored procedure, 163
  XP_ReadErrorLog system stored procedure, 164
  XP_SubDirs system stored procedure, 162
**fn_helpcollations function, 192**
**fn_listextendedproperty function, 192**
**fn_serversharedrives function, 192**
**fn_trace_geteventinfo function, 192**
**fn_trace_getfilterinfo function, 192**
**fn_trace_getinfo function, 192**
**fn_trace_gettable function, 192**
**fn_virtualfilestats function, 192**
**fn_virtualservernodes function, 192**

**FOR trigger, 206**
replaced by AFTER trigger, 206
**FOREIGN KEY constraints, 124**
**FORWARD_ONLY**
direction for cursor, 68
**FROM clause**
FETCH statement, 71
**full model**
recovery model for database, 81

# G

**generic stored procedures, 131**
problems with, 131
**get_sid function**
0x80000000 status bit, 143
sp_getsid stored procedure, 143
**GETDATE() function, 180**
non-deterministic functions, 184
**GLOBAL scope**
scope for cursor, 67
system stored procedures, 136
user defined functions, 195
**global tables, 144**
creating using sp_ prefix, 144
**global views, 144**
creating using sp_ prefix, 144
**Go keyword, 48**
as command terminator, 48
batch operations and, 48
Batch separator option, 49
not T-SQL command, 48
**Go option**
SQL Server Debugger, 60
**GOTO label**
decisions, 25
flow control of stored procedures, 25
**GRANT action**
object permissions, 226
**graphical view of execution plan, 39**
Display Estimated Execution Plan option, 39
Query Analyzer, 39
Show Execution Plan option, 39
**group accounts**
permissions issues, 223
**grouping stored procedures, 129**
example, 129
not good practice, 130
**guest user**
advantages of deleting, 225, 231

# H

**halting execution**
flow control of stored procedures, 26
SQL Server Agent, 26

**WAITFOR() function, 26**
**hardware issues**
concurrency, 92
**high performance stored procedures, 115**
see also optimizing stored procedures.
example, 118
SET NOCOUNT ON option, 119
**hives**
Windows registry, 153

# I

**IF UPDATE test**
firing triggers on INSERT or UPDATE action, 205
**IF...ELSE decision processing**
flow control of stored procedures, 22
**immediate update subscriber**
nested trigger option, 214
replication, 214
**implicit transactions, 88**
compared to explicit transactions, 88
**in-built functions, 180**
AVG() function, 180
COUNT() function, 180
GETDATE() function, 180
inspecting with Query Analyzer, 180
ISNULL() function, 180
scalar valued functions, 186
TABLE data type, 192
**index**
creating index using deterministic function, 183
**indirect recursion triggers, 215**
example, 215
**INSERT action**
firing triggers, 205
**inserted table**
conceptual tables for triggers, 204
**INSTEAD OF trigger, 198, 209**
assigning to views, 209
compared to AFTER trigger, 209
CREATE TRIGGER statement for, 203
description, 209
**INT data type**
using in stored procedures, 31
**intent locks, 94**
**INTO clause**
FETCH statement, 71, 72
**ISNULL() function, 180**
**isolation**
ACID properties, 82
**isolation levels**
READCOMMITTED, 98
READUNCOMMITTED, 98
REPEATABLEREAD, 98
SERIALIZABLE, 13, 98
SQL Server concurrency controls, 96
syntax, 98

# K

key locks, 93
key-range locks, 93
keys
  Windows registry, 153
KEYSET
  type of cursor, 68

# L

LOCAL scope
  reasons for preferring, 81
  scope for cursor, 67
locks
  blocking, 94
  deadlocks, 95
  hints for locks, 95
  optimistic locking, 101
  pessimistic locking, 100
  SQL Server concurrency controls, 93
  table of lock modes, 94
  table of lock types, 93
  transactions and, 108
logic
  encapsulating logic in stored procedures, 112
logical unit of work, optimistic locking, 101, 106
  description, 106
  example, 106
login ID's
  permissions issues, 224
  sysxlogins table, 224
loops
  flow control of stored procedures, 25
  WHILE loop, 25

# M

merge replication, 214
  triggers, 214
Merge Replication stored procedures
  removing stored procedures to prevent buffer overflow, 243
Meta Data Services stored procedures
  removing stored procedures to prevent buffer overflow, 243
Microsoft Distributed Transaction Co-ordinator service
  see MSDTC.
Microsoft Visual SourceSafe
  see Visual SourceSafe.
mining system stored procedures, 150
MSDTC
  BEGIN DISTRIBUTED TRANSACTION command, 87

distributed transactions, 87
multiple statement stored procedures
  execution plan, 43
    Query Analyzer, 43
multi-statement table function
  description, 190
  example, 191
  syntax, 190
  TABLE data type, 188
  table variables, 190

# N

naming stored procedures, 17
  avoiding sp_ prefix, 17
  renaming using sp_rename, 19
nested stored procedures, 27, 131
  @@NESTLEVEL function, 27, 131
  problems with, 28, 131
  recursion, 27
nested trigger option
  immediate update subscriber, 214
  queued update subscriber, 214
nesting transactions
  @@TRANCOUNT variable, 84
  simple transactions, 84
networking
  stored procedures, 11
NOLOCK hint, 95
non-deterministic functions, 182
  converting non-deterministic function to deterministic, 183
  DATEADD() function, 185
  DATEPART() function, 185
  description, 182
  GETDATE() function, 184
  user defined functions, 182
Northwind example database
  restoring to default condition, 31
NOT FOR REPLICATION option
  creating triggers, 203
NVARCHAR parameter
  XP_Test_Mapi_Profile system stored procedure, 172

# O

Object Browser
  debugging stored procedures, 58
  inspecting in-built functions, 181
object ownership
  DBO owning objects, 229
    compared to alternative, 229
    security problems, 229
  parts of named object, 228
  permissions issues, 228
  sp_changeobjectowner system stored procedure, 228

**object permissions**
DENY action, 226
GRANT action, 226
permissions issues, 226
REVOKE action, 226
syntax, 226
**OBJECTPROPERTY**
checking if function is deterministic or not, 182
**objects**
tracing object creation and deletion, 168
**Open method**
SqlConnection class, 117
**OPEN statement**
accessing cursors from code, 70
**operator cost**
execution plan, 45
**OPTIMISTIC**
updatability of cursor, 69
**optimistic locking**
coding for integrity and concurrency, 101
logical unit of work, 101, 106
reasons for preferring, 108
row based scheme, 101, 102
checking all fields, 102
date-time column, 102
timestamp column, 102
unchecked scheme, 101
**optimizing stored procedures, 35**
see also high performance stored
procedures.
dynamic SQL in stored procedures, 50
execution plan, 38
cost, 44
stored procedure execution plan, 42
understanding execution plan, 44
SET NOCOUNT ON option, 35
example of using, 37
WITH RECOMPILE clause, 37
reasons for using, 38
**OS (Operating System) issues**
concurrency, 92
**Outlook**
SQL Mail and, 170
**OUTPUT method**
returning values from stored procedures, 29
**OUTPUT parameter**
XP_FileExists system stored procedure, 163
**overflows**
SQL buffer overflow, 243

**P**

**page locks, 93**
**PAGLOCK hint, 95**
**parameters**

return parameters in error handling, 56
stored procedures, 18, 20, 131
avoiding too many parameters, 132
matching input and ouput parameters, 31
**Parameters collection**
compared to REPLACE() function, 238
sp_executesql system stored procedure,
237, 238
SQL injection attack solutions, 237
**password column**
sysxlogins table, 224
**passwords**
attacking with PWDCOMPARE() function, 224
comparing with PWDCOMPARE() function, 224
generating random password, 223
sa password, 223
**pausing execution**
flow control of stored procedures, 26
SQL Server Agent, 26
WAITFOR() function, 26
**performance tuning**
administration and stored procedures, 120
**permissions issues**
database objects, 225
group accounts, 223
guidelines for setting permissions, 231
login ID's, 224
object ownership, 228
object permissions, 226
roles, 227
SQL injection attacks, 239
SQL Server Debugger, 58
SQL Server security vulnerabilities, 223
statement permissions, 226
user accounts, 223
user ID's, 225
**pessimistic locking**
coding for integrity and concurrency, 100
**phantom rows, 97**
**port 1433**
security problems, 221
**POWER() function**
COLUMNS_UPDATED test, 206
**procedure execution article**
serializable procedure execution article, 13
stored procedures and replication, 13
**PUBLIC role, 227**
advantages of removing, 228
SQL injection attacks, 239
**pubs example database**
restoring to default condition, 31
**PWDCOMPARE() function**
attacking passwords, 224
comparing passwords, 224
**PWDENCRYPT() function**
SQL buffer overflow, 243

# Q

**queries**
  guidelines for using, 108
**Query Analyzer**
  execution plan
    graphical view of execution plan, 39
    multiple statement stored procedures, 43
    stored procedure execution plan, 42
    textual view of execution plan, 41
  inspecting in-built functions, 180
  Object Browser, 181
  restoring example databases to default
    condition, 31
  SQL injection attack example, 234
  SQL Server Debugger, 57
  system stored procedures, 6
**query cost**
  execution plan, 44
**queued update subscriber**
  nested trigger option, 214
  replication, 214

# R

**RAISERROR statement**
  compared to return parameters, 56
  error handling, 55
  example of using, 56
  syntax, 55
  triggers, 211
**RAND() function**
  building complex result set, 76
**READ_ONLY**
  updatability of cursor, 68
**READCOMMITTED**
  isolation levels, 98
**READUNCOMMITTED**
  isolation levels, 98
**recompiling stored procedures, 19**
  sp_recompile system stored procedure, 20
  WITH RECOMPILE clause, 20
    optimizing stored procedures, 37
**recovery model for database**
  bulk-logged model, 81
  full model, 81
  simple model, 81
  transactions, 81
**recursion**
  nested stored procedures, 27
    @@NESTLEVEL function, 27
    problems with, 28
  triggers, 215
    direct recursion triggers, 215
    indirect recursion triggers, 215
  XP_SendMail system stored procedure, 170
**RECURSIVE_TRIGGERS option**

    direct recursion triggers, 215
**recycled procedures**
  checking data integrity, 15
**referential integrity, 15**
  triggers, 217
**REGEDIT.EXE program**
  Windows registry, 153
**REGEDT32.EXE program**
  Windows registry, 153
**registry**
  see Windows registry.
**Remove All Breakpoints option**
  SQL Server Debugger, 60
**repeatable reads, 97**
**REPEATABLEREAD**
  isolation levels, 98
**REPLACE() function**
  compared to Parameters collection, 238
  SQL injection attack solutions, 237
**replication**
  immediate update subscriber, 214
  merge replication, 214
  queued update subscriber, 214
  snapshot replication, 214
  stored procedures, 12
    procedure execution article, 13
  transactional replication, 214
  triggers, 213
  WITH ENCRYPTION triggers, problems with, 215
**Restart option**
  SQL Server Debugger, 60
**result set**
  formatting result set using cursors, 73
    complex result set, 76
    field formatting, 73
**RETURN method**
  returning values from stored procedures, 28
**return parameters**
  compared to RAISERROR statement, 56
  error handling, 56
**RETURNS statement**
  creating user defined functions, 181
**REVOKE action**
  object permissions, 226
**roles**
  compared to user ID's, 227
  permissions issues, 227
  PUBLIC role, 227
  sp_addrolemember system stored
    procedure, 227
  sp_helprole system stored procedure, 227
  sysmembers table, 227
  sysusers table, 227
**ROLLBACK TRANSACTION command**
  savepoints, 90
  simple transactions, 82
  triggers, 211
    description of ROLLBACK, 212

**row based scheme, optimistic locking, 101, 102**
checking all fields, 102
date-time column, 102
example, 102
timestamp column, 102
**row locks, 93**
**ROWLOCK hint, 95**
**Run to Cursor option**
SQL Server Debugger, 60

# S

**sa password, 223**
auditing use, 223
generating random password, 223
**savepoints**
ROLLBACK TRANSACTION command, 90
transactions, 86
stored procedures, 90
**scalar valued functions, 186**
description, 186
in-built functions, 186
user defined functions, 186
constraints, 187
**scan for startup procs config option**
sp_configure system stored procedure, 16
**schema binding**
deterministic functions, 194
requirements, 193
user defined functions, 193
WITH SCHEMABINDING statement, 193
**schema locks, 94**
**scope for cursor, 67**
ALTER DATABASE command, 67
DATABASEPROPERTYEX() function, 68
GLOBAL scope, 67
LOCAL scope, 67
**SCROLL**
direction for cursor, 68
**SCROLL_LOCKS**
updatability of cursor, 69
**security, 219**
0x80000000 status bit security issues, 139
data encryption, 242
need for security, 219
SQL Server vulnerabilities, 220
mis-configuration, 220
SQL buffer overflow, 243
SQL injection attacks, 234
SSL, 244
stored procedures, 51, 219
data validation, 51
dynamic SQL in stored procedures, 50
encrypted stored procedures, 239
improving database security, 121
**SERIALIZABLE**
isolation levels, 13, 98
**serializable procedure execution article**
stored procedures and replication, 13

**Server Network Utility**
changing server settings, 222
**SET NOCOUNT ON option**
example of using, 37
high performance stored procedures, 119
optimizing stored procedures, 35
**SET SHOWPLAN_TEXT command**
textual view of execution plan, 40
**set-based operations**
compared to cursors, 66
**SetCert tool, 244**
using SSL encryption, 245
**setup problems**
permissions issues, 223
security holes, 221
SQL Server security vulnerabilities, 220
**shared locks, 94**
**Show Execution Plan option**
graphical view of execution plan, 39
**simple model**
recovery model for database, 81
**simple transactions, 82**
BEGIN TRANSACTION command, 82
COMMIT TRANSACTION command, 82
distributed transactions, 87
nesting transactions, 84
ROLLBACK TRANSACTION command, 82
syntax, 82
**single row of data**
returning values from stored procedures, 30
**single statement table function**
example, 188
TABLE data type, 188
**snapshot replication, 214**
**source control systems**
stored procedures, 18
Visual SourceSafe, 18
**sp_ prefix**
avoiding in naming stored procedures, 17
creating global tables and views, 144
extended stored procedures, 136
system stored procedures, 7, 136
**sp_addlogin system stored procedure, 147**
**sp_addrole system stored procedure, 148, 233**
**sp_addrolemember system stored procedure, 148, 227**
**sp_adduser system stored procedure, 148, 233**
**sp_attach_db system stored procedure, 146**
**sp_change_users_login system stored procedure, 146**
**sp_changedbowner system stored procedure, 146**
**sp_changeobjectowner system stored procedure, 228**
**sp_configure system stored procedure, 145, 195**
scan for startup procs config option, 16
**sp_cycle_errorlog system stored procedure, 148**
exanple of using, 166

sp_dboption system stored procedure, 145
sp_depends system stored procedure, 193
  renaming stored procedures, 19
sp_detach_db system stored procedure, 146
sp_executesql system stored procedure, 149
  Parameters collection, 237, 238
sp_getsid stored procedure
  get_sid function, 143
sp_grantdbaccess system stored procedure, 148
sp_grantlogin system stored procedure,
  147, 232
sp_help system stored procedure, 147
sp_helpdb system stored procedure, 147
sp_helprole system stored procedure, 227
sp_helpserver system stored procedure, 147
sp_helptext system stored procedure, 147
sp_instance_regread system stored
  procedure
  using, 166
sp_lock system stored procedure, 145
sp_password system stored procedure, 145
sp_procoption system stored procedure, 147
  running stored procedure on start up, 16,
    127, 128
  using, 166
sp_recompile system stored procedure
  recompiling stored procedures, 20
sp_rename system stored procedure, 146
  renaming stored procedures, 19
sp_spaceused system stored procedure, 146
sp_start_job system stored procedure, 150
sp_stop_job system stored procedure, 150
sp_trace extended stored procedures
  tracing object creation and deletion, 169
sp_trace_setevent extended stored procedure
  executing code at start up, 128
sp_trace_setstatus extended stored
  procedure
  executing code at start up, 128
sp_validatelogins system stored procedure, 150
sp_who2 system stored procedure, 145
sp_xml_preparedocument system stored
  procedure, 148
sp_xml_removedocument system stored
  procedure, 148
special cursor syntax, 67
  cursor source, 69
  data updatability for cursor, 69
  direction for cursor, 68
  scope for cursor, 67
  type of cursor, 68
  updatability of cursor, 68
  warnings for cursor, 69
SQL buffer overflow
  DBCC statements, 243
  PWDENCRYPT() function, 243
  removing stored procedures to prevent
    buffer overflow, 243

  Merge Replication stored procedures, 243
  Meta Data Services stored procedures, 243
  SQL Server security vulnerabilities, 243
SQL injection attacks
  deleting database table, 236
  examples, 234
  permissions issues, 239
  problems with, 234
  PUBLIC role, 239
  solutions, 237
    Parameters collection, 237
    REPLACE() function, 237
  SQL Server security vulnerabilities, 234
SQL Mail
  guidelines for using, 170
  Outlook and, 170
  system stored procedures, 169
  XP_SendMail system stored procedure, 169
    bullet-proofing XP_SendMail, 172
    recursion, 170
  XP_SMTP_SendMail stored procedure, 172
SQL Server Agent
  flow control of stored procedures, 26
SQL Server concurrency controls, 93
  isolation levels, 96
  locks, 93
SQL Server Debugger, 57
  debug options, 60
    Auto Rollback option, 60
    Go option, 60
    Remove All Breakpoints option, 60
    Restart option, 60
    Run to Cursor option, 60
    Step Into option, 60
    Step Out option, 60
    Step Over option, 60
    Stop Debugging option, 60
    Toggle Breakpoint option, 60
  debugging stored procedure, 58
  permissions issues, 58
  Query Analyzer, 57
SQL Server security vulnerabilities, 220
  mis-configuration, 220
    permissions issues, 223
    setup problems, 220
  SQL buffer overflow, 243
SqlCommand class
  CommandText property, 117
  Connection property, 117
  ExecuteReader method, 117
SqlConnection class
  Open method, 117
SSL, 244
  CA, 244
  installing SSL certificate, 244
  SetCert tool, 244
  using SSL encryption, 245
statement permissions
  permissions issues, 226
STATIC
  type of cursor, 68

**status column**
  0x80000000 status bit, 137
  system stored procedures, 136
**Step Into option**
  SQL Server Debugger, 60
**Step Out option**
  SQL Server Debugger, 60
**Step Over option**
  SQL Server Debugger, 60
**Stop Debugging option**
  SQL Server Debugger, 60
**stored procedures, 5**
  see also system stored procedures.
  advantages, 6
  bad practice, 129
  batch operations, 78
  calling stored procedures, 17
    performance issues, 17
  commenting stored procedures, 18
  compared to CHECK constraints, 17, 124
  compared to extended stored procedures, 136
  compared to triggers, 126, 213
  compared to T-SQL code
    data validation, 122
    database security, 122
    performance, 115, 118
  compared to user interface data validation, 125
  compared to user defined functions, 179, 194
  creating stored procedures, 9
    CREATE PROCEDURE statement, 9
    deferred name resolution, 10
    storing stored procedure, 10
  debugging, 57
    SQL Server Debugger, 57, 58
  definition, 6
  design principles, 13
  dynamic SQL in stored procedures, 50
  error handling, 52
  extended stored procedures, 6
  flow control, 21
    BEGIN...END code blocks, 21
    decisions, 22
    loops, 25
    pausing and halting execution, 26
  generic stored procedures, 131
  grouping stored procedures, 129
  introduction, 5
  modifying stored procedures, 19
    ALTER PROCEDURE statement, 19
  multiple statement stored procedures, 43
  naming stored procedures, 17
  nested stored procedures, 27, 131
  networking, 11
  optimizing stored procedures, 35
    execution plan, 38
  parameters, 18, 20, 131
    avoiding too many parameters, 132
    matching input and ouput parameters, 31
  performance gain, 11
    cached query plans, 11
  reasons for using, 11, 111

  data validation, 122
  encapsulating logic in stored procedures, 112
  executing code at start up, 127
  improving database security, 121
  improving performance, 115
  simplifying administration, 120
  simplifying deployment, 120
  recompiling stored procedures, 19
  recycled procedures, 15
  removing stored procedures to prevent
    buffer overflow, 243
  replication, 12
    procedure execution article, 13
  returning values, 28
    error handling, 30
    OUTPUT method, 29
    RETURN method, 28
    single row of data, 30
  running on start up, 16, 127
  security, 51, 219
    data validation, 51
    encrypted stored procedures, 239
    improving database security, 121
  source control systems, 18
  strategy for data encryption, 242
  system stored procedures, 6, 135
  transactions, 88
    savepoints, 90
  triggers, 9, 198
  user defined functions, 9
  user stored procedures, 8
**SUBSTRING() function**
  COLUMNS_UPDATED test, 206
**syscomments table**
  database objects, 225
  encrypted stored procedures, 240
    storage of stored procedure, 240
  storing stored procedure, 10
**sysdepends table**
  storing stored procedure, 10
**sysmembers table**
  roles, 227
  user ID's, 227
**sysobjects table**
  database objects, 225
  encrypted stored procedures, 240
  storing stored procedure, 10
**system stored procedures, 6, 135**
  categories of system stored procedures, 149
  checking data integrity, 15
    DBCC statements, 15
  complex tasks, performing, 166
  creating system stored procedures, 7, 140
    0x80000000 status bit, 140
    care in using, 140
    documentation, 141
    example, 141
    naming guidelines, 140
  definition, 136
  effects of setting 0x80000000 status bit, 138
  Enterprise Manager, 7

**system stored procedures (continued)**
  extended stored procedures, 136
    undocumented features, 152
  GLOBAL scope, 136
  introduction, 6, 135
  limited documentation, 135
  list of important documented system
    stored procedures, 145
  mining system stored procedures, 150
  Query Analyzer, 6
  sp_ prefix, 7, 136
  SQL Mail, 169
  status column, 136
    0x80000000 status bit, 137
  tracing object creation and deletion, 168
  undocumented features, 137, 142, 151
    extended stored procedures, 152
    file system stored procedures, 161
    get_sid function, 143
    Windows registry system stored procedures, 152
    xp_ prefix, 136
**sysusers table**
  roles, 227
  user ID's, 227
**sysxlogins table**
  login ID's, 224
  password column, 224

# T

**TABLE data type, 188**
  avoiding returning from stored procedure, 30
  definition, 188
  in-built functions, 192
  multi-statement table function, 188, 190
    example, 191
    table variables, 190
  single statement table function, 188
    example, 188
  user defined functions, 188
**table locks, 93**
**table variables**
  multi-statement table function, 190
**tables**
  assigning triggers, 198
  conceptual tables for triggers, 204
  deleting table by SQL injection attack, 236
**TABLOCK hint, 95**
**TABLOCKX hint, 95**
**temporary tables**
  cursors and, 74, 77, 78, 80
**textual view of execution plan, 40**
  Query Analyzer, 41
  SET SHOWPLAN_TEXT command, 40
**thick arrows as cost measure**
  example, 46
  execution plan, 45
**timestamp column**
  optimistic locking row based scheme, 102

reasons for preferring, 108
**TINYINT parameter**
  XP_AvailableMedia system stored procedure, 161
**Toggle Breakpoint option**
  SQL Server Debugger, 60
**tracing object creation and deletion**
  sp_trace extended stored procedures, 169
  system stored procedures, 168
  XP_Trace system stored procedures, 169
**transactional replication, 214**
  triggers, 214
**transactions, 65**
  ACID properties, 82
  definition, 65
  description, 81
  explicit transactions, 88
  guidelines for using, 90
  implicit transactions, 88
  locks and, 108
  recovery model for database, 81
  stored procedures, 88
    savepoints, 90
  syntax, 82
    distributed transactions, 87
    savepoints, 86
    simple transactions, 82
  triggers, 90
    AFTER trigger, 207
**triggers, 9, 197**
  @@ROWCOUNT variable, 211
  actions and, 203
    ordering trigger actions, 208
  AFTER trigger, 198, 206
    complex AFTER trigger, 208
  assigning to tables, 198
  assigning to views, 198
  bad practice, 216
  cascading triggers, 210
  COMMIT TRANSACTION command, 211
  compared to CHECK constraints, 127, 212
  compared to stored procedures, 126, 213
  conceptual tables, 204
  creating triggers, 202
    CREATE TRIGGER statement, 202
    NOT FOR REPLICATION option, 203
  data validation, 126
  definition, 198
  disabling trigger, 198
  domain integrity, 212, 217
  dropping trigger, 198
  entity integrity, 216
  firing on INSERT or UPDATE action, 205
    COLUMNS_UPDATED test, 205
    IF UPDATE test, 205
  FOR trigger, 206
  good practice, 216
  INSTEAD OF trigger, 198, 209
  nested trigger option, 214
  performance issues, 198, 201
  RAISERROR statement, 211

**triggers (continued)**
  reasons for using, 200
    data integrity, 200
  recursion, 215
    direct recursion triggers, 215
    indirect recursion triggers, 215
  referential integrity, 217
  replication, 213
    merge replication, 214
    transactional replication, 214
  require deferred updates, 202
  ROLLBACK TRANSACTION command, 211
    description of ROLLBACK, 212
  transactions, 90
  WITH ENCRYPTION triggers, 215
**T-SQL code**
  compared to stored procedures
    data validation, 122
    database security, 122
    performance, 115, 118
**type of cursor, 68**
  DYNAMIC, 68
  FAST_FORWARD, 68
  KEYSET, 68
  STATIC, 68
**TYPE_WARNING**
  warnings for cursor, 69

**U**

**UDFs**
  see user defined functions.
**unchecked scheme, optimistic locking, 101**
**updatability of cursor, 68**
  data updatability for cursor, 69
  OPTIMISTIC, 69
  READ_ONLY, 68
  SCROLL_LOCKS, 69
**UPDATE action**
  firing triggers, 205
**update locks, 94**
**user accounts**
  permissions issues, 223
**user defined functions, 9**
  compared to cursors, 66
  compared to stored procedures, 179, 194
  converting non-deterministic function to
    deterministic, 183
  creating, 181
    CREATE FUNCTION statement, 181
    example, 183
    RETURNS statement, 181
  description, 179
  deterministic functions, 182
  GLOBAL scope, 195
  history in SQL Server, 180
  non-deterministic functions, 182
  scalar valued functions, 186
    constraints, 187

  schema binding, 193
    WITH SCHEMABINDING statement, 193
  TABLE data type, 188
    multi-statement table function, 188, 190
    single statement table function, 188
**user ID's**
  compared to roles, 227
  DBO, 225
  permissions issues, 225
  sysmembers table, 227
  sysusers table, 227
**user interface data validation, 125**
  compared to stored procedures, 125
  security risks, 125
**user stored procedures, 8**

**V**

**validation**
  see data validation.
**values**
  returning from stored procedures, 28
    error handling, 30
    OUTPUT method, 29
    RETURN method, 28
    single row of data, 30
  Windows registry, 153
**VARCHAR data type**
  using in stored procedures, 31
**variable based cursors, 70**
**view**
  assigning triggers, 198
    INSTEAD OF trigger, 209
  creating index using deterministic function, 183
**Visual SourceSafe**
  stored procedures, 18

**W**

**WAITFOR() function**
  care in using, 26
  flow control of stored procedures, 26
**warnings for cursor, 69**
  TYPE_WARNING, 69
**WHILE loop**
  flow control of stored procedures, 25
  syntax, 25
**Windows registry, 152**
  care in modifying, 152
  description, 153
  hives, 153
  introduction, 152
  keys, 153
  REGEDIT.EXE program, 153
  REGEDT32.EXE program, 153
  values, 153

**Windows registry system stored procedures, 152**
XP_Instance_Reg extended stored procedures, 160
XP_RegAddMultiString system stored procedure, 158
XP_RegDeleteKey system stored procedure, 157
XP_RegDeleteValue system stored procedure, 158
XP_RegEnumKeys system stored procedure, 156
XP_RegEnumValues system stored procedure, 157
XP_RegRead system stored procedure, 153
XP_RegWrite system stored procedure, 155
**WITH ENCRYPTION clause**
encrypted stored procedures, 239
**WITH ENCRYPTION triggers**
problems with replication, 215
triggers, 215
**WITH MARK clause**
BEGIN TRANSACTION command, 83
**WITH RECOMPILE clause**
CREATE PROCEDURE statement, 20
optimizing stored procedures, 37
reasons for using, 38
recompiling stored procedures, 20
specifying as part of execution, 38
syntax, 37
**WITH SCHEMABINDING statement**
user defined functions, 193
**wrapper script**
XP_SMTP_SendMail stored procedure, 173

# X

**xp_ prefix**
extended stored procedures, 136
system stored procedures, 136
**XP_AvailableMedia system stored procedure**
code for using, 161
file system stored procedures, 161
TINYINT parameter, 161
**XP_CmdShell system stored procedure, 148**
**XP_DirTree system stored procedure**
code for using, 162
file system stored procedures, 162
**XP_FileExists system stored procedure**
code for using, 163
file system stored procedures, 163
OUTPUT parameter, 163
**XP_FixedDrives system stored procedure**
code for using, 163
file system stored procedures, 163
**XP_Instance_Reg extended stored procedures**
Windows registry system stored procedures, 160

**XP_LoginInfo system stored procedure, 149**
**XP_MSVer system stored procedure, 147**
**XP_ReadErrorLog system stored procedure**
code for using, 165
file system stored procedures, 164
parameters, 164
syntax, 164
**XP_RegAddMultiString system stored procedure**
code for using, 159
guidelines for using, 159
limited usage, 159
Windows registry system stored procedures, 158
**XP_RegDeleteKey system stored procedure**
care in using, 157
code for using, 157
Windows registry system stored procedures, 157
**XP_RegDeleteValue system stored procedure**
code for using, 158
guidelines for using, 158
Windows registry system stored procedures, 158
**XP_RegEnumKeys system stored procedure**
code for using, 156
Windows registry system stored procedures, 156
**XP_RegEnumValues system stored procedure**
code for using, 157
guidelines for using, 157
Windows registry system stored procedures, 157
**XP_RegRead system stored procedure**
code for using, 154
guidelines for using, 155
Windows registry system stored procedures, 153
**XP_RegRemoveMultiString system stored procedure**
code for using, 159
guidelines for using, 159
Windows registry system stored procedures, 159
**XP_RegWrite system stored procedure**
code for using, 155
guidelines for using, 156
Windows registry system stored procedures, 155
**XP_SendMail system stored procedure, 148**
bullet-proofing XP_SendMail, 172
XP_Test_Mapi_Profile system stored procedure, 172
compared to XP_SMTP_SendMail stored procedure, 173
recursion, 170
SQL Mail, 169
**XP_SMTP_SendMail stored procedure**
compared to XP_SendMail system stored procedure, 173
implementing, 172

**XP_SMTP_SendMail stored procedure (continued)**
    SQL Mail, 172
    wrapper script, 173
**XP_SubDirs system stored procedure**
    code for using, 162
    file system stored procedures, 162

**XP_Test_Mapi_Profile system stored procedure**
    bullet-proofing XP_SendMail, 172
    NVARCHAR parameter, 172
**XP_Trace system stored procedures, 150**
    tracing object creation and deletion, 169

# forums.apress.com

JOIN THE APRESS FORUMS AND BE PART OF OUR COMMUNITY. You'll find discussions that cover topics of interest to IT professionals, programmers, and enthusiasts just like you. If you post a query to one of our forums, you can expect that some of the best minds in the business—especially Apress authors, who all write with *The Expert's Voice™*—will chime in to help you. Why not aim to become one of our most valuable participants (MVPs) and win cool stuff? Here's a sampling of what you'll find:

## DATABASES
**Data drives everything.**

Share information, exchange ideas, and discuss any database programming or administration issues.

## INTERNET TECHNOLOGIES AND NETWORKING
**Try living without plumbing (and eventually IPv6).**

Talk about networking topics including protocols, design, administration, wireless, wired, storage, backup, certifications, trends, and new technologies.

## JAVA
**We've come a long way from the old Oak tree.**

Hang out and discuss Java in whatever flavor you choose: J2SE, J2EE, J2ME, Jakarta, and so on.

## MAC OS X
**All about the Zen of OS X.**

OS X is both the present and the future for Mac apps. Make suggestions, offer up ideas, or boast about your new hardware.

## OPEN SOURCE
**Source code is good; understanding (open) source is better.**

Discuss open source technologies and related topics such as PHP, MySQL, Linux, Perl, Apache, Python, and more.

## PROGRAMMING/BUSINESS
**Unfortunately, it is.**

Talk about the Apress line of books that cover software methodology, best practices, and how programmers interact with the "suits."

## WEB DEVELOPMENT/DESIGN
**Ugly doesn't cut it anymore, and CGI is absurd.**

Help is in sight for your site. Find design solutions for your projects and get ideas for building an interactive Web site.

## SECURITY
**Lots of bad guys out there—the good guys need help.**

Discuss computer and network security issues here. Just don't let anyone else know the answers!

## TECHNOLOGY IN ACTION
**Cool things. Fun things.**

It's after hours. It's time to play. Whether you're into LEGO® MINDSTORMS™ or turning an old PC into a DVR, this is where technology turns into fun.

## WINDOWS
**No defenestration here.**

Ask questions about all aspects of Windows programming, get help on Microsoft technologies covered in Apress books, or provide feedback on any Apress Windows book.

**HOW TO PARTICIPATE:**

Go to the Apress Forums site at **http://forums.apress.com/**.

Click the New User link.